BLACK AMERICA SERIES

BLACK LIFE IN WEST CENTRAL ILLINOIS

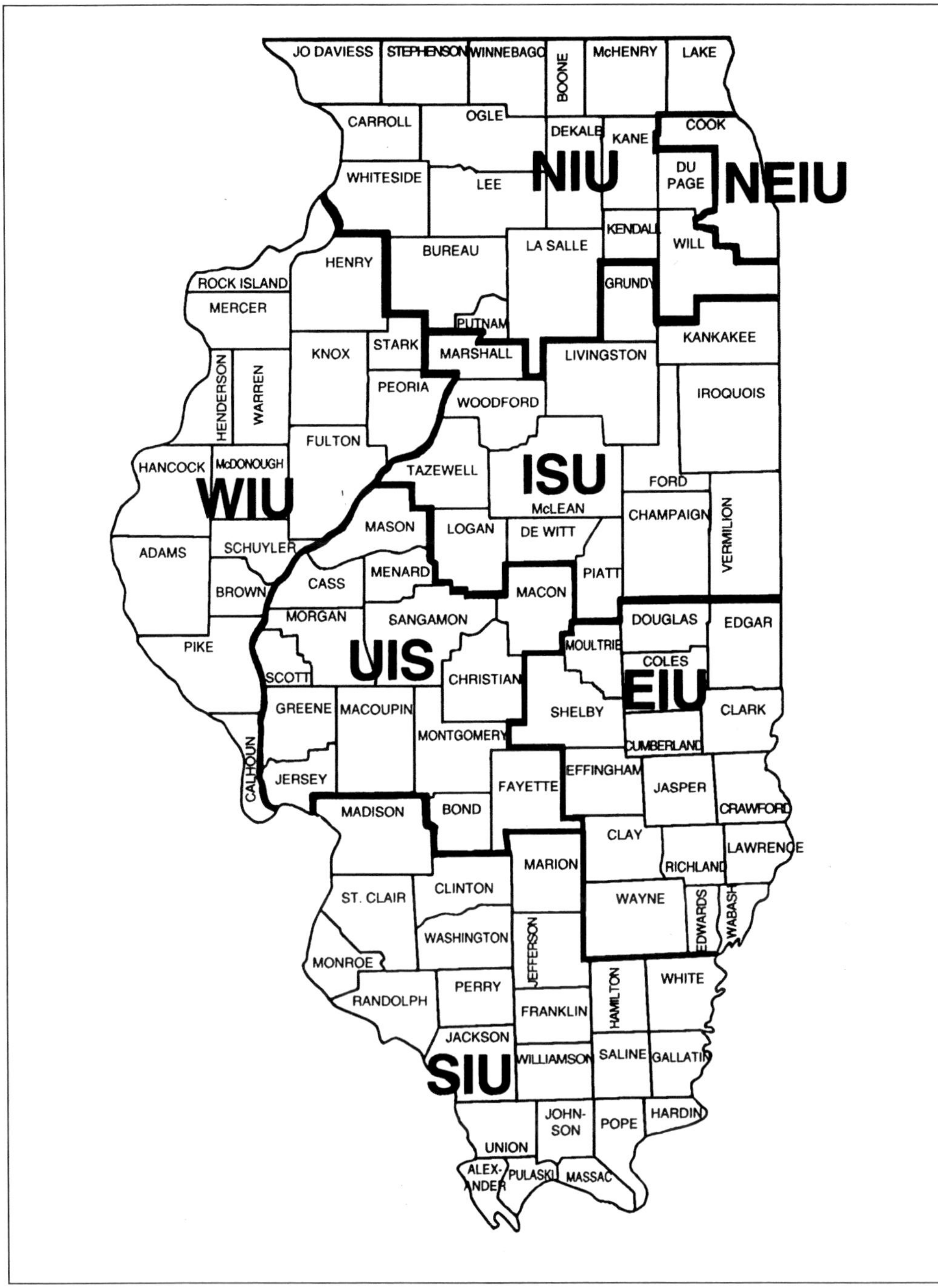

This map of the state of Illinois depicts the official regions of the state's geographical division, according to the Illinois State Archives for its Illinois Regional Archives Depository System (IRAD). Each region of the state has an (IRAD) that is housed in one of the state-supported universities in the area. Western Illinois University (WIU) is the site for west central Illinois and the 16 counties covered in this profile of *Black Life in West Central Illinois*. (Courtesy of IRAD, Western Illinois University.)

BLACK AMERICA SERIES

BLACK LIFE IN WEST CENTRAL ILLINOIS

Felix L. Armfield
Preface by Rev. C.T. Vivian

ARCADIA PUBLISHING

ISBN 978-0-7385-0792-7

Published by Arcadia Publishing
Charleston, South Carolina

Printed in the United States of America

Library of Congress Catalog Card Number: 2001089282

For all general information contact Arcadia Publishing at:
Telephone 843-853-2070
Fax 843-853-0044
E-Mail sales@arcadiapublishing.com
For customer service and orders:
Toll-Free 1-888-313-2665

Visit us on the Internet at www.arcadiapublishing.com

Contents

PREFACE

I was made in western Illinois. I have traveled all over this country and a good part of the world. When asked, "Where were you from?" and I reply, "Illinois," they do not ask, they assume or simply say, "Chicago." According to my mood, I tell the full story—Macomb, Illinois.

They are startled that African Americans lived in western Illinois. I assure them that outside of Chicago there is a place called Illinois. Then I become the object of curiosity and they ask, "Did it affect you?" It is asked in a way that assumes I had to overcome my life in western Illinois.

I simply smile, but in my head and under my breastplate there is a rush of positive thoughts and good feelings. Even the negatives in my lifetime proved to be of great value. At the same time it taught me to live in a racist society, it also taught me how good people can be, regardless of race. It also taught me that money was not a determiner of worth, again, regardless of race. However, it hurt to see people like me with so much talent not having a chance to use it.

As a small child my mother would travel to Kankakee to visit friends. They loved to fish and do night-long crawdad hunting. What a time. The big bands came to the Tri Cities of Rock Island and over into Davenport and Fort Madison, Iowa. All western Illinois' African-American population met there. We could not go to dances in Macomb, even when the band was Cab Calloway.

There were places we could not go to. When I won the county marble contest and it was announced that the regional was to be held in Beardstown, my mother would not allow me to go for fear, rightly so, of bodily harm. Yet one of the finest people I ever met was a competitor in the high jump named Churchhill, from Rushville, Illinois.

My high school experiences were the most important of my life. I was the president or an officer of almost every organization at Macomb High School. I was admired and we had great times together, but I was never invited to a party. It was explained to me that the other students' parents would not allow a black person into "mixed parties—male, female."

Another high school experience was very important. A group of elite students from the University High School inducted me into a group of several fine intellectuals. I remember them now: I saw another part of life that affirmed my dreams and inner-self.

My parents had moved to Macomb from Missouri when I was six years old so I could go to better schools. They chose Macomb so I could enter first grade and "go on to college." This saved me and so many like me from western Illinois. While partial acceptance there gave a good sense of self and offered a clear analysis of American culture, I had to move to obtain a job and be totally accepted as a full human being.

It was in Peoria, Illinois, that I found my first professional job, my wife, and started a family. I learned non-violent direct action in Peoria. A group of white students and other African Americans opened lunch counters that prepared me to work with Martin King ten years later. I was one of those who helped open Caterpillar tractor company to African Americans. Later, one of us became president of the union.

I often think of that time in western Illinois. I can now add what it means to go back to the school and be given an honorary doctorate. I share a special feeling in knowing a building is named after poetess Gwendolyn Brooks, when the head of the English department would not allow me to join the English Club; in knowing there is a department of African-American studies when a few years ago African-American women were not allowed to stay in the dormitory, and so stayed at my grandmother's house instead.

I would have happily spent my life and raised a family in western Illinois, if only custom and tradition had been willing to accept me at the level of my humanity. I feel we both lost.

Rev. C.T. Vivian

Acknowledgments

Too often, historians work in isolation of the larger communities. This project has convinced me of the need to do otherwise. I found a community of willing and often eager individuals to assist me in this endeavor of discovering black life throughout west central Illinois. It has proven to be a rather fruitful journey, despite earlier notions from some that this project could not be done given the misguided belief that the documents did not exist. I found numerous treasures as I began to comb through the unearthed histories of west central Illinois.

While gathering the materials and documents necessary to piece together this pictorial history, I acquired an enormous debt to a great number of people throughout west central Illinois. When I first approached the Provost and vice president of Academic Affairs at Western Illinois University, Dr. Burt Witthuhn, about some financial assistance to jump-start this project, never did I imagine that his office would completely embrace this endeavor and urge me to bring it to full completion. Many thanks to Dr. Witthuhn and Dr. Eric Stifler from the Provost office at Western Illinois University for being ever so supportive of this work and of me. Marla Vizdal from the Archives and Special Collections at Western Illinois University Library proved to be a major resource for me starting in 1995, when I joined the faculty at Western Illinois University. Everyone in visual productions at Western Illinois University eagerly assisted me with this project from the very beginning. They restored life to several documents through their understanding of modern technology. I also acquired a cheerleader and a lifelong friend in Mary Beth Roderick of Macomb, Illinois. Mary Beth's influence was very much a driving force in convincing me that this work must be done. She did so in a manner that only Mary Beth has the power to do. Last but certainly not least, Belinda J. Carr, Director of the Gwendolyn Brooks Culture Center at Western Illinois University, was my anchor not only for this endeavor but also for everything I undertook in west central Illinois from 1995–2000.

When I sent out the call for materials asking individuals and organizations to search their vaults for what I assumed would be scraps of black history, I found a community of people who were seemingly awaiting my call. Those who came forth with materials that have helped to comprise this work were indeed scattered across the dotted landscape of west central Illinois. Ms. Millie Hall, librarian and local historian-extraordinaire of Peoria, Illinois, proved to be a walking and breathing history text. She walked me through the Greater Peoria area and allowed me to have access to information that without her would have been virtually impossible. James Thomas was also very helpful as he assisted my efforts in Peoria as well. Ms. Millie (as I refer to her) was just the person that I needed to fulfill this task of obtaining access into that community. There is no greater referral in Peoria than Ms. Millie Hall. The same can be said of Ms. Kathryn Harris, the Director of the Illinois State Historical Library of Springfield, Illinois. Ms. Kathryn (again, as I refer to her) is always on the job when it comes to giving black history a voice and greater visibility.

There were several individuals from university archives and historical societies that provided me with lessons on local folklore and histories from across west central Illinois as well. The Schuyler County Jail Museum and Historical Society was most efficient. The ladies of the organization were very eager to not only share their history with me, but they also told me stories that only they would have known about black life, in Rushville in particular. Eighty-eight-year-old Ms. Lavina Walton exposed me to black life in Rushville, from the first arrivals to the cemetery plots. The ladies of Rushville convinced me in profound ways that history itself does not have a race assigned to it. This mostly all-white women's organization embraced me and welcomed me into their establishment with open arms. As a matter of fact, Rushville was one of the places that I was told time and again that I would not find any black history. Well, my discoveries have proven otherwise. I was elated to discover that not only had black life existed in Rushville, but that painstaking efforts had been made to preserve it by the Schuyler County Historical Society.

Thanks to all the individuals and persons who came to my aid to make this synthesis possible, including: Evelyn Eifert, President of the Schuyler County Historical Society; Terry Ransom, local expert on the underground railroad; Patricia A. Tomczak, Associate Librarian Quincy University; Carley Robison, Archivist, Knox College; Donna Hill, Special Collections Assistant, Augustana College Library; Steve Abrams, Owner, Abrams Barber Shop, Galesburg; Stacey Cordery, Archivist and Historian, Monmouth College; and the Pike County Historical Society. This work would not have been possible had the above mentioned persons and organizations not assisted me. I am also grateful to Buffalo State College for offering me a reduced teaching load spring semester 2000, which allowed me the time to complete this project and work on other research endeavors. There is a bit of each person who provided me with assistance within the body of the work. However, I take full responsibility for any of the works' shortcomings.

INTRODUCTION

When I first joined the faculty of Western Illinois University in the fall of 1995, I began the tedious task of collecting traces of African-American life locally through paper documents. I soon discovered that black life in west central Illinois had come at quite a premium. I had managed to know most of the local history of Macomb, Illinois, within a year's time. Soon thereafter, I developed a course through the departments of history and African American Studies entitled "Black Material Culture." The students were encouraged to think regionally so that a bigger picture could emerge. Afterwards a fieldwork course was developed, and students began digging locally for more layers of black life. It was at this point that more contacts began to emerge. I spent the summer of 2000 traveling throughout west central Illinois and visiting with local libraries, colleges, and universities in the region. I even managed to visit several archives, met with local and public historians, visited local museums and historical societies, and ultimately visited several cemeteries in search of black life—even if it was sporadic.

As the State of Illinois received its charter for statehood in 1818, and Euro-American settlers came to the state, so too did African-American settlers come to this "free" state within the Union. Though the vast majority of African Americans who came to Illinois during its early history were attached to Euro-American families from the East and Southeast, they accompanied the earliest settlers to the state nonetheless. African Americans settled in practically every area of the state, beginning with the much-talked-about permanent settlement in Chicago of John Baptiste Pointe DuSable. Though Chicago is not the first Illinois settlement, it is looked to as the first African-American settlement within the territory prior to statehood.

West Central Illinois traces African-American life from the very earliest settlements in the area. Sixteen counties make up what is considered west central Illinois today. Pike County, Illinois, was first settled by "Free Frank" McWorter, an African American who eventually purchased the freedom of his entire family and moved them all to an area once called New Philadelphia, Illinois, in Pike County during the 1830s. McWorter settled in this portion of the state just as Euro-American settlers were coming into the area. Considering that many portions of west central Illinois were not settled until the 1830s, it is safe to assume that African Americans were just as eager to discover the New Frontier as their Euro-American counterparts.

Despite African Americans' desires to help settle the frontier state, they were not often afforded such opportunities. The 1830s engrossed American society with the fever of antebellum obsession. Though it was declared that Illinois and all of the Northwest Territory were to be non-slave states when admitted into the Union, unpaid servitude continued to thrive in some locales. As late as 1845, bills of sales for slaves could be placed in Adams County, Illinois. Quincy, Illinois, usually considered a strong anti-slavery area, became a mixed kaleidoscope of what American society reflected in this period of early Illinois statehood and antebellum America.

In the midst of this small burgeoning society of the 1840s and '50s, some African Americans managed to survive in hostile areas throughout west central Illinois. McDonough County founders declared that no African Americans were welcome in the town of Macomb. After the passage of the Fugitive Slave Law in 1850, Macomb was a noted slave catcher's hangout until the close of the Civil War. It lay strategically between the towns of Galesburg and Quincy, which provided those escaping enslaved persons access to the Mississippi River. Despite this declaration, one known African-American male did live in McDonough County before 1865. He had come to the area accompanying a white American family from the East. The family settled just outside of town in the 1840s. Jack McCord, commonly referred to as "Jack the Black Man" of John McCord, worked the family farm and no doubt attended to other needs and concerns of the McCord family throughout his life. Jack McCord was rather endeared by the McCord family, as he was buried in the family plot on the farm in McDonough County. This was much talked about in the local newspaper of the day, as it was uncommon for African Americans and Euro-Americans to share the same burial grounds. This also made Jack McCord the first African American to be buried in McDonough County.

After the Civil War ended in 1865, African-American men and women began to lay claims to settlement in several areas of west central Illinois. Immediately after the war, African Americans began to establish homes, businesses, organizations, and churches that attest to their presence in the sparsely populated area of the state. In 1899, Western Illinois State Normal School (now Western Illinois University) was established at Macomb, Illinois, as the first state-supported public institution of higher learning in the area. The children of some of Macomb's first black families made use of the institution from the very beginning. In just a few years of its opening, black students from as far away as Quincy began to make use of the institution. In 1923, Leala Burnett graduated with a two-year teaching degree and was the first African American to graduate that institution.

By the time of the Great Depression in 1929 and into the 1930s, several African-American families were in west central Illinois. Some came to areas such as Macomb expecting relief from the harsh realities of the economic depression that had engulfed the nation. Civil Rights activist C.T. Vivian tells that he and his family migrated to the area in the 1930s from Missouri, so he would have greater chances to receive a college education at Western Illinois University. The area of West Central Illinois witnessed numerous black families come and go during the twentieth century. In spite of such an increase and decrease, African Americans continued to be a part of the dotted landscape of west central Illinois. This photographic synthesis will serve as a brief overview of African-American existence in west central Illinois, starting with statehood in 1818.

There are numerous aspects of black life that are not covered here, as I am well aware. Some areas of west central Illinois never responded to my call for materials. Some did not provide the type of documentation that could be used here. Most of the documents provided here were discovered through my own initiative and/or those that came forth from the numerous individuals who provided them from libraries, archives, museums, and historical societies throughout the region.

One

BEFORE FREEDOM CAME

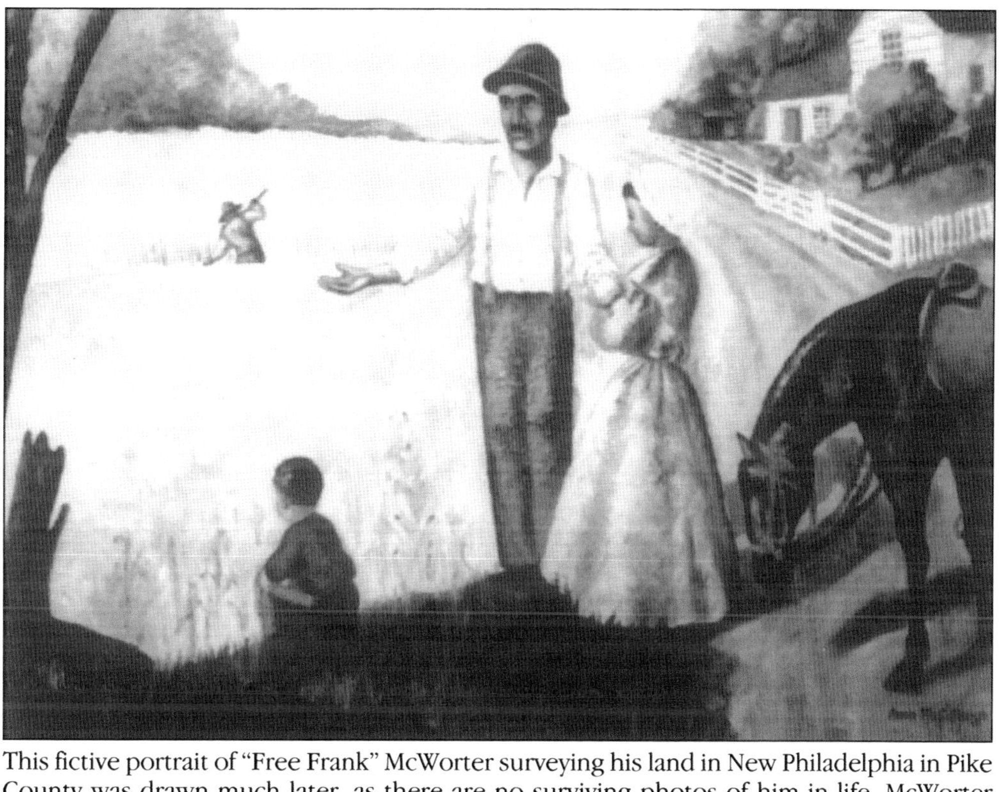

This fictive portrait of "Free Frank" McWorter surveying his land in New Philadelphia in Pike County was drawn much later, as there are no surviving photos of him in life. McWorter settled in Pike County, Illinois, in 1830. He was a rather prosperous farmer and was able to purchase the liberty of a total of 16 family members during his lifetime. McWorter died at New Philadelphia in 1854. The Illinois Emancipation Centennial Commission commissioned this drawing, done by Anna McCullough. (Photo courtesy of the Illinois State Historical Library.)

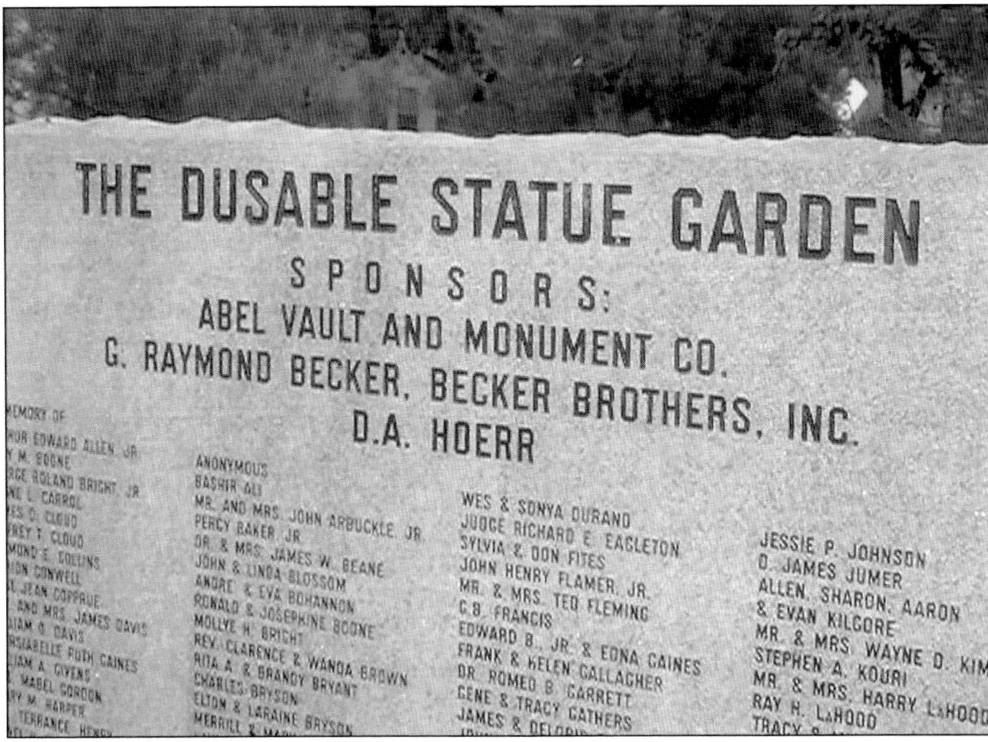

The DuSable Statue Garden was erected in the city of Peoria in 1994. Local artist Preston Jackson was the sculptor of the statue. (Photo courtesy of AAMCC.)

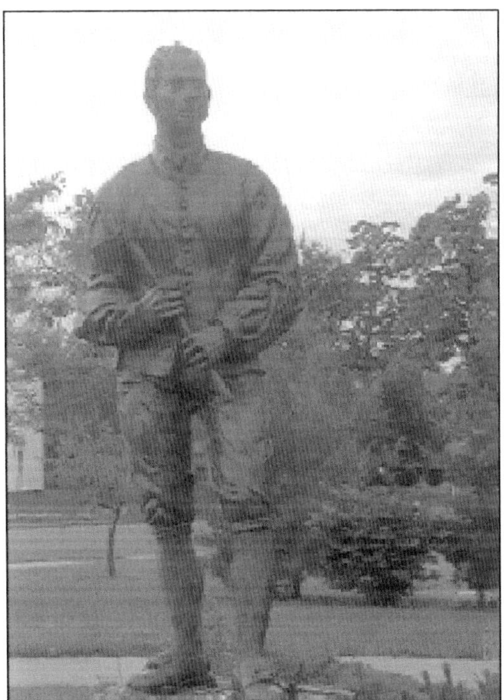

This statue of John Baptiste Pointe DuSable stands in Peoria. DuSable first sailed up the Peoria River and settled in the city of Peoria for a period of about seven years prior to his migration on to what became Chicago. (Photo courtesy of African American Museum and Culture Center—AAMCC, Peoria, Illinois.)

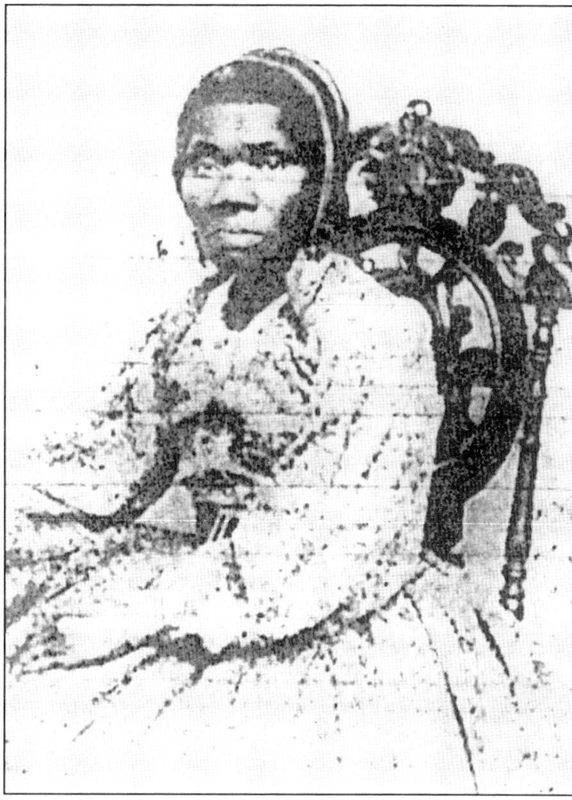

This is Jemime Hall, and she arrived in Warren County as many early African Americans did in the early settlements of the area. She came to Warren County in 1836, with the Aleri Rodgers family. Hall is buried in the Rodgers plot in the Sugar Tree Grove Cemetery. (Photo courtesy of Warren County Historical Library.)

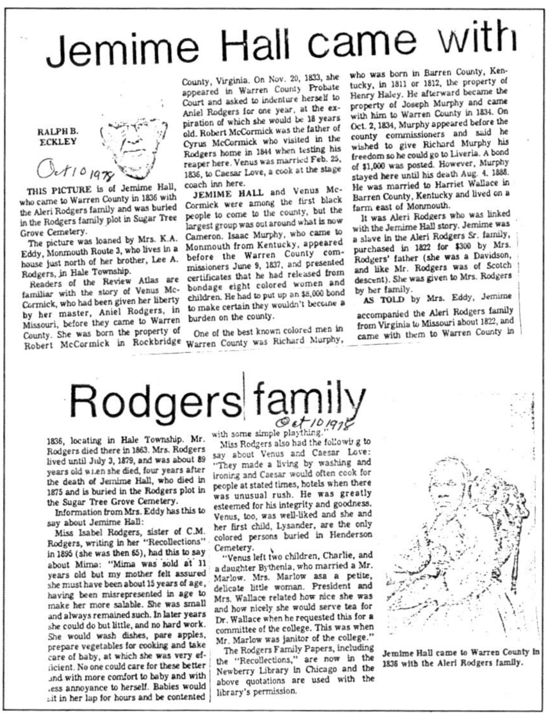

Jemime Hall came with Rodgers family

RALPH B. ECKLEY

Oct 10 1978

THIS PICTURE is of Jemime Hall, who came to Warren County in 1836 with the Aleri Rodgers family and was buried in the Rodgers family plot in Sugar Tree Grove Cemetery.

The picture was loaned by Mrs. K.A. Eddy, Monmouth Route 3, who lives in a house just north of her brother, Lee A. Rodgers, in Hale Township.

Readers of the Review Atlas are familiar with the story of Venus McCormick, who had been given her liberty by her master, Aniel Rodgers, in Missouri, before they came to Warren County. She was born the property of Robert McCormick in Rockbridge County, Virginia. On Nov. 20, 1833, she appeared in Warren County Probate Court and asked to indenture herself to Aniel Rodgers for one year, at the expiration of which she would be 18 years old. Robert McCormick was the father of Cyrus McCormick who visited in the Rodgers home in 1844 when testing his reaper here. Venus was married Feb. 25, 1836, to Caesar Love, a cook at the stage coach inn here.

JEMIME HALL and Venus McCormick were among the first black people to come to the county, but the largest group was out around what is now Cameron. Isaac Murphy, who came to Monmouth from Kentucky, appeared before the Warren County commissioners June 9, 1837, and presented certificates that he had released from bondage eight colored women and children. He had to put up an $8,000 bond to make certain they wouldn't become a burden on the county.

One of the best known colored men in Warren County was Richard Murphy, who was born in Barren County, Kentucky, in 1811 or 1812, the property of Henry Haley. He afterward became the property of Joseph Murphy and came with him to Warren County in 1834. On Oct. 2, 1834, Murphy appeared before the county commissioners and said he wished to give Richard Murphy his freedom so he could go to Liveria. A bond of $1,000 was posted. However, Murphy stayed here until his death Aug. 4, 1888. He was married to Harriet Wallace in Barren County, Kentucky and lived on a farm east of Monmouth.

It was Aleri Rodgers who was linked with the Jemime Hall story. Jemime was a slave in the Aleri Rodgers Sr. family, purchased in 1822 for $300 by Mrs. Rodgers' father (she was a Davidson, and like Mr. Rodgers was of Scotch descent). She was given to Mrs. Rodgers by her family.

AS TOLD by Mrs. Eddy, Jemime accompanied the Aleri Rodgers family from Virginia to Missouri about 1822, and came with them to Warren County in 1836, locating in Hale Township. Mr. Rodgers died there in 1863. Mrs. Rodgers lived until July 3, 1879, and was about 89 years old when she died, four years after the death of Jemime Hall, who died in 1875 and is buried in the Rodgers plot in the Sugar Tree Grove Cemetery.

Oct 10 1978

Information from Mrs. Eddy has this to say about Jemime Hall:

Miss Isabel Rodgers, sister of C.M. Rodgers, writing in her "Recollections" in 1895 (she was then 65), had this to say about Mima: "Mima was sold at 11 years old but my mother felt assured she must have been about 15 years of age, having been misrepresented in age to make her more salable. She was small and always remained such. In later years she could do but little, and no hard work. She would wash dishes, pare apples, prepare vegetables for cooking and take care of baby, at which she was very efficient. No one could care for these better and with more comfort to baby and with less annoyance to herself. Babies would sit in her lap for hours and be contented with some simple plaything."

Miss Rodgers also had the following to say about Venus and Caesar Love: "They made a living by washing and ironing and Caesar would often cook for people at stated times, hotels when there was unusual rush. He was greatly esteemed for his integrity and goodness. Venus, too, was well-liked and she and her first child, Lysander, are the only colored persons buried in Henderson Cemetery.

"Venus left two children, Charlie, and a daughter Bythenia, who married a Mr. Marlow. Mrs. Marlow asa a petite, delicate little woman. President and Mrs. Wallace related how nice she was and how nicely she would serve tea for Dr. Wallace when he requested this for a committee of the college. This was when Mr. Marlow was janitor of the college."

The Rodgers Family Papers, including the "Recollections," are now in the Newberry Library in Chicago and the above quotations are used with the library's permission.

Jemime Hall came to Warren County in 1836 with the Aleri Rodgers family.

This news article was placed in the local newspaper on October 10, 1978. (Document courtesy of Warren County Historical Library.)

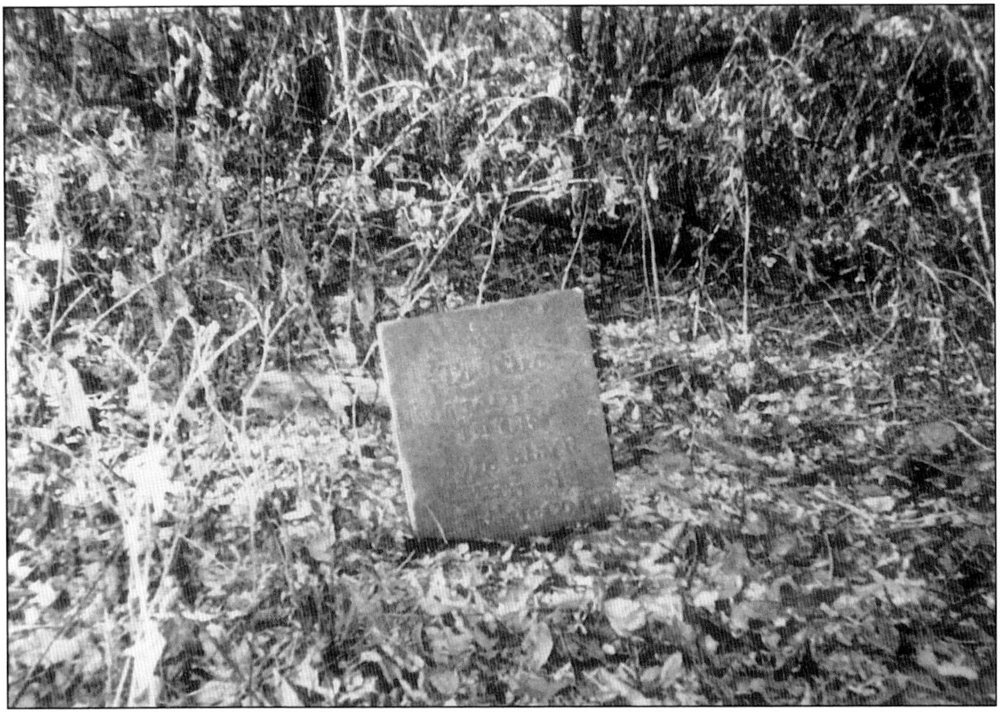

This tombstone that time has eroded marks the final resting place of Jack McCord of McDonough County. McCord was referred to by the locals as "Jack the Black Man" of John McCord. Many locals still refer to him today as such. McCord was the first African American to be buried in McDonough County. He too came to the area accompanying a white family from the East. (Photo courtesy of Archives and Special Collections, Western Illinois University Library.)

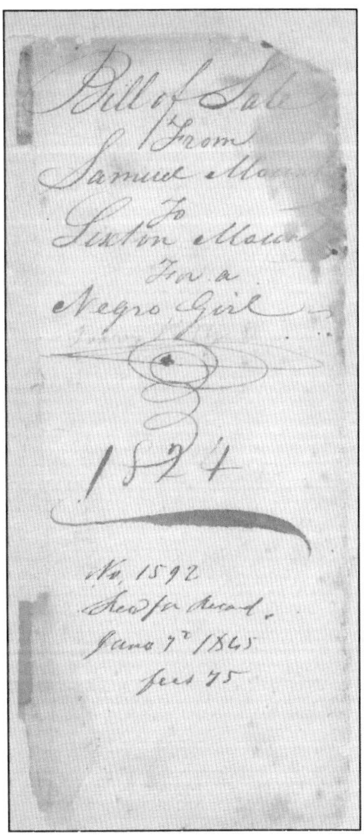

Bill of Sale
From
Samuel Mou
To
Sexton Mou
For a
Negro Girl

1824

No. 1592
Rec'd for record
June 7th 1845
fees 75

In the 1840s, numerous white settlers from the eastern United States settled in and around Adams County. Its access to the Mississippi River made for lucrative business ventures. However, many that settled were hard on their luck and were steeped in financial misfortunes in the East and sought financial relief through the sale of human property that often accompanied them. This bill of sale between Samuel Mount and Sexton Mount for a "Negro Girl" is revealing about the status of African Americans arriving in this "free state." (Photo courtesy of IRAD, Western Illinois University.)

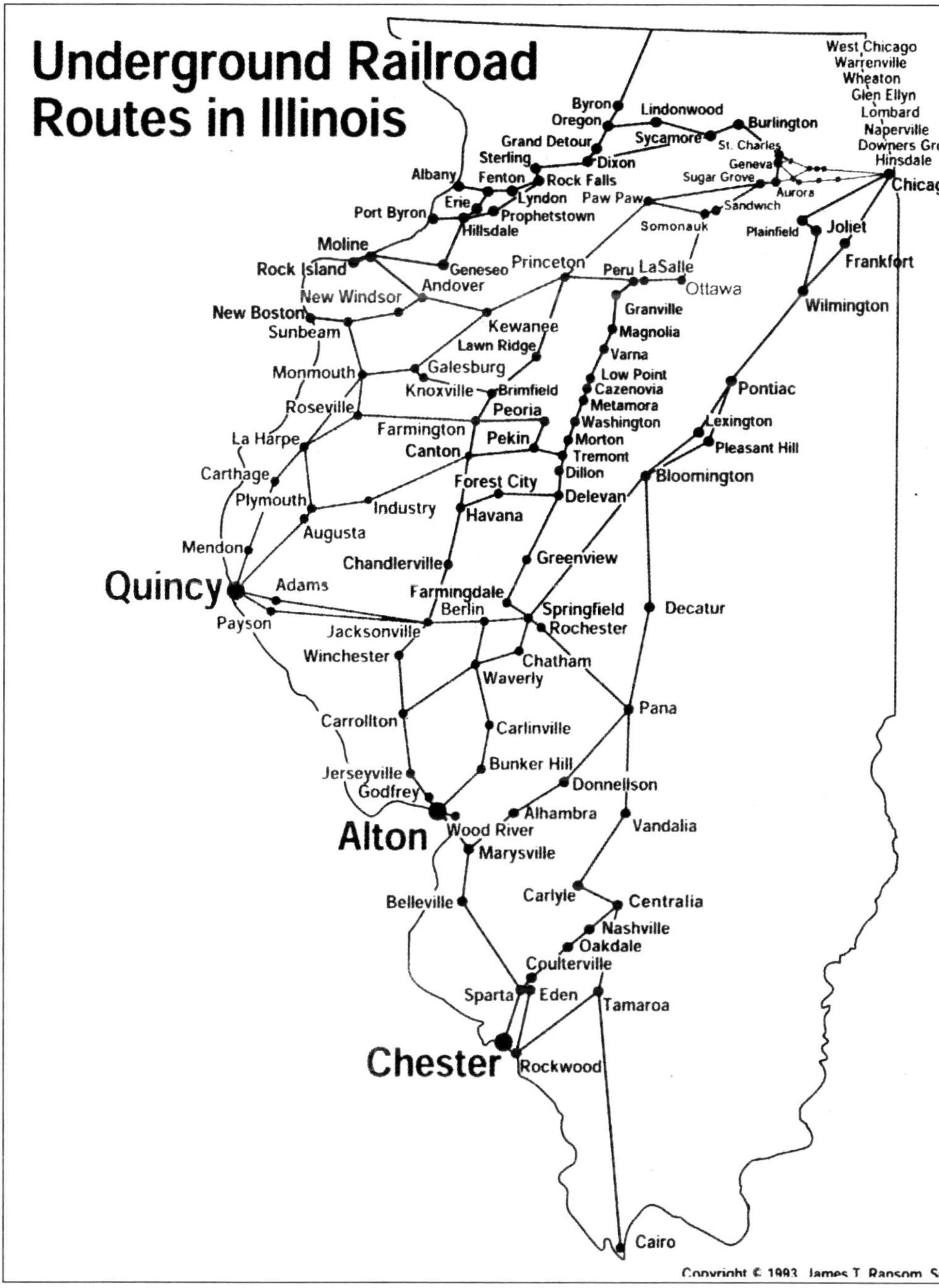

After the passage of the 1850 Fugitive Slave Law Act, many places in west central Illinois provided shelter for those escaping enslaved persons to make their way towards the Mississippi River and on to freedom. This rather detailed map illustrates the routes traveled by African Americans through the state of Illinois seeking freedom that lay on the other side of the Mississippi River. (Document courtesy of James T. Ransom Sr. and the Illinois State Historical Library.)

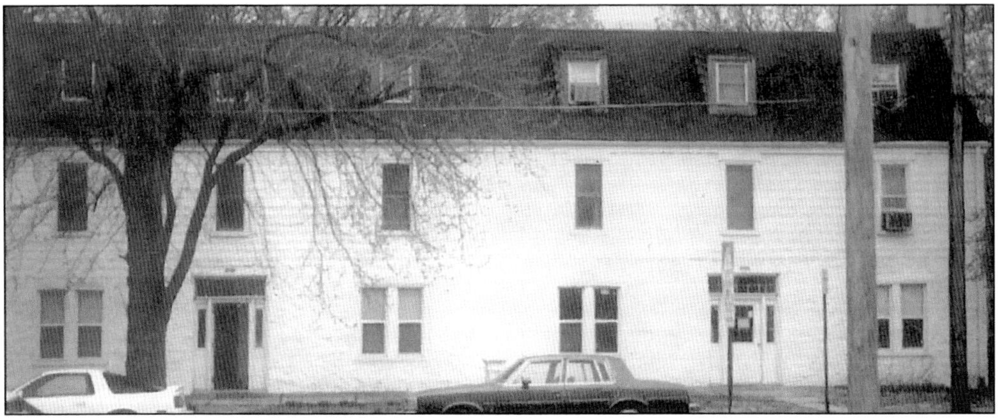

The Old Stone House in Alton has been documented as a station on the Underground Railroad. Local historian Terry Ransom continues to be a leading authority on the Underground Railroad in Illinois. (Photo courtesy of Terry Ransom.)

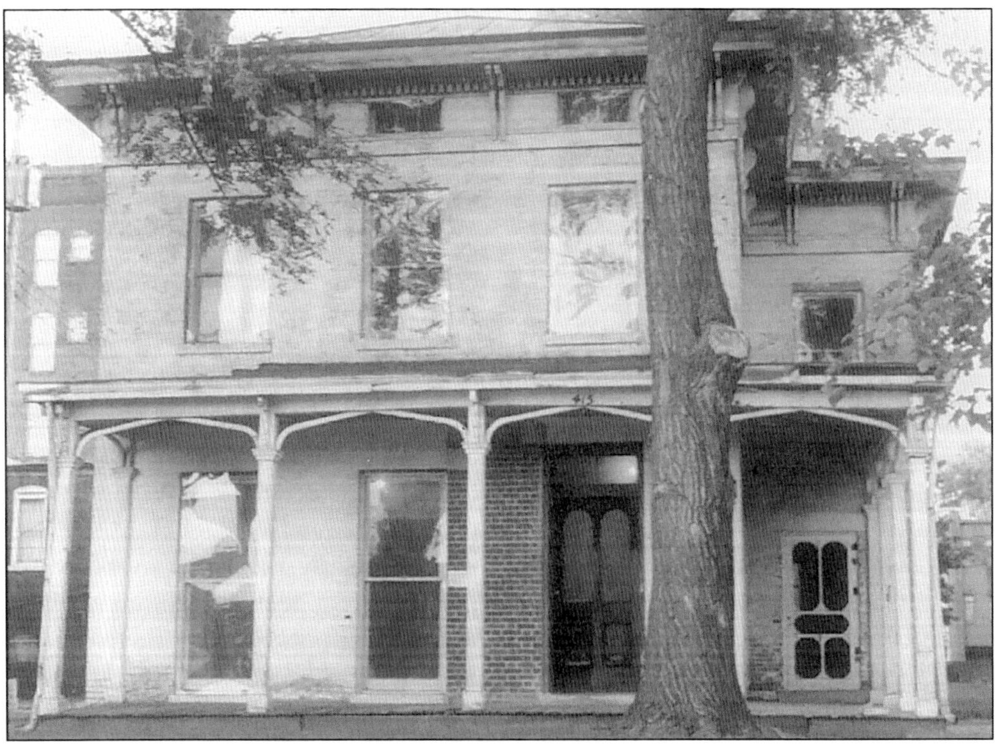

The Eells house is one of the most noted homes in west central Illinois for its activity in helping fugitives to freedom. It is reported that the home of Dr. Richard Eells harbored many fugitive slaves in Quincy. (Photo courtesy of Terry Ransom.)

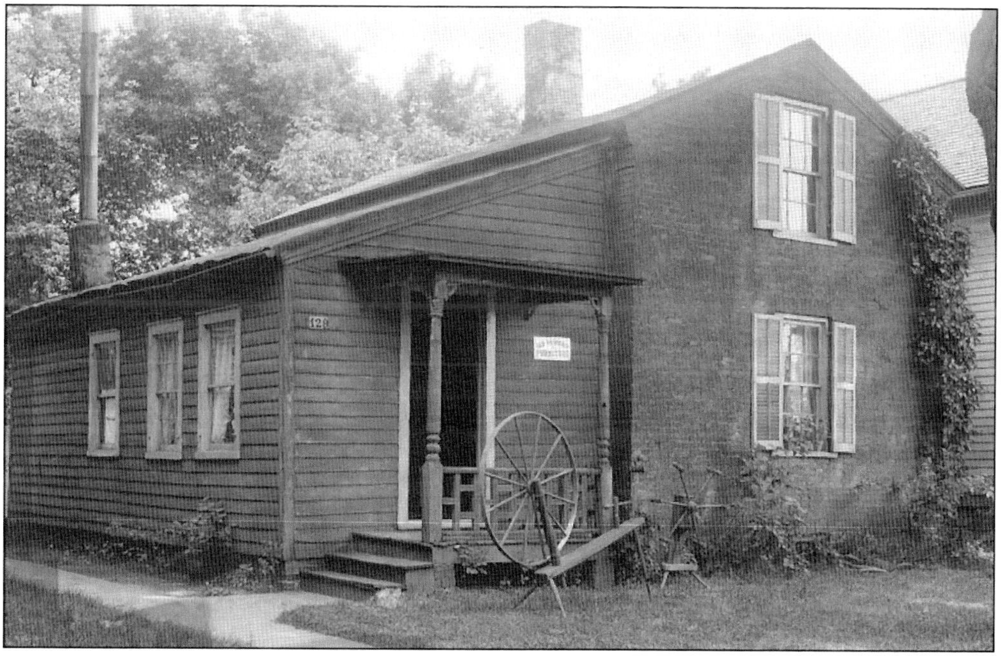

This structure at the time of these photographs had become an antique store *c.* 1910. It is widely reported that it was a major stop on the Underground Railroad in Knox County, at Galesburg. (Photo courtesy of Knox College Archives, Galesburg, Illinois.)

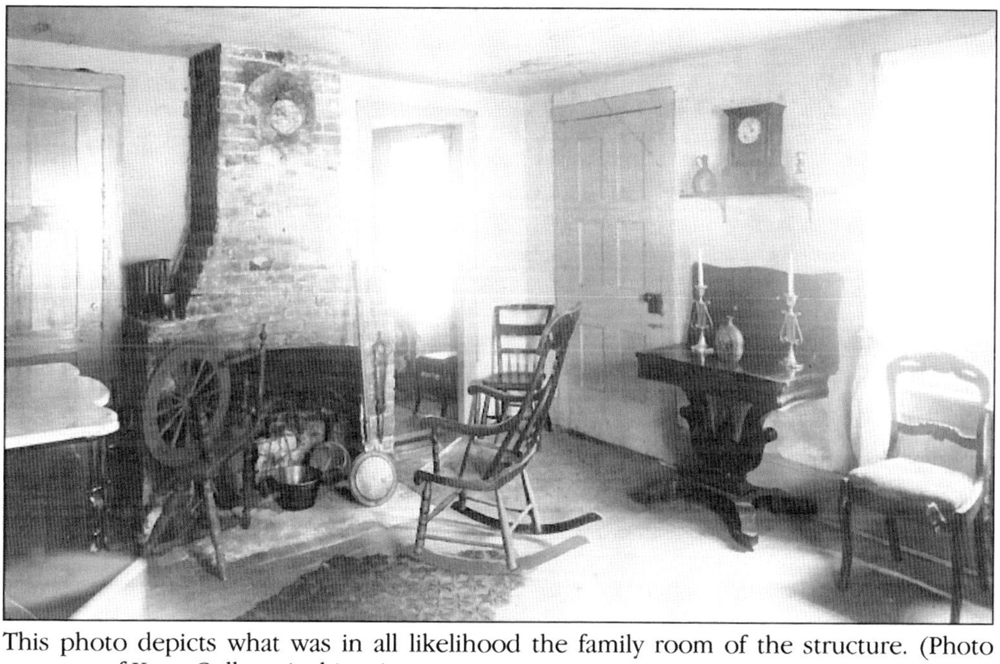

This photo depicts what was in all likelihood the family room of the structure. (Photo courtesy of Knox College Archives.)

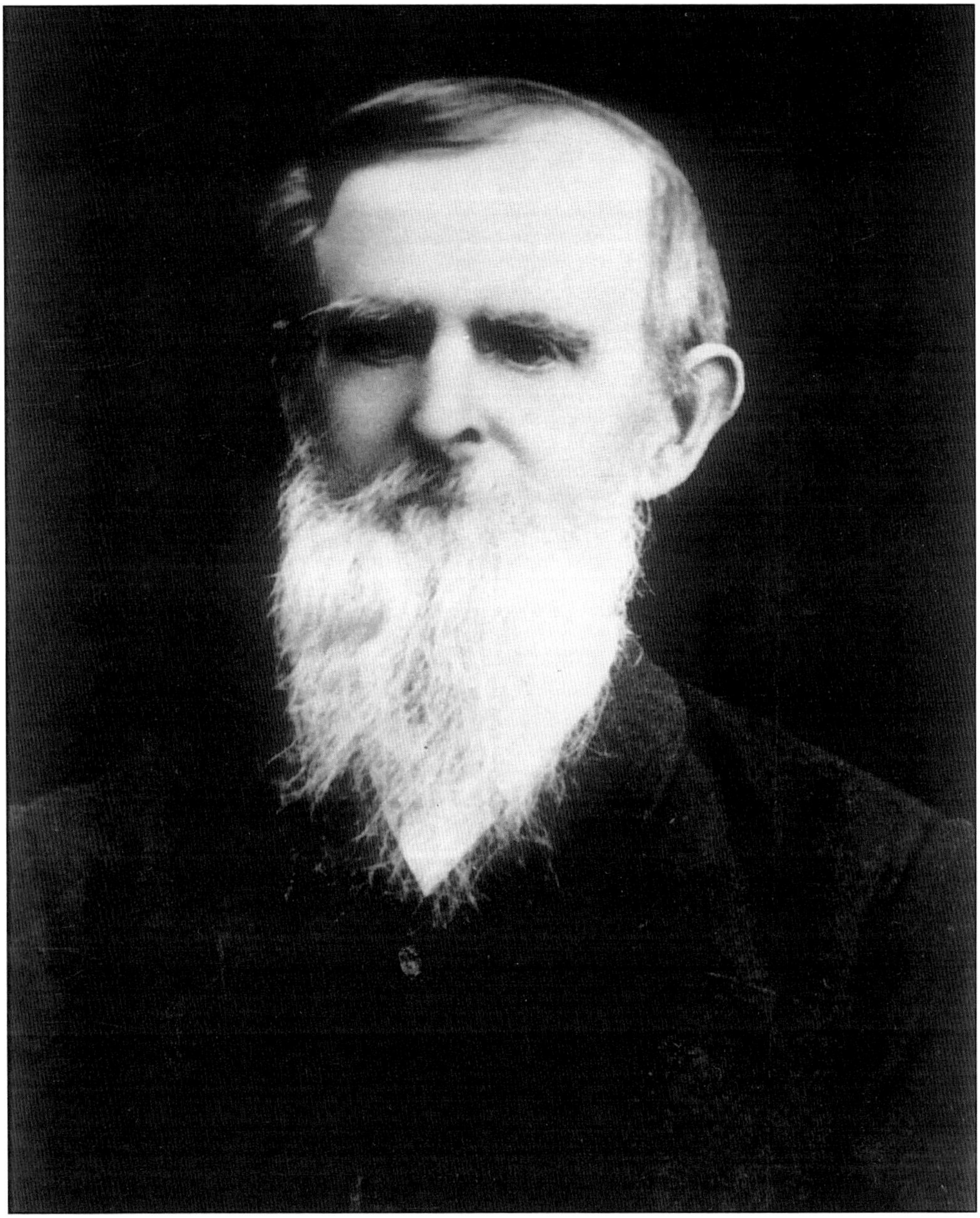

The Allison family of McDonough County is widely reported to have assisted escaping enslaved persons on their journey into freedom. The Allisons lived outside the town borders and harbored many at their farm, which was located south of Macomb. The family home later belonged to Andrew Haines Allison. (Photo courtesy of Archives and Special Collections, Western Illinois University Library.)

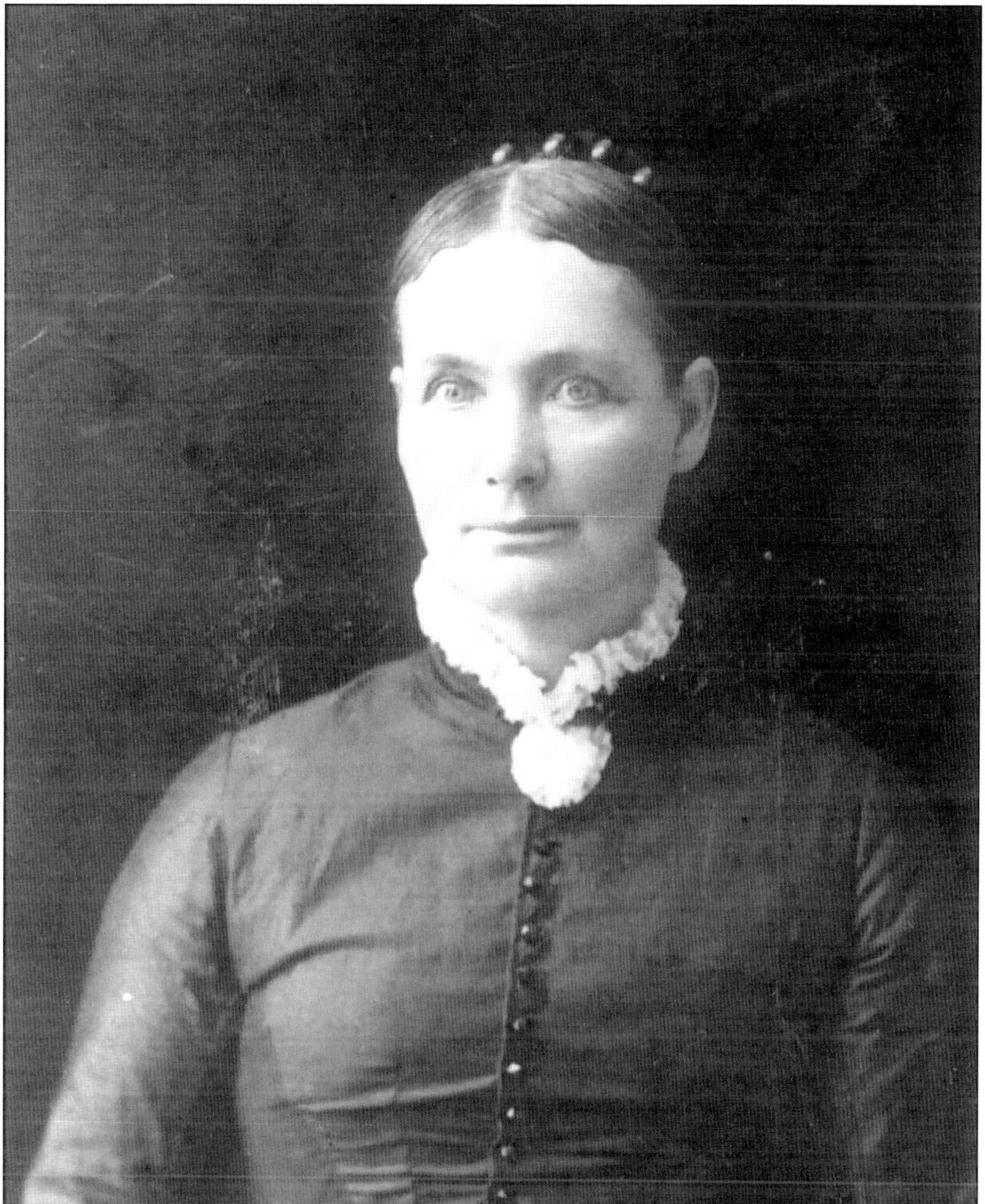

Lucinda Brown Allison, wife of Andrew, was a supporter of the anti-slavery activities of the area. (Photo courtesy of Archives and Special Collections, Western Illinois University Library.)

Macomb Negro Born In Slavery Reviews Life As He Nears 94

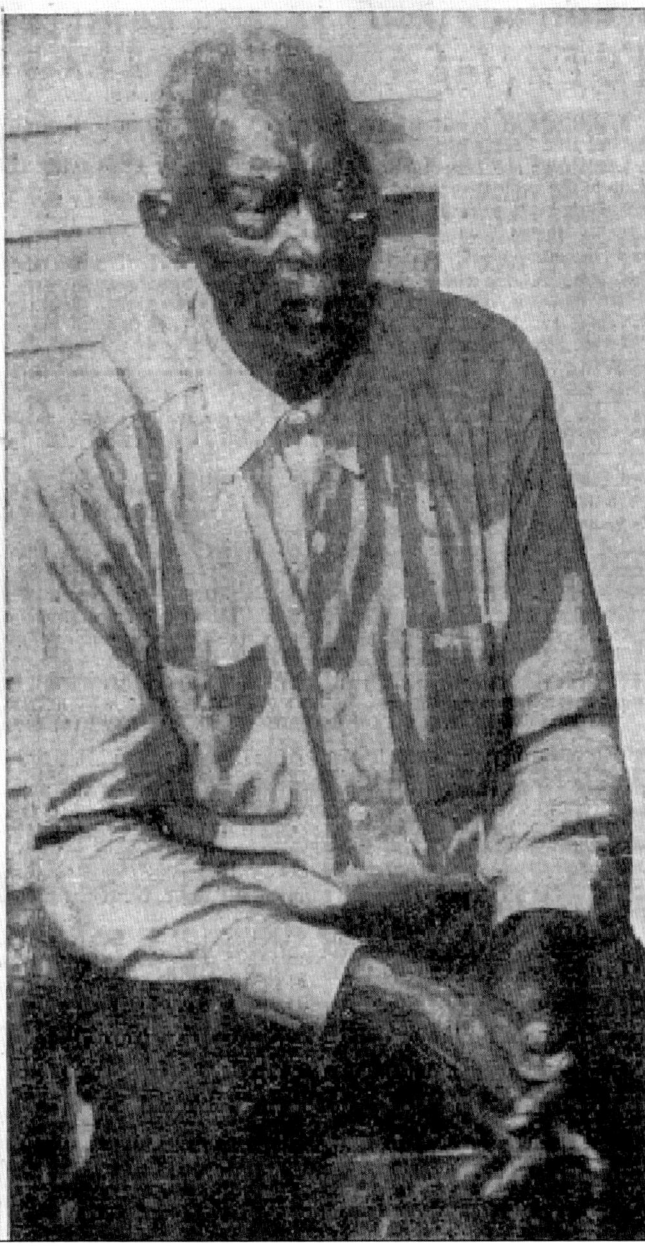

Sanford Daniels, Macomb's oldest negro and one of the first of his race to come to the Macomb community, is approaching his 94th birthday.

Daniels lives in two small rooms built at the rear of the A.M.E. Church, 320 N. Mechanic St. Incidentally, he helped build that church.

Born into a slave family just before the Civil War started, Daniels can recall numerous incidents of his childhood.

"I can remember when our master stood up on a rock out in front of our cabin and read a notice about the end of the war and telling us we were free because of President Lincoln's proclamation," he said. "We stayed right there as there was no place to go. That was when I was about five or six years old and we were living near Mexico, Mo."

Parents Sold.

Daniels was born Dec. 18, 1860, in Kentucky. When he was about a year old his parents were traded to a new master near Mexico, Mo. Enroute there, he said, the group he was with met a slave trader who was transporting a group of colored people, chained together, to another part of the country. Daniels' father, Milford, was sold for $[illegible] to the trader, separating the family, he said. However, his mother's master became so concerned over the trade that he had someone ride in pursuit of the slave trader group later in the day and his father was bought back so he could accompany them on to Missouri.

After the slaves were freed, Daniels' family decided to locate in McDonough County and work for a man by the name of Major Yocum who lived in the Pennington Point community. The Daniels' family, which included the parents and five boys and girls, rode the train to Bardolph and walked about seven miles from there to the Yocum farm, he said. The Daniels knew Yocum when he liv-

Sanford Daniels and his family were the first African Americans to settle in McDonough County after the Civil War in 1867. Though Daniels was born enslaved in Kentucky, he and his wife and children migrated to Macomb after the Civil War. (Photo courtesy of Archives and Special Collections, Western Illinois University Library.)

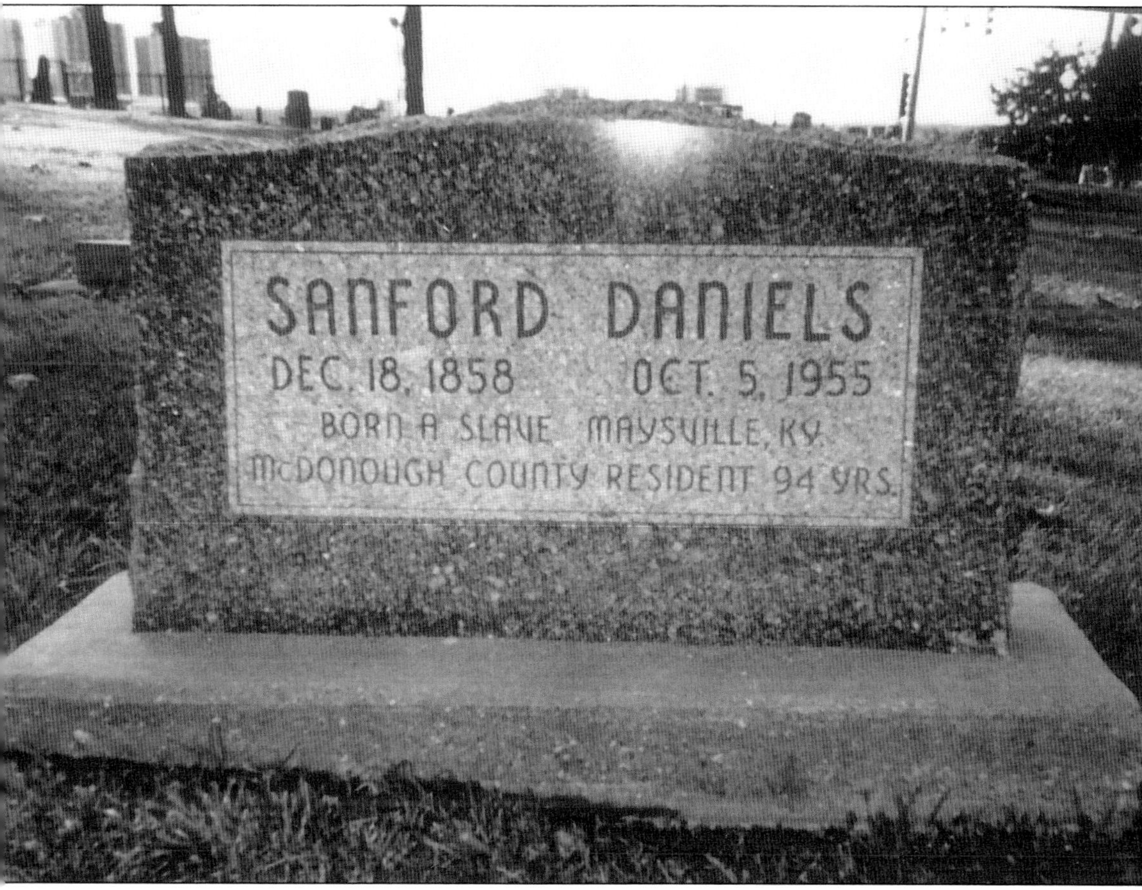

Sanford Daniels lived in Macomb for almost 100 years. His family placed a more modern tomb at his grave later in the twentieth century. (Photo courtesy of Archives and Special Collections, Western Illinois University Library.)

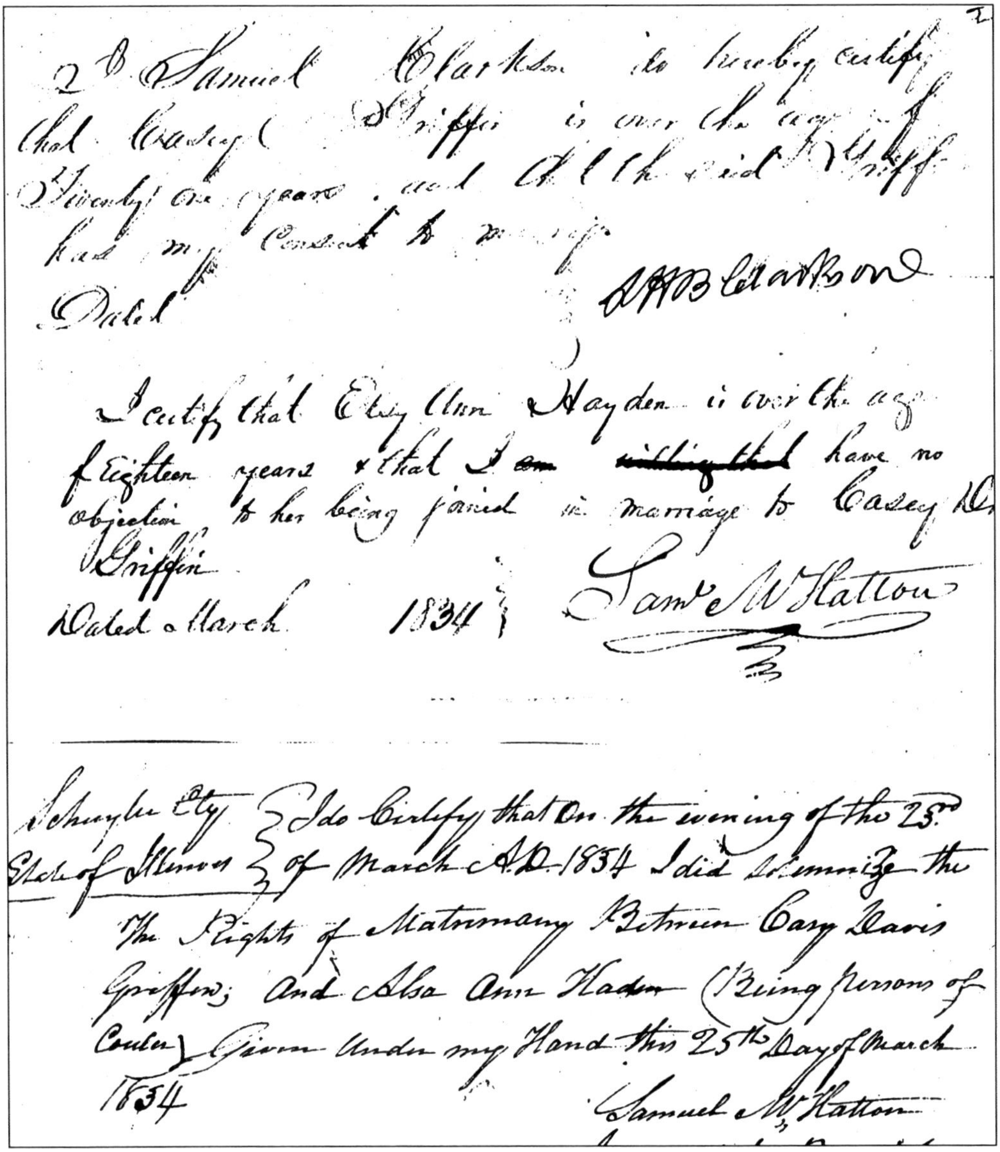

I Samuel Clarkson do hereby certify that Casey D. Griffin is over the age of Twenty one years and that the said Griffin had my consent to marry

Dated

Saml Clarkson

I certify that Elsy Ann Hayden is over the age of Eighteen years & that I am ~~willing that~~ have no objection to her being joined in marriage to Casey D. Griffin

Dated March 1834

Saml W Hatton

Schuyler Cty State of Illinois } I do Certify that On the evening of the 25th of March A.D. 1834 I did Solemnize the The Rights of Matrimony Between Cary Davis Griffin; And Alsa Ann Hadin (Being persons of Coulor) Given Under my Hand this 25th Day of March 1834

Samuel W Hatton

While most African Americans came to west central Illinois after the Civil War as free individuals, some came during the antebellum era when their freedoms were ambiguous at best. The following documents attest to the fact that African Americans seeking to marry before 1865 in the "free" state of Illinois could not do so without the written consent of a white male. This document is a written statement by two white men granting their permission for African Americans Casey Griffin and Elsy Ann Hayden to be joined in marriage in 1834, at Rushville in Schuyler County. It reads as such: "I Samuel Clarkson do hereby certify that Casey Griffin is over the age of Twenty one years and that the said Griffin has my consent to marry." Signed Clarkson.

Latter statement: "I certify that Elsy Ann Hayden is over the age of eighteen years and that I have no objection to her being joined in marriage to Casey D. Griffin. Dated March 1834: Signed Sam W. Hatton." The document further notes that they were persons of "color." (Document is courtesy of the Schuyler County Jail Museum and Historical Society.)

State of Illinois }
Schuyler County } The People of the state of Illinois

To any person lawfully authorized to solemnize Marriage Greeting: You are hereby Licensed and permitted to celebrate and certify the rites of marriage between Mr. Casey D. Griffin and Miss Elsy Ann Hayden and for so doing this shall be your sufficient warrant.

Witness Hart Fellows clerk of the County Commissioners Court of said County at Rushville this 2nd day of March A.D. 1834, the seal of said Court being hereunto affixed.

Hart Fellows Clk.

This official document was registered and filed at the county commissioner's office in Rushville, recording the marriage on March 2, 1834, of Casey D. Griffin and Elsy Ann Hayden. Unfortunately no photographs of the two have survived. (Document is courtesy of Schuyler County Jail Museum and Historical Society.)

MARRIAGE LICENSE WAS GRANTED, On the 9th *day of* February, *A. D. 18*36,

to Ceasar Love, *and* Venice McCormic, *now both of this County.*
People of color.

Clerk.

STATE OF ILLINOIS, } *Sct.*
Warren County. }

Deputy.

I HEREBY CERTIFY, That on the 25th *day of* February, *A. D. 18*36, *I joined in the state of matrimony Mr.* Caesar Love, *and Miss* Venice McCormic, *according to the usual custom and laws of the State of Illinois.*

Given under my hand and seal this 25th *day of* February *A. D. 18*36.

Returned, registered and filed, February 25th, *18*36. James C. Bruce. (SEAL)

Several other African-American couples were joined in matrimony in west central Illinois before 1865, indicating that blacks were indeed a part of the early settlements in this area. Ceasar Love and Venice McCormic (people of color) were married in Warren County on February 25, 1836. (Document courtesy of Warren County Historical Library.)

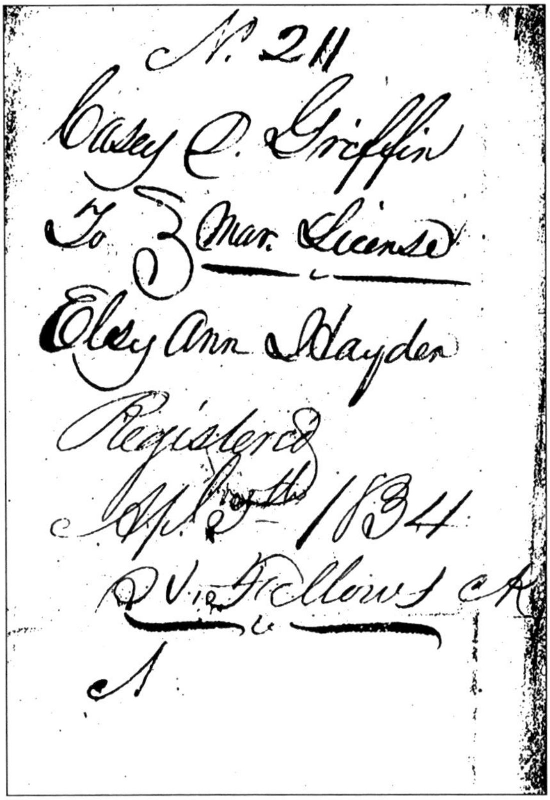

No. 211
Casey C. Griffin
To
Mar. License
Elsey Ann Hayden
Registered
Apl 5th 1834
D. V. Fellows Clk

This was also listed in the county records as document No. 211. (Document is courtesy of Schuyler County Jail Museum and Historical Society.)

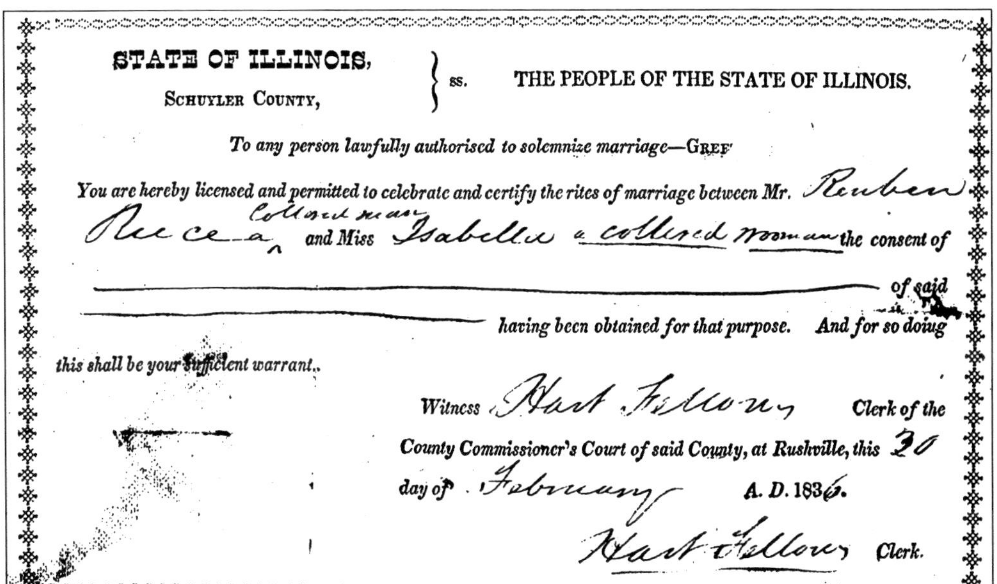

STATE OF ILLINOIS, } ss. THE PEOPLE OF THE STATE OF ILLINOIS.
SCHUYLER COUNTY,

*To any person lawfully authorised to solemnize marriage—*GREE

You are hereby licensed and permitted to celebrate and certify the rites of marriage between Mr. Reuben Reece a colored man *and Miss* Isabella a colored woman *the consent of* ____ *of said* ____ *having been obtained for that purpose. And for so doing this shall be your sufficient warrant.*

Witness Hart Fellows *Clerk of the County Commissioner's Court of said County, at Rushville, this* 30 *day of* February *A. D.* 1836.

Hart Fellows *Clerk.*

Reuben Reece (colored man) and Isabella (a colored woman) were married on the last day of February 1836, in Rushville. (Document courtesy of Schuyler County Jail Museum and Historical Society.)

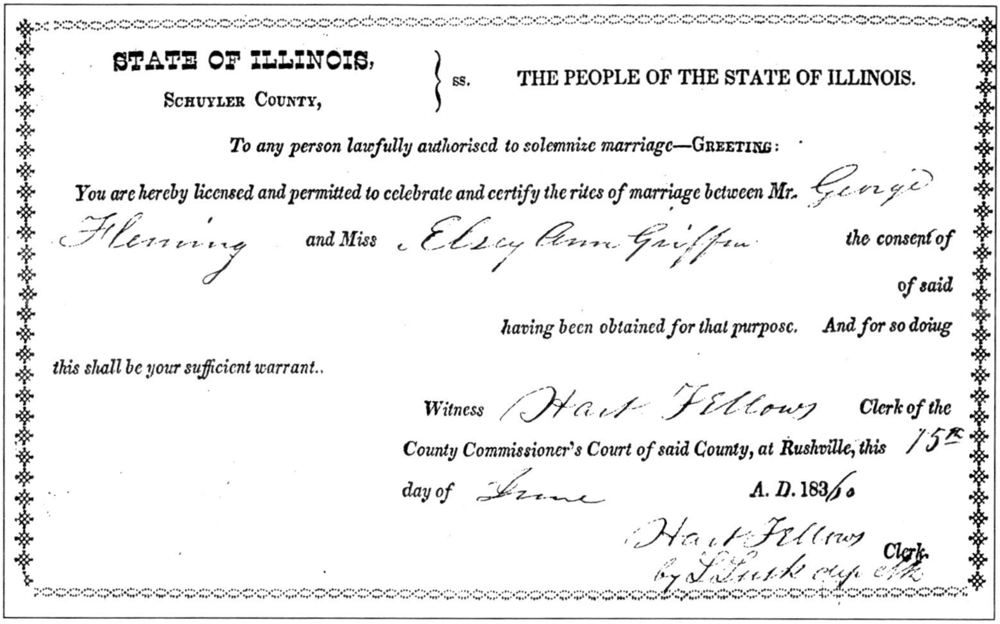

STATE OF ILLINOIS, } ss. THE PEOPLE OF THE STATE OF ILLINOIS.
SCHUYLER COUNTY,

To any person lawfully authorised to solemnize marriage—GREETING:

You are hereby licensed and permitted to celebrate and certify the rites of marriage between Mr. George Fleming *and Miss* Elsey Ann Griffin *the consent of of said having been obtained for that purpose. And for so doing this shall be your sufficient warrant.*

Witness Hart Fellows *Clerk of the County Commissioner's Court of said County, at Rushville, this* 15th *day of* June *A. D. 183*6

Hart Fellows Clerk.
by [illegible] dep. clk

On June 15, 1836, George Fleming and Elsey Ann Griffin were married at Rushville. (Document courtesy of Schuyler County Jail Museum and Historical Society.)

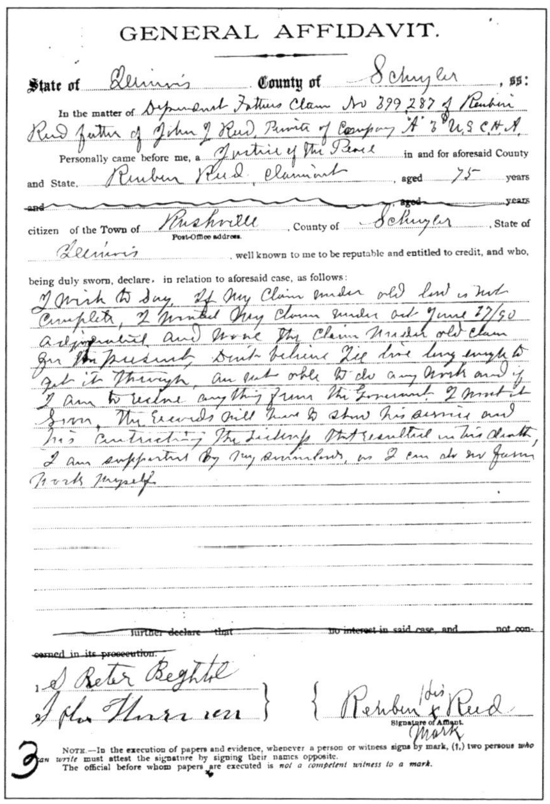

GENERAL AFFIDAVIT.

State of Illinois County of Schuyler, ss:

In the matter of Dependent Fathers Claim No 399,287 of Reuben Reed father of John J Reed Private of Company "A" 3 U.S.C.H.A.

Personally came before me, a Justice of the Peace in and for aforesaid County and State, Reuben Reed, claimant, aged 75 years ~~and aged years~~ citizen of the Town of Rushville, County of Schuyler, State of Illinois, well known to me to be reputable and entitled to credit, and who, being duly sworn, declare, in relation to aforesaid case, as follows:

I wish to say, If my Claim under old law is not Complete, I wanted my Claim under act June 27/90 adjudicated and none the Claim under old Claim for the present. Dont believe I'll live long enough to get it through, am not able to do any work and if I am to receive anything from the Government I must it soon, The Records will have to show his service and his contracting the sickness that resulted in his death, I am supported by my [illegible], as I can do no farm work myself.

~~further declare that no interest in said case, and not concerned in its prosecution.~~

1 S Peter Beghtol
2 John Warren

Reuben his X mark Reed
Signature of Affiant.

NOTE.—In the execution of papers and evidence, whenever a person or witness signs by mark, (X,) two persons who can write must attest the signature by signing their names opposite.
The official before whom papers are executed is *not a competent witness to a mark.*

This is Reuben Reed, the father of John R. Reed, who was a Private of Company "A," 3rd United States Colored Heavy Artillery (U.S.C.H.A.) during the Civil War. Reuben Reed was 75 years old in 1890, and was unable to work and needed credit with the town of Rushville. He placed his mark (X) on the General Affidavit in order to use his land as collateral. (Document courtesy of Schuyler County Jail Museum and Historical Society.)

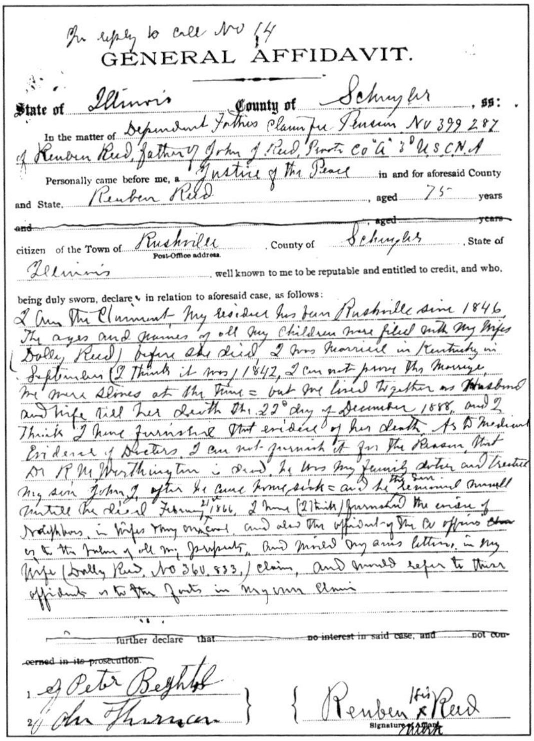

In reply to call No 64

GENERAL AFFIDAVIT.

State of Illinois, County of Schuyler, ss:

In the matter of Dependent Fathers Claim for Pension No 399 287 of Reuben Reed, father of John J. Reed, Pvt Co "A" 3d U.S.C.H.A.

Personally came before me, a Justice of the Peace in and for aforesaid County and State, Reuben Reed, aged 75 years

citizen of the Town of Rushville, County of Schuyler, State of Illinois, well known to me to be reputable and entitled to credit, and who, being duly sworn, declares in relation to aforesaid case, as follows:

I am the Claimant, my residence has been Rushville since 1846. The ages and names of all my children were filed with my wifes (Dolly Reed) before she died. I was married in Kentucky in September (I think it was) 1842, I can not prove the marriage, we were alone at the time = but we lived together as husband and wife till her death the 22d day of December 1888, and I think I have furnished that evidence of her death. As to medical evidence of doctors, I can not furnish it for the reason that Dr R. M. Worthington is dead, he was my family doctor and treated my son John J. after he came home sick = and he remained unwell untill he died February 21 1866. I have (I think) furnished the evidence of neighbors in wifes claim, and also the affidavit of the Co officers as to the value of all my property, and would refer to their affidavits as to other facts in my own claim

further declare that no interest in said case, and not concerned in its prosecution.

1 J Peter Beghtol
2 John Thurman

Reuben his x mark Reed
Signature of Affiant.

Here Reuben Reed discussed the fact that he settled in Rushville, Illinois, in 1846, and that his wife Dolly Reed died in 1888. He also mentioned the fact that he was married in the state of Kentucky in 1842. He goes on to further discuss the fact that the doctor who had cared for Dolly and the rest of his family could in fact offer his story creditability. (Document courtesy of Schuyler County Jail Museum and Historical Society.)

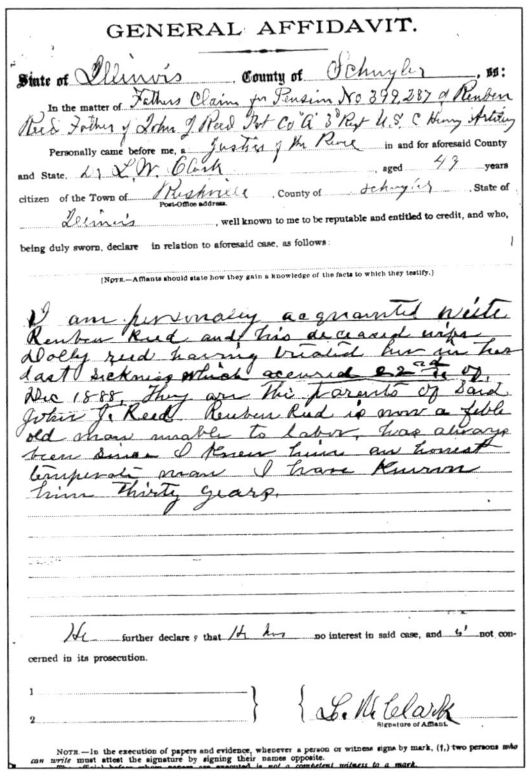

GENERAL AFFIDAVIT.

State of Illinois, County of Schuyler, ss:

In the matter of Fathers Claim for Pension No 399,287 of Reuben Reed Father of John J Reed Pvt Co "A" 3d Regt U.S.C Heavy Artillery

Personally came before me, a Justice of the Peace in and for aforesaid County and State, Dr L.W. Clark, aged 47 years

citizen of the Town of Rushville, County of Schuyler, State of Illinois, well known to me to be reputable and entitled to credit, and who, being duly sworn, declare in relation to aforesaid case, as follows:

(Note.—Affiants should state how they gain a knowledge of the facts to which they testify.)

I am personaly acquainted with Reuben Reed and his deceased wife Dolly reed having treated her in her last sickness which accured 22d of Dec 1888. They are the parents of said John J. Reed. Reuben Reed is now a feble old man unable to labor, was always been since I knew him an honest temperate man I have known him thirty years.

He further declare that he has no interest in said case, and is not concerned in its prosecution.

1

2

L. W. Clark
Signature of Affiant.

Note.—In the execution of papers and evidence, whenever a person or witness signs by mark, (†,) two persons who can write must attest the signature by signing their names opposite.

This document is the doctor's statement. It reads as follows: "I am personally acquainted with Reuben Reed and his deceased wife Dolly Reed having treated her in her last sickness which occurred 22nd of December, 1888. They are the parents of said John J. Reed. Reuben Reed is now a feble (sic.) old man unable to labor. Has always been since I knew him an honest temperate man I have known him thirty years. Sign: Dr. L.W. Clark. (Document courtesy of Schuyler County Jail Museum and Historical Society.)

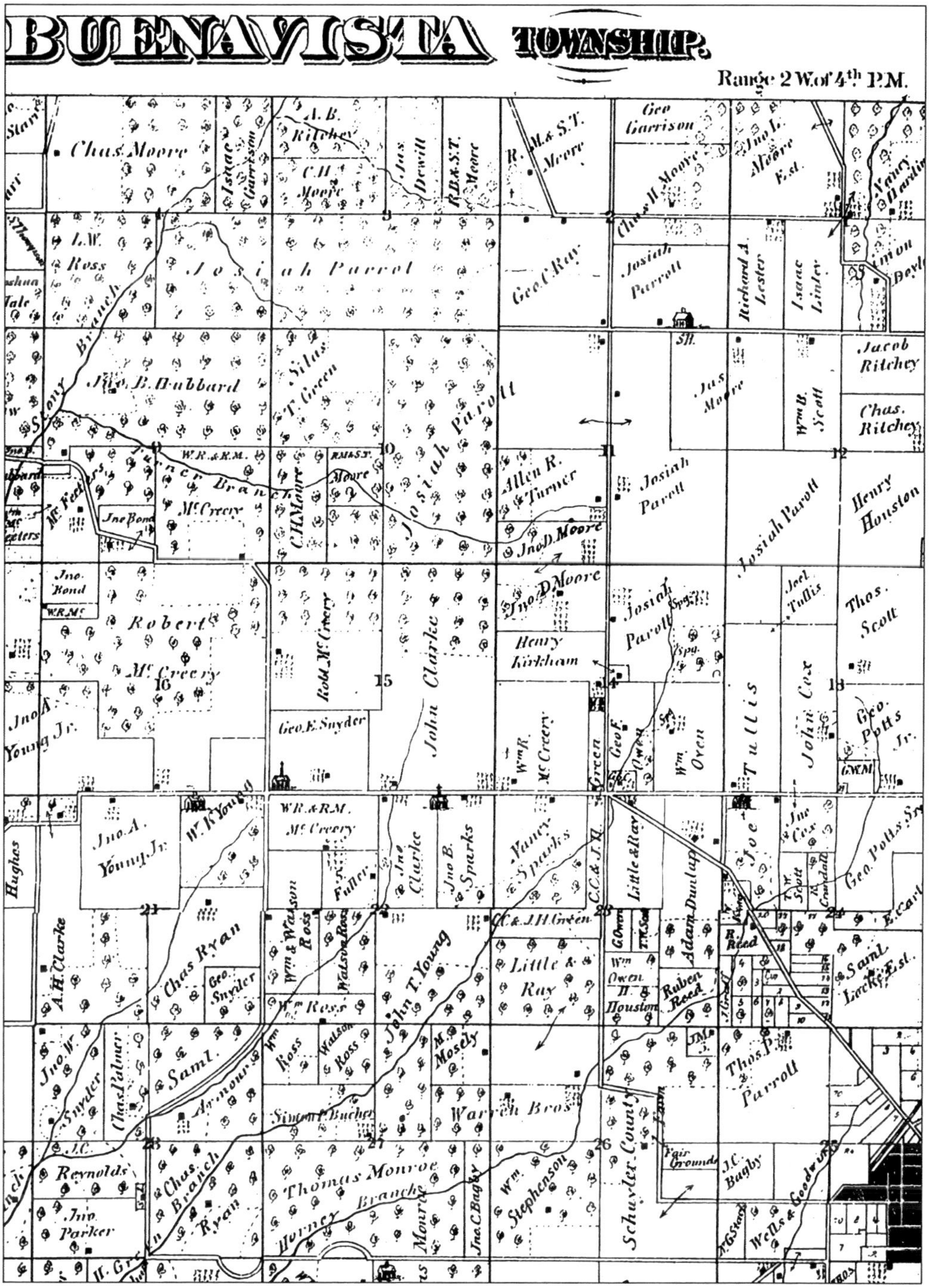

This map of the Buena Vista Township, of which Rushville was a part, illustrates the property and land plots owned by the citizens of Rushville at the time that the Reed family resided there. (Document courtesy of Schuyler County Jail Museum and Historical Society.)

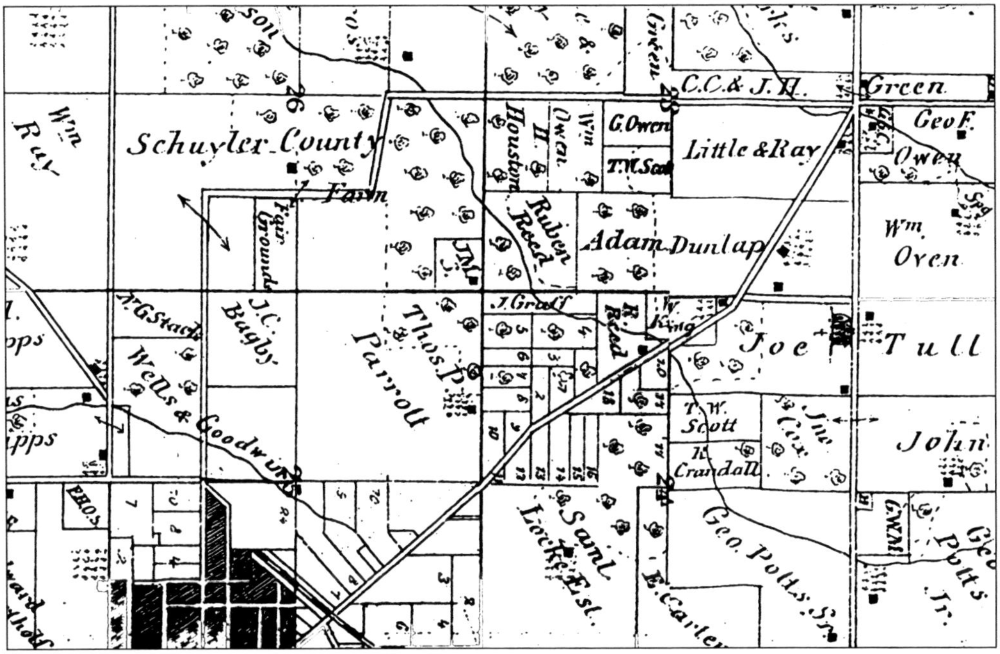

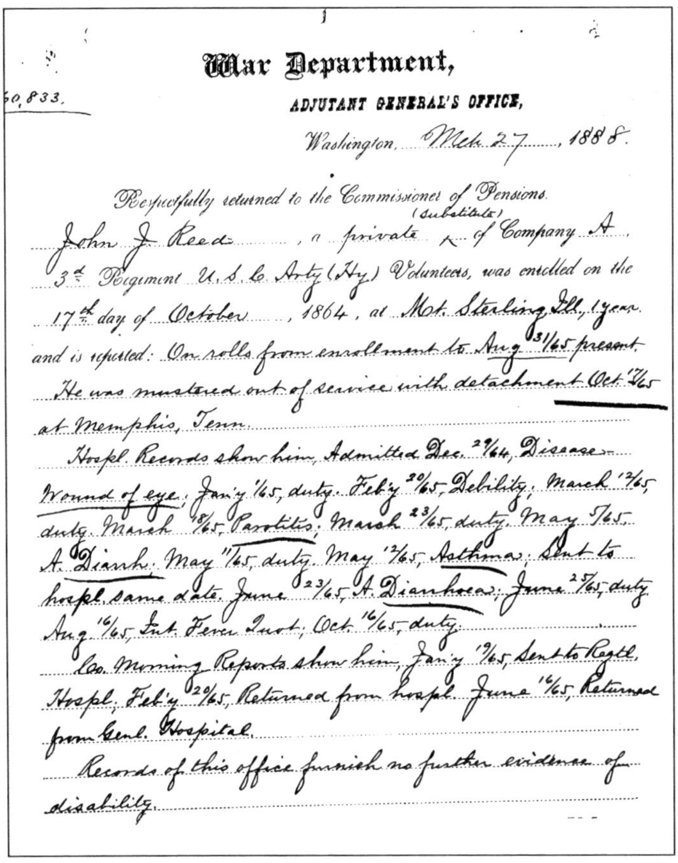

60,833.

War Department,

ADJUTANT GENERAL'S OFFICE,

Washington, Mch 27, 1888.

Respectfully returned to the Commissioner of Pensions.

John J. Reed, a private (substitute) of Company A, 3d Regiment U.S.C. Arty (Hy) Volunteers, was enrolled on the 17th day of October, 1864, at Mt. Sterling Ill, 1 year and is reported: On rolls from enrollment to Aug 31/65 present. He was mustered out of service with detachment Oct 7/65 at Memphis, Tenn.

Hospl. Records show him, Admitted Dec. 29/64, Disease Wound of eye; Jan'y 1/65, duty. Feb'y 20/65, Debility; March 12/65, duty. March 18/65, Parotitis; March 23/65, duty. May 5/65, A. Diarrh. May 11/65, duty. May 12/65, Asthma; Sent to hospl same date. June 23/65, A. Diarrhoea; June 25/65, duty. Aug 16/65, Int. Fever Quot; Oct. 16/65, duty.

Co. Morning Reports show him, Jan'y 19/65, Sent to Regtl. Hospl. Feb'y 20/65, Returned from hospl. June 16/65, Returned from Genl. Hospital.

Records of this office furnish no further evidence of disability.

This document provides a closer view of the land plots that were owned by Reuben Reed of Rushville. (Document courtesy of the Schuyler County Jail Museum and Historical Society.)

This document from the war department records John J. Reed's time spent in the military during the Civil War. He enrolled in October 1864, and was discharged October 1865, at Memphis, Tennessee. This document is further revealing of the illnesses that Reed suffered during war that was not unlike many other Civil War soldiers. (Document courtesy of the Schuyler County Jail Museum and Historical Society.)

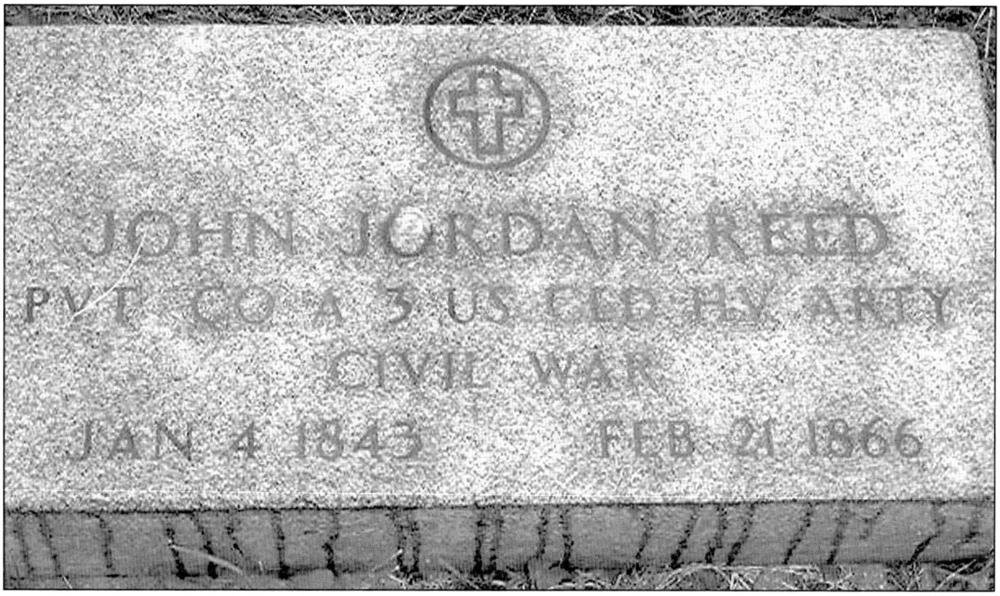

John Jordan Reed was laid at his final resting-place in the Rushville, Illinois, cemetery. His war injuries and illnesses consumed him at the family home on February 21, 1866. (Photo courtesy of the author.)

On June 11, 1889, at the age of 73, Reuben Reed also petitioned for the pension from his son's service in the "war of the rebellion." (Document courtesy of the Schuyler County Jail Museum and Historical Society.)

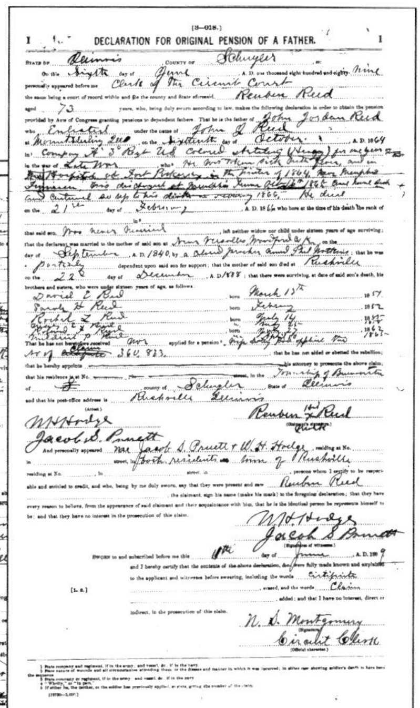
DECLARATION FOR ORIGINAL PENSION OF A FATHER.

State of Illinois, County of Schuyler

On this Sixth day of June, A.D. one thousand eight hundred and eighty-nine personally appeared before me Clerk of the Circuit Court ... Reuben Reed aged 73 years ... That he is the father of John Jordan Reed who enlisted under the name of John J Reed ... in Company A 3rd Regt US Colored Artillery (Heavy) ...

on the 21st day of February, A.D. 1866 ...

Reuben Reed

W.H. Hodge
Jacob S. Pruett

N. D. Montgomery
Circuit Clerk

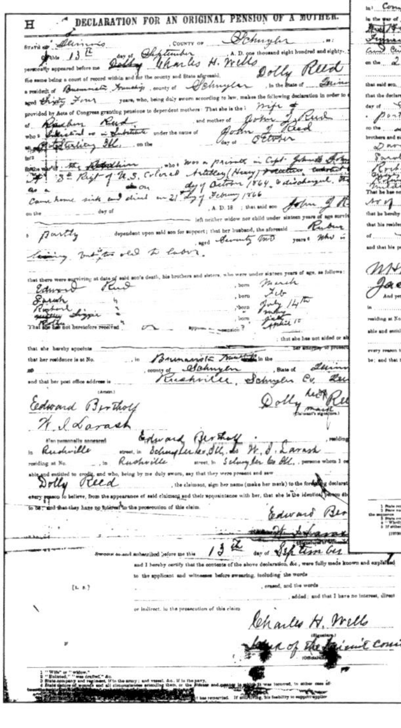
DECLARATION FOR AN ORIGINAL PENSION OF A MOTHER.

State of Illinois, County of Schuyler

... 13th day of September ... Charles H. Wells ... Dolly Reed ... aged Sixty Four years ... that she is the wife of Reuben Reed and mother of John J Reed ... 3rd Regt of U.S. Colored Artillery (Heavy) ... Came home sick and died on 21st day of February 1866 ...

Edward Berthof
H. I. Larash

Dolly Reed

Charles H. Wells
Clerk of the Circuit Court

On September 13, 1867, his mother Dolly Reed filed for the pension owed her for her son's service in the "war of the rebellion." (Document courtesy of the Schuyler County Jail Museum and Historical Society.)

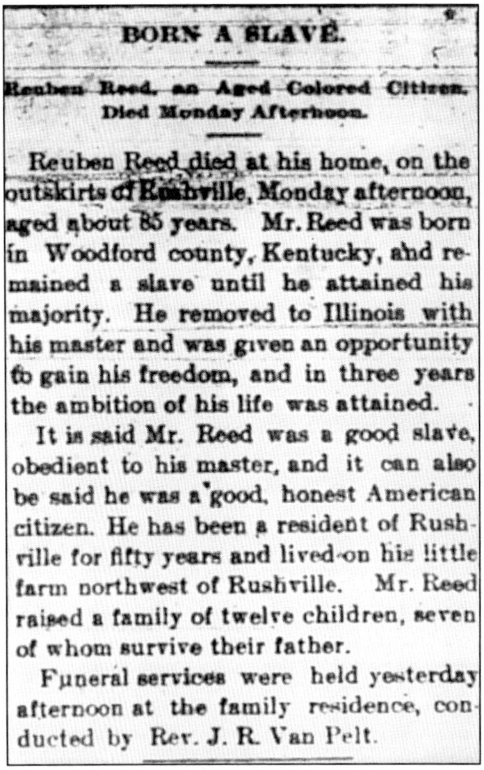

BORN A SLAVE.

Reuben Reed, an Aged Colored Citizen, Died Monday Afternoon.

Reuben Reed died at his home, on the outskirts of Rushville, Monday afternoon, aged about 85 years. Mr. Reed was born in Woodford county, Kentucky, and remained a slave until he attained his majority. He removed to Illinois with his master and was given an opportunity to gain his freedom, and in three years the ambition of his life was attained.

It is said Mr. Reed was a good slave, obedient to his master, and it can also be said he was a good, honest American citizen. He has been a resident of Rushville for fifty years and lived on his little farm northwest of Rushville. Mr. Reed raised a family of twelve children, seven of whom survive their father.

Funeral services were held yesterday afternoon at the family residence, conducted by Rev. J. R. Van Pelt.

Reuben Reed lived out the remaining years of his life just on the outskirts of the town of Rushville. *The Rushville Times* made note of his passing on May 22, 1902, at the age of 87, according to his tombstone. (Document courtesy of the Schuyler County Jail Museum and Historical Society.)

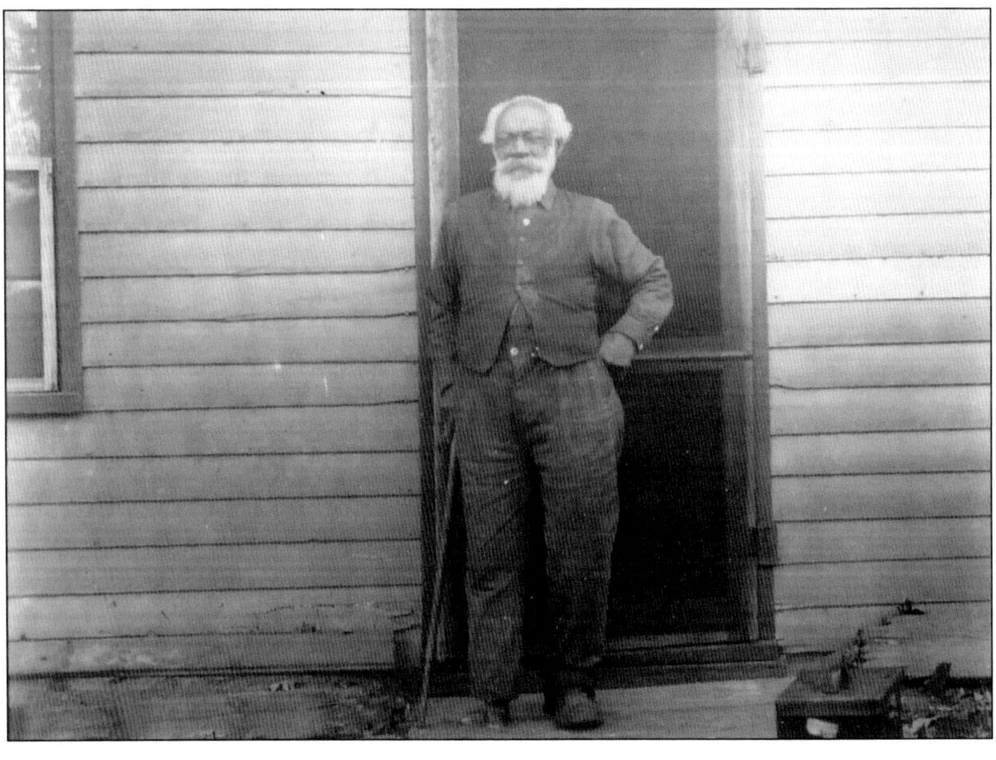

Charley Wilson is believed to be the only African American to have ever lived at Port Byron in Rock Island County. It is widely reported that while helping with the local elections to elect William McKinley to the presidency, Wilson was shot in the leg. This led to him living with a peg leg later in life. He became a very well respected "veterinary doctor" in the local area after the war. (Photo courtesy Special Collections, Augustana College Library, Rock Island, Illinois.)

Two

SERVING FAMILY, COMMUNITY, AND MILITARY

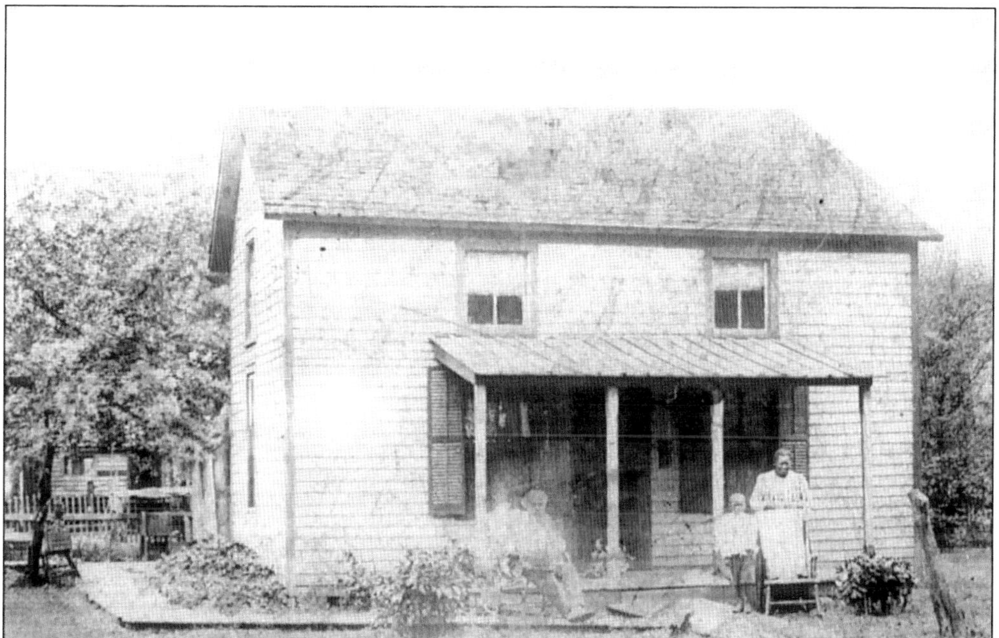

The Daniels family of Macomb was the first African-American family to settle in Macomb after the Civil War. Their home was at the corner of Mechanic and Pierce Streets on the east end of town. The Daniels settled in Macomb in 1867. (Courtesy of the Archives and Special Collections, Western Illinois University Library.)

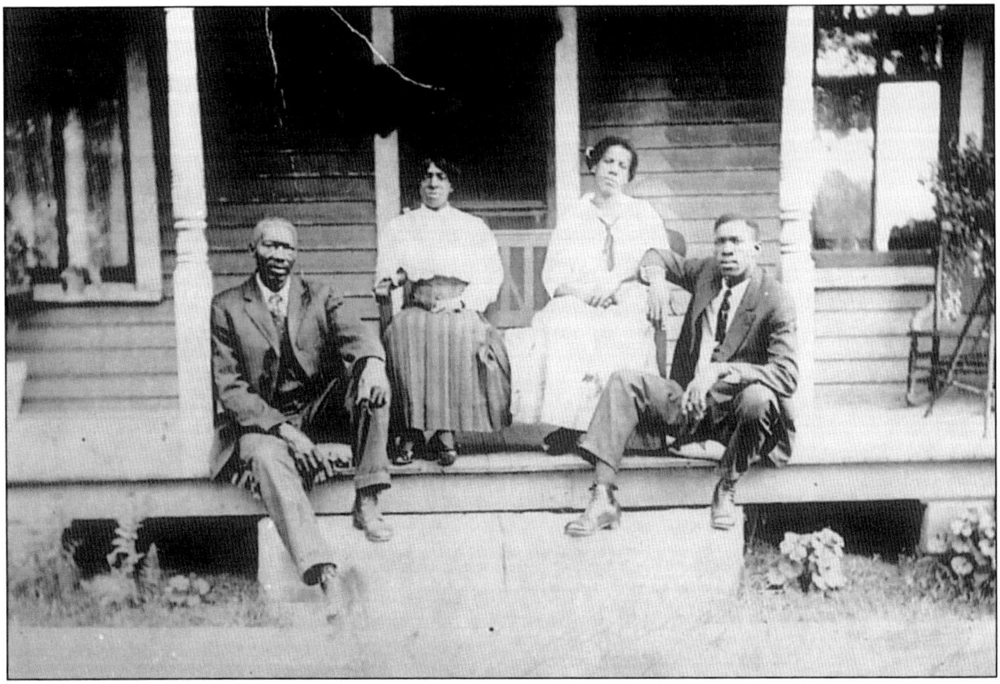

Here the Daniels family poses for a group shot. From left to right are: Sanford, wife Millie Daniels, stepdaughter, and Joseph Daniels Sr. This photograph was taken in 1921. (Courtesy of the Archives and Special Collections, Western Illinois University Library.)

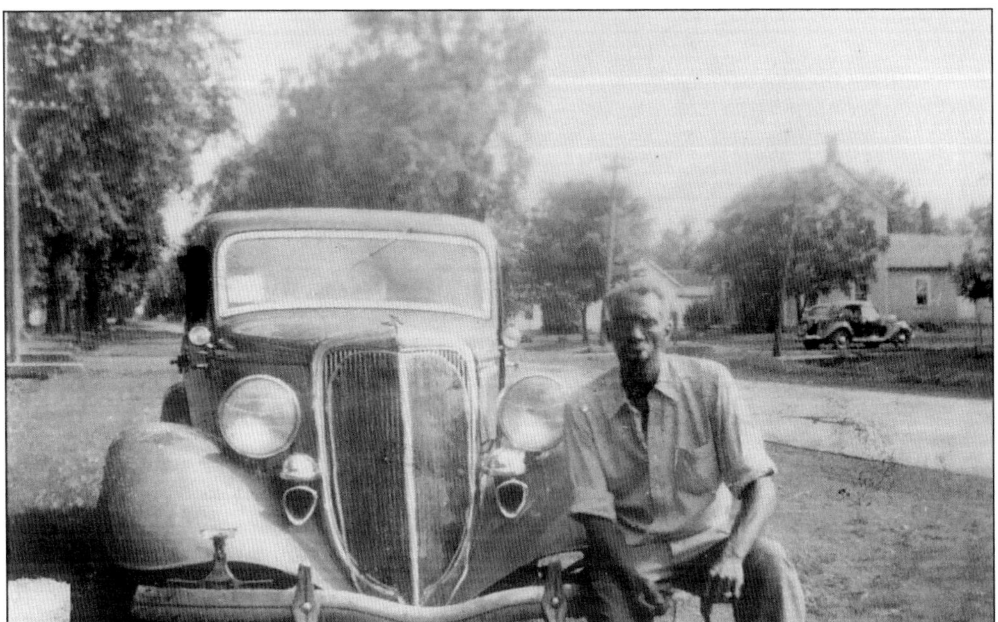

Joseph Daniels poses on the family car in 1940. Local legend reports that the Daniels were the first African Americans to own an automobile in the town of Macomb. (Courtesy of the Archives and Special Collections, Western Illinois University.)

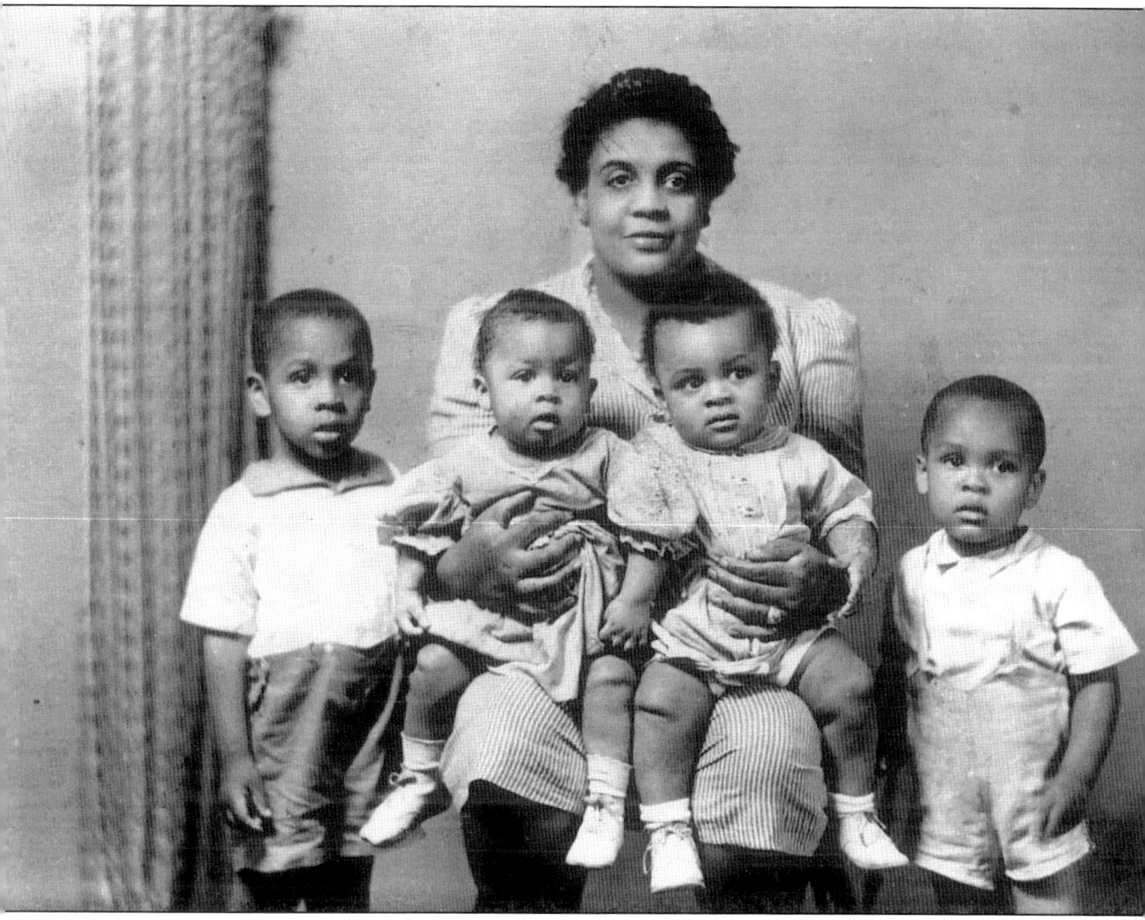

The Thorpes and Coopers were some of Macomb's earliest black families. Pearl Cooper Thorpe posed with her four children. They are, from left to right: Lewis, Ardith, Aaron, and Wayman Thorpe. (Courtesy of the Archives and Special Collections, Western Illinois University.)

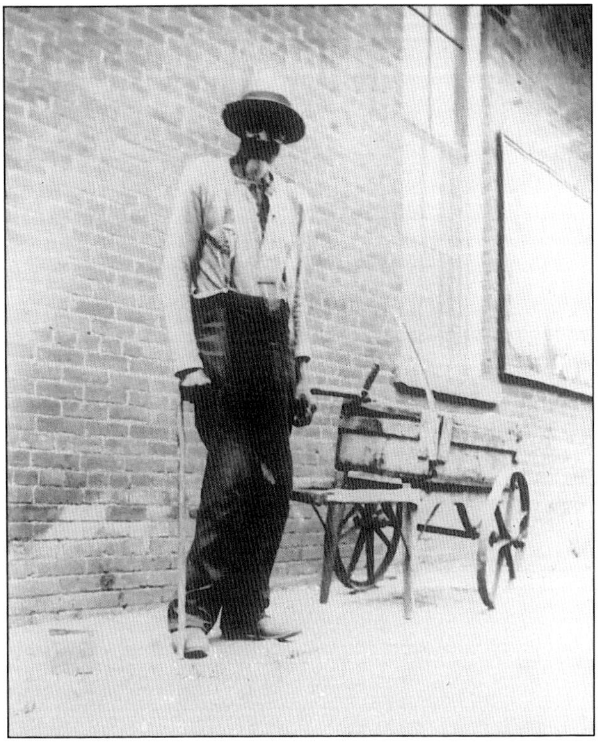

Peter Cooper was the patriarch of the Cooper family of Macomb. (Courtesy of the Archives and Special Collections, Western Illinois University Library.)

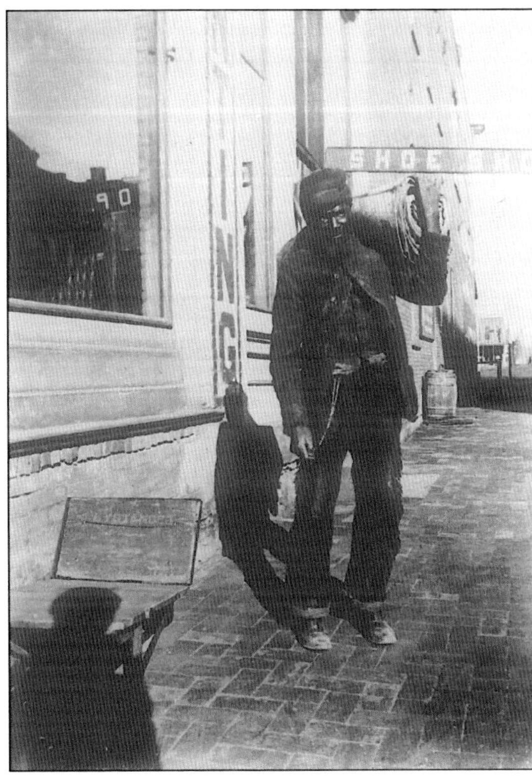

Nathan Thorpe was the patriarch of the Thorpe family and the town of Macomb's flag bearer for major events such as Flag Day, Fourth of July, and Memorial Day parades. Here he is pictured with the flag rolled up, being carried over his shoulder. (Courtesy of the Archives and Special Collections, Western Illinois University.)

An unidentifiable woman of Macomb is pictured at the turn of the nineteenth and into the twentieth century. This photograph was discovered amongst the Daniels family pictorial collection. (Courtesy of the Archives and Special Collections, Western Illinois University Library.)

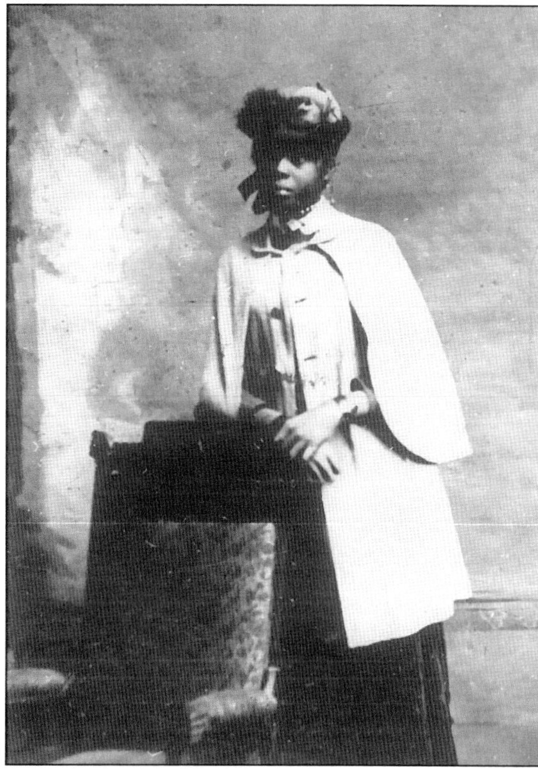

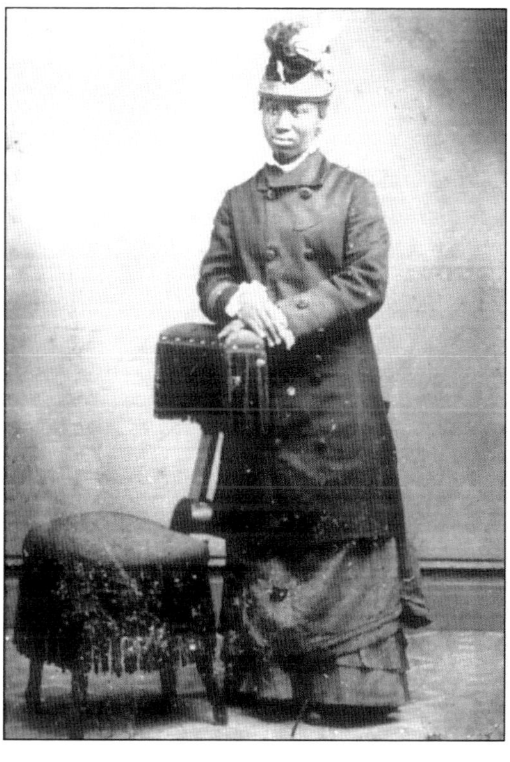

This is another unidentifiable woman of Macomb at the turn of the twentieth century. The photograph was discovered amongst the Daniels family pictorial collection. (Courtesy of the Archives and Special Collections, Western Illinois University Library.)

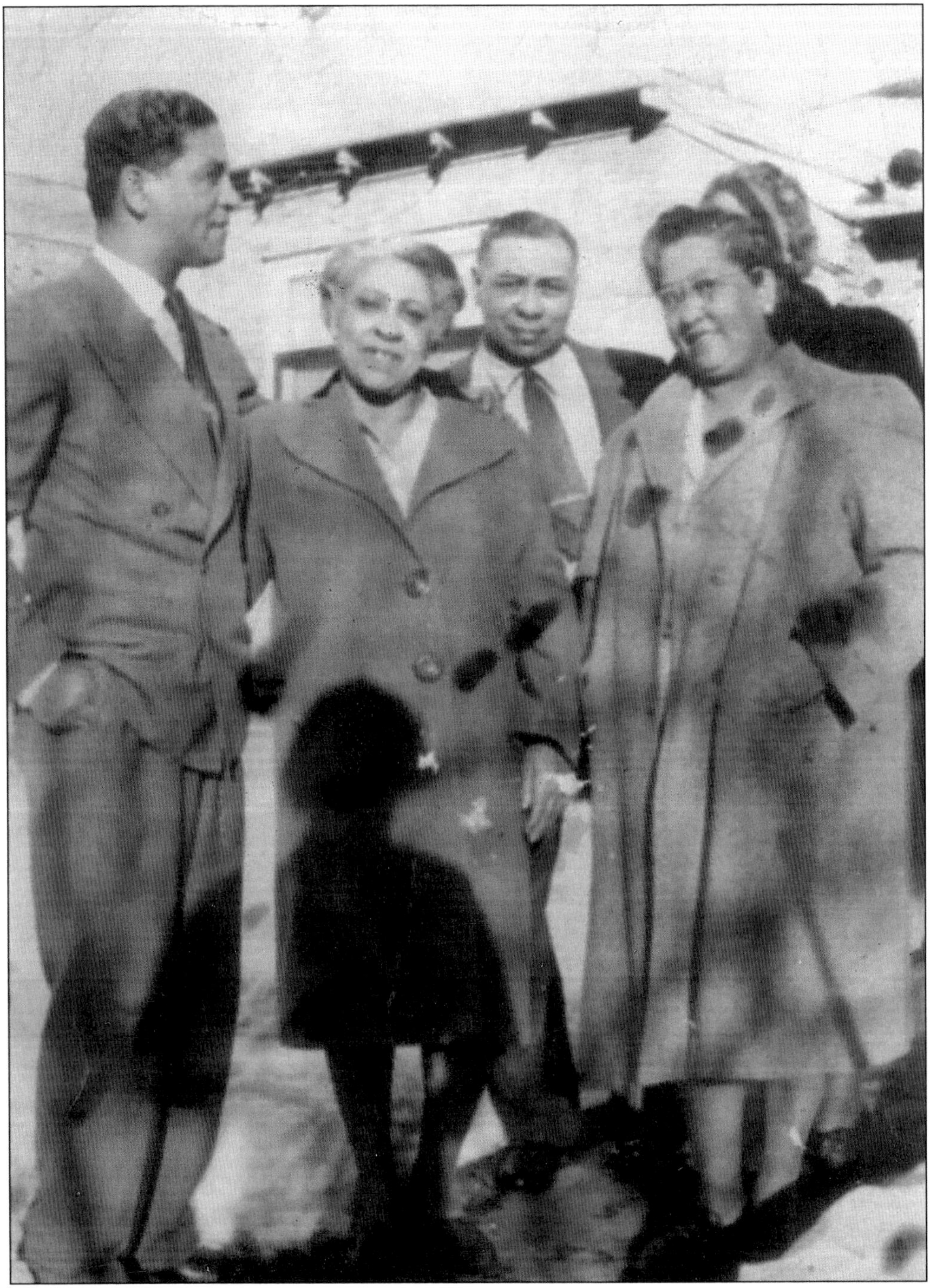

Ethel Thorpe and her siblings are pictured at a family gathering, date unknown. The Thorpes are a long-standing family in the Macomb community. From left to right are: Gilbert Broach Thorpe, Ethel Thorpe, Will Ashby Thorpe, hidden is Edna Thorpe King, and Naomi Thorpe Hutson. (Courtesy of the Archives and Special Collections, Western Illinois University Library.)

A group of women pose in Macomb, Illinois, but none could be identified. This photograph was discovered amongst the Daniels family pictorial collection. (Courtesy of the Archives and Special Collections, Western Illinois University Library.)

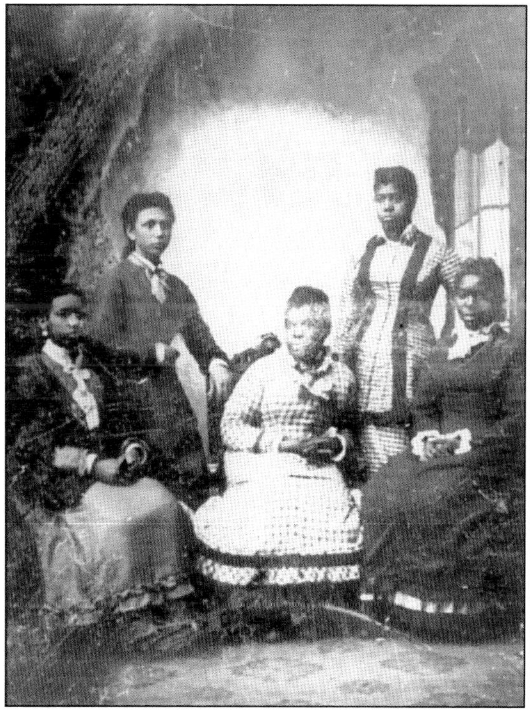

This is an unidentifiable family that was settled in Galesburg by the late nineteenth century. (Courtesy of Knox College Archives, Galesburg, Illinois.)

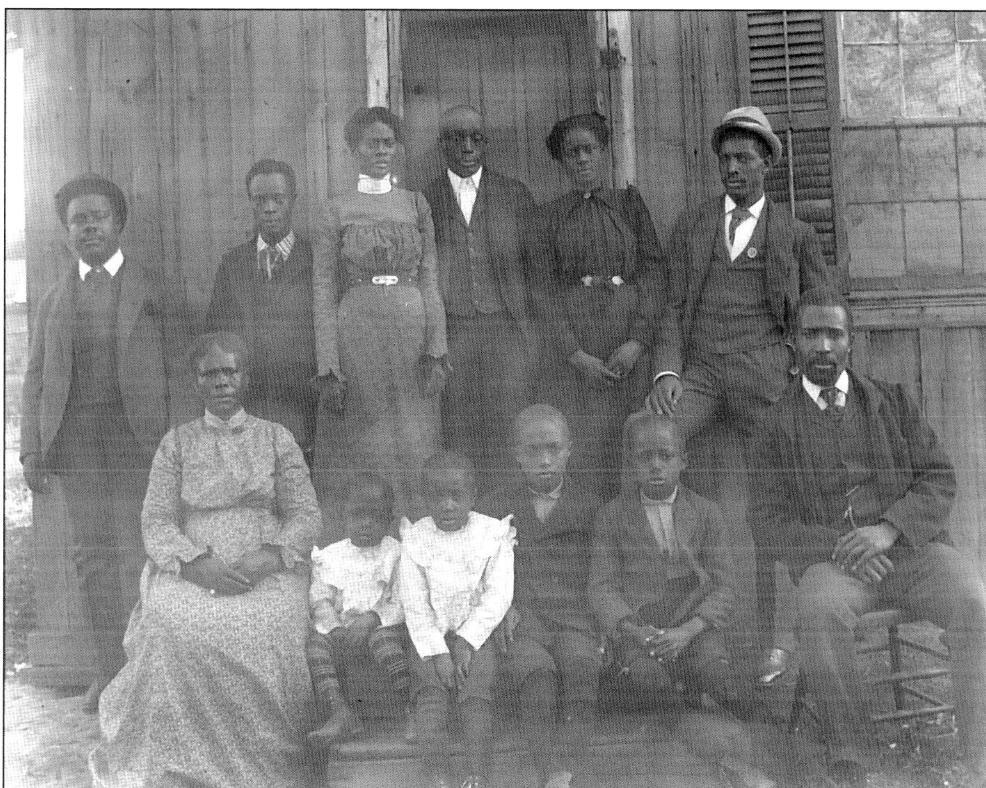

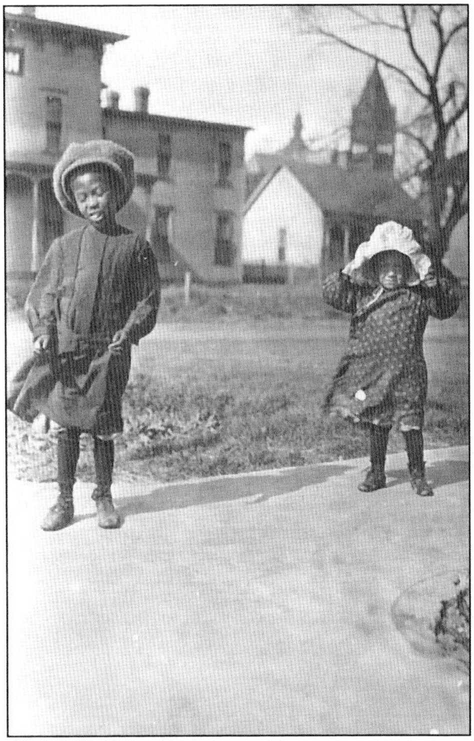

Two girls are shown here playing in Galesburg. (Courtesy of Knox College Archives, Galesburg, Illinois.)

Three young African-American boys are pictured playing in an open field area in Galesburg. (Courtesy of Knox College Archives, Galesburg, Illinois.)

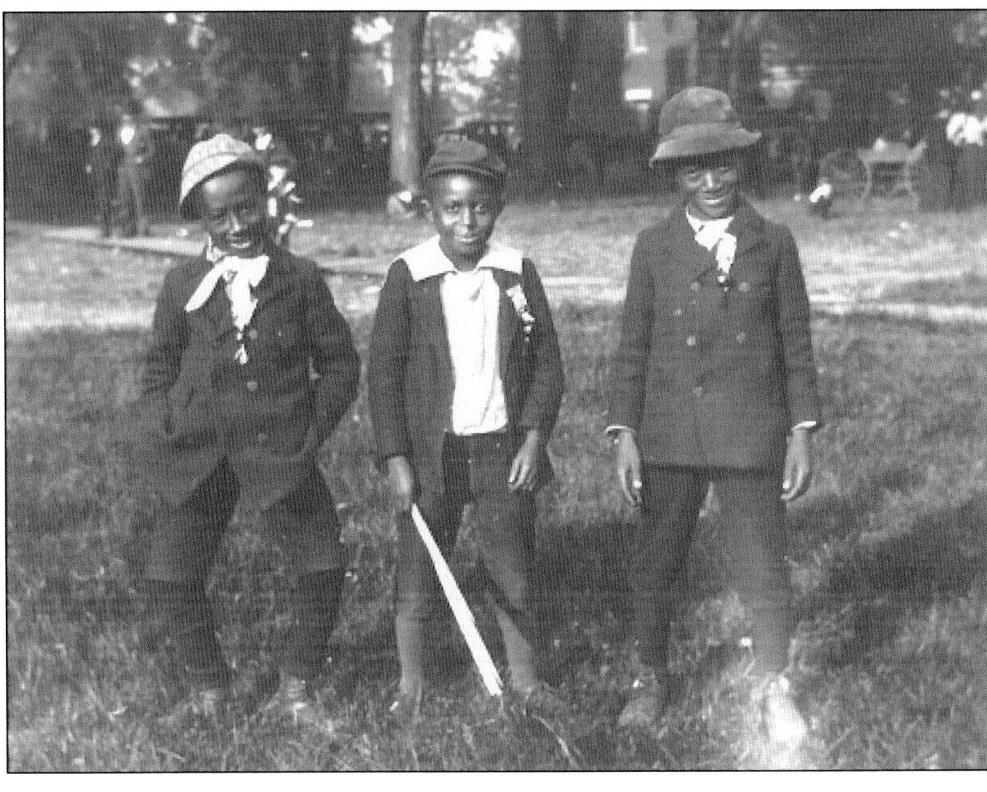

This little one was labeled "Happy Boy" amongst the collection. (Courtesy of Knox College Archives, Galesburg, Illinois.)

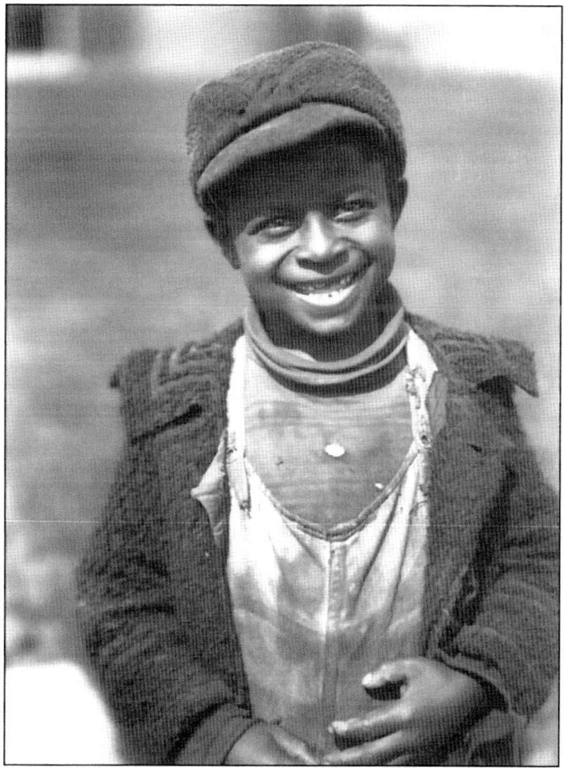

Here two women and a man pose for the camera at their family home in Galesburg early in the twentieth century. (Courtesy of Knox College Archives, Galesburg, Illinois.)

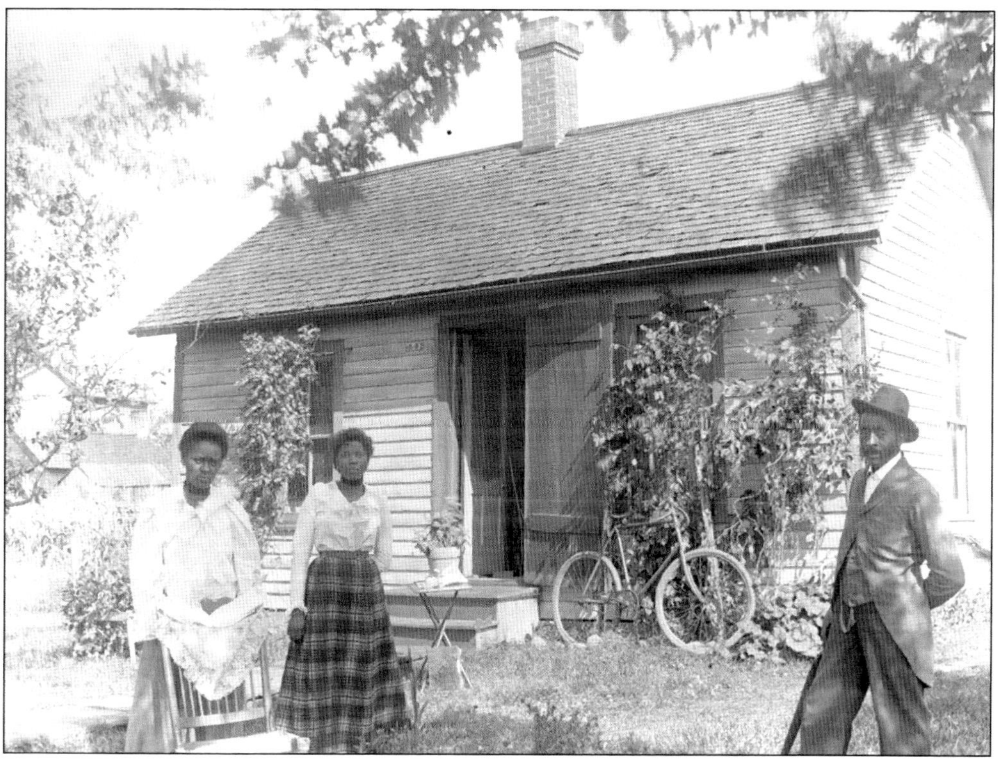

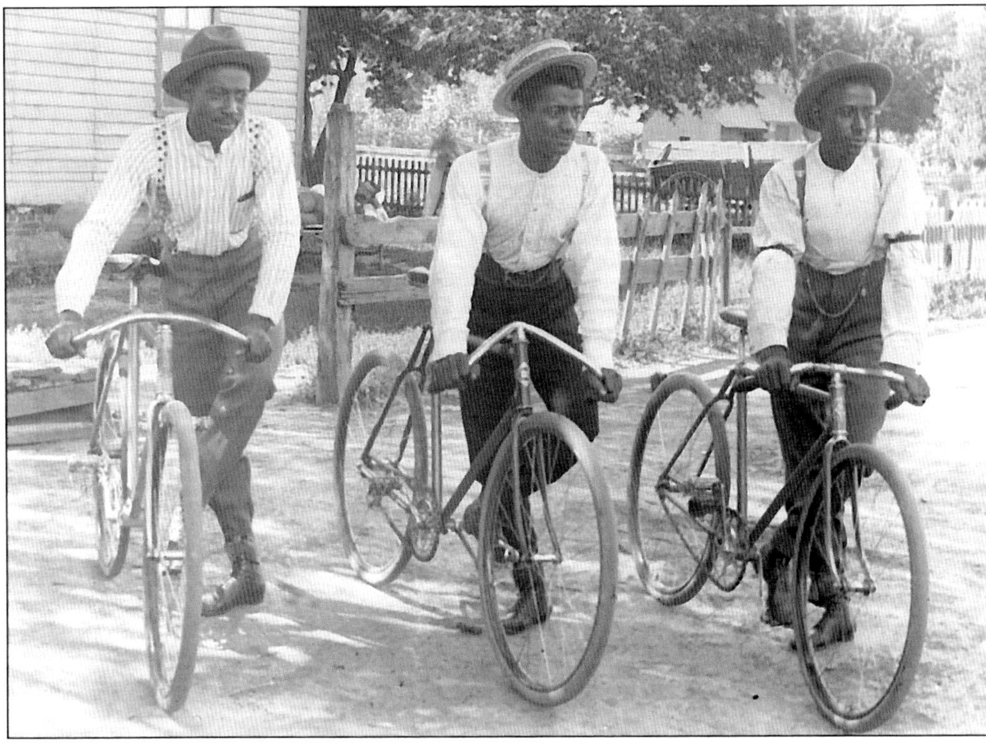

Three young men are pictured showing off their bicycles, possibly preparing for a race in Galesburg. (Courtesy of Knox College Archives, Galesburg, Illinois.)

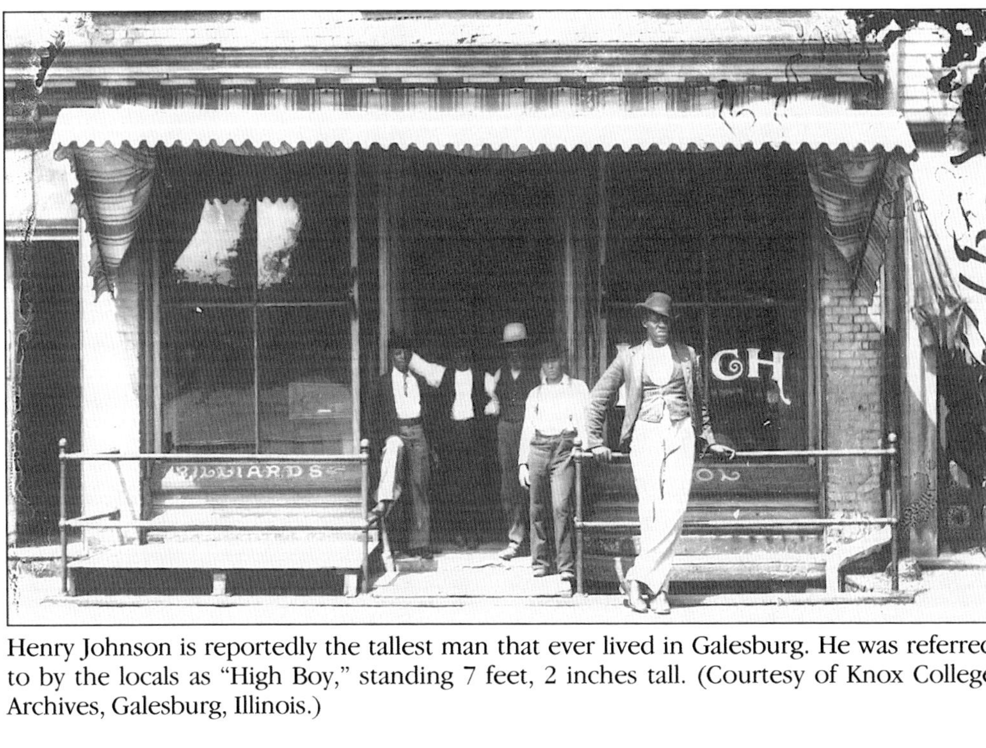

Henry Johnson is reportedly the tallest man that ever lived in Galesburg. He was referred to by the locals as "High Boy," standing 7 feet, 2 inches tall. (Courtesy of Knox College Archives, Galesburg, Illinois.)

HIGH-BOY ATTRACTS ATTENTION

Galesburg's Colored Giant Is Viewed With Interest at Moline.

The Moline Republican-Journal has this to say of a well-known Galesburg citizen:

"It would have been nice if the Plow company had had its new sky-scraper up, just as a comparison to Henry Johnson, a colored man, who is the tallest man who has visited Moline. Perhaps this is a little stretched—but so is Johnson. He has attracted considerable attention on our streets the past few days. He is known as the 'High Boy,' and this is not a misnomer, for he measures 7 feet net, and with his shoes on his height is 7 feet 2 inches. He is 26 years old and weighs 260 pounds, and looks it, though his feet rattle around in No. 7 shoes, indicating that a small beginning oftimes has a big ending, figuring fro mthe ground up. Mr. Johnson is from Galesburg, and is the giant of his family. His father is a short man, yet heavy, and his mother is a medium-sized woman. He was born in Galesburg, and told a Journal reporter that he was always an overgrown boy. He enjoys the best of health, and notwithstanding his giant proportions, enjoys life.

"His chief occupation since he has been big enough to earn his own livelihood has been in the advertising line, and for some time he has been in the service of the 'Adlake' Bicycle company, riding a specially built wheel for advertising purposes. At Galesburg he led the street fair as one of the chief productions of that city, and attracted attention which gave him a reputation as the giant of Illinois. Since then his services have been in demand. He is a very pleasant gentleman and a good conversationalist,and it is possible that he may be engaged to take part in our free street fair.

"There are a great many possibilities for a man of his size, and yet his extreme height has its drawbacks, and these sometimes prove quite expensive. It isn't every hotel that can accommodate him with a bed, nor can he borrow his neighbor's clothes.

"He has been enjoying a visit to the family of Charles Anderson, on Fourteenth street near Fourth avenue, who recently moved here from Galesburg. The 'High Boy' leaves here for home this evening."

Henry Johnson was viewed as a novelty. He attracted much attention throughout west central Illinois. Upon one visit to Moline, the local newspaper ran this story about his visit. (Courtesy of Knox College Archives, Galesburg, Illinois.)

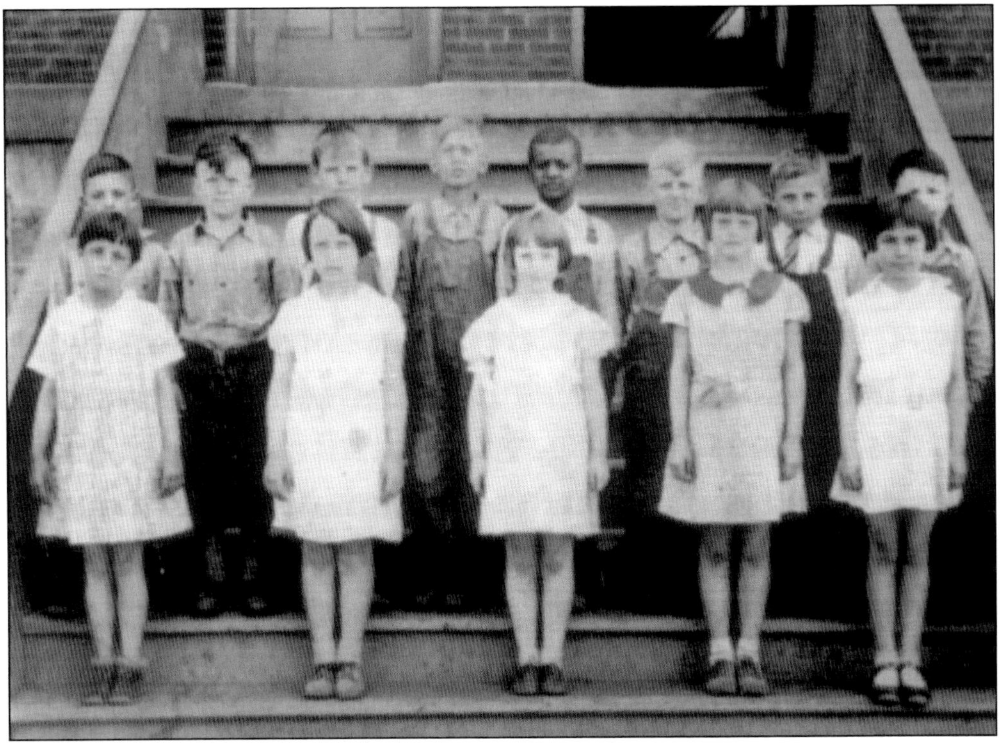

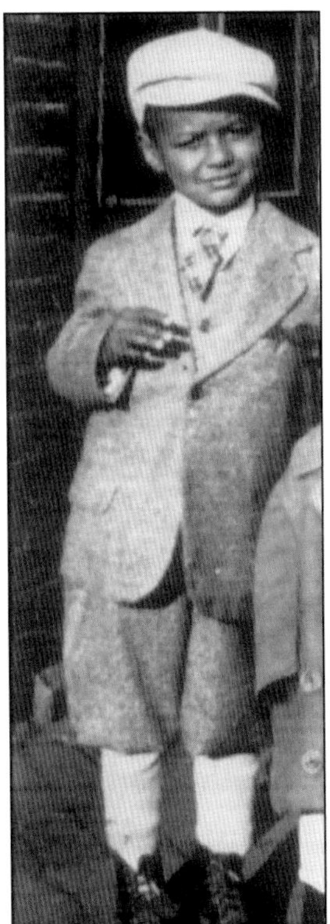

Civil Rights Pioneer and Activist C.T. Vivian is pictured as a schoolboy in Macomb, Illinois. C.T. Vivian, his mother, and his grandmother moved to Macomb in the 1930s, as the family sought to escape the harsh realities of the Depression in the city of St. Louis, Missouri. (Courtesy of C.T. Vivian Personal Collection.)

Civil Rights Activist C.T. Vivian is shown dressed up in his Sunday best in Macomb. (Courtesy of C.T. Vivian Personal Collection.)

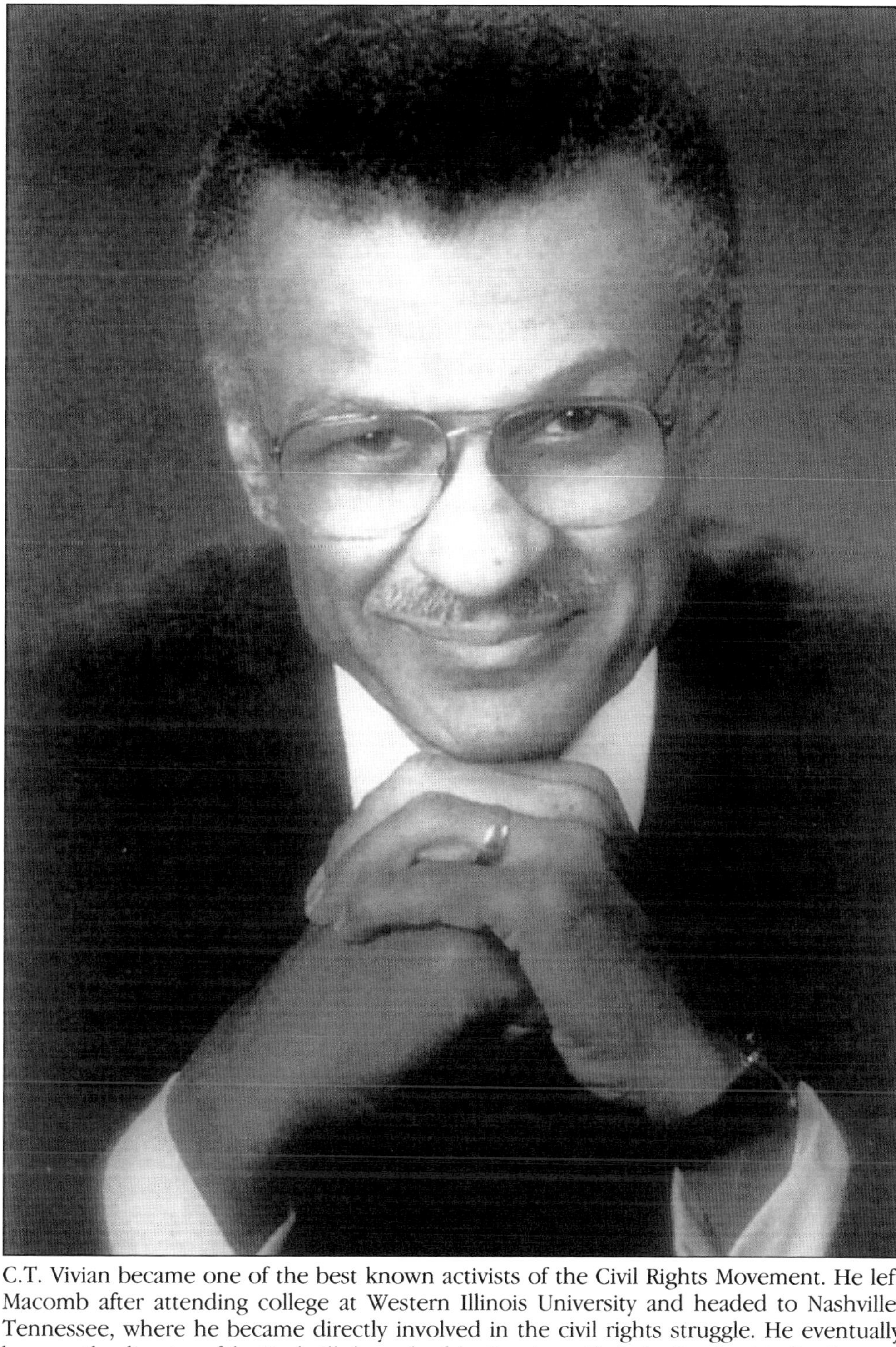

C.T. Vivian became one of the best known activists of the Civil Rights Movement. He left Macomb after attending college at Western Illinois University and headed to Nashville, Tennessee, where he became directly involved in the civil rights struggle. He eventually became the director of the Nashville branch of the Southern Christian Leadership Conference (SCLC). (Courtesy of C.T. Vivian Personal Collection.)

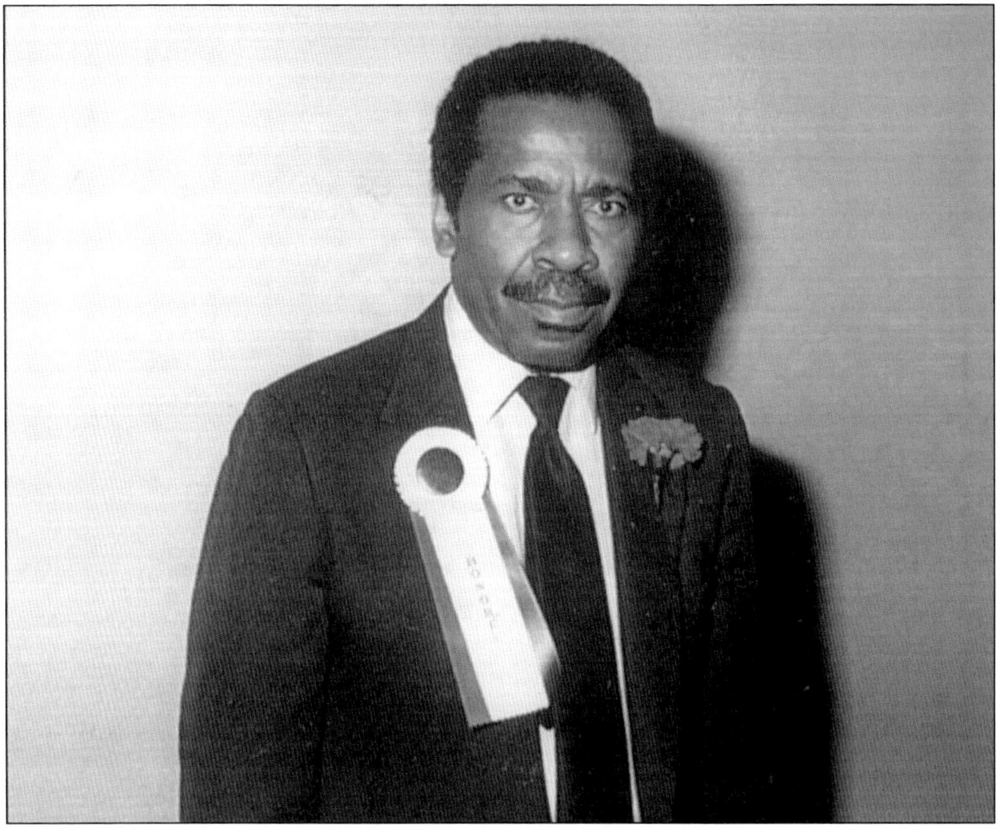

John Gwynn Jr. was president of the Peoria, Illinois, branch of the NAACP, and eventually he became the president of the Illinois Conference of the NAACP Branches. He was perhaps the most well known leader of the Peoria NAACP Branch, leading the group during the turbulent '60s. (Courtesy of African American Hall of Fame Museum Collection, Peoria, Illinois.)

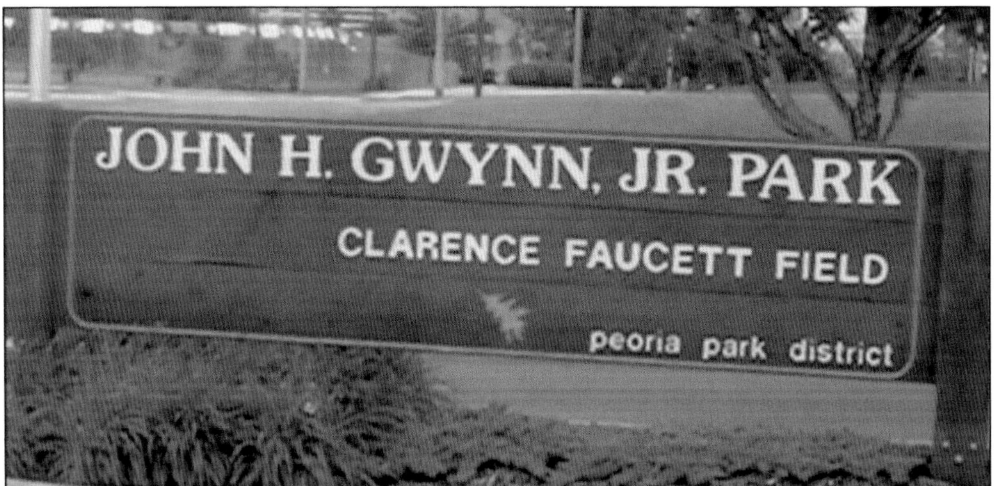

John H. Gwynn Jr. is remembered throughout the city of Peoria by this park named in his honor. (Courtesy of the author.)

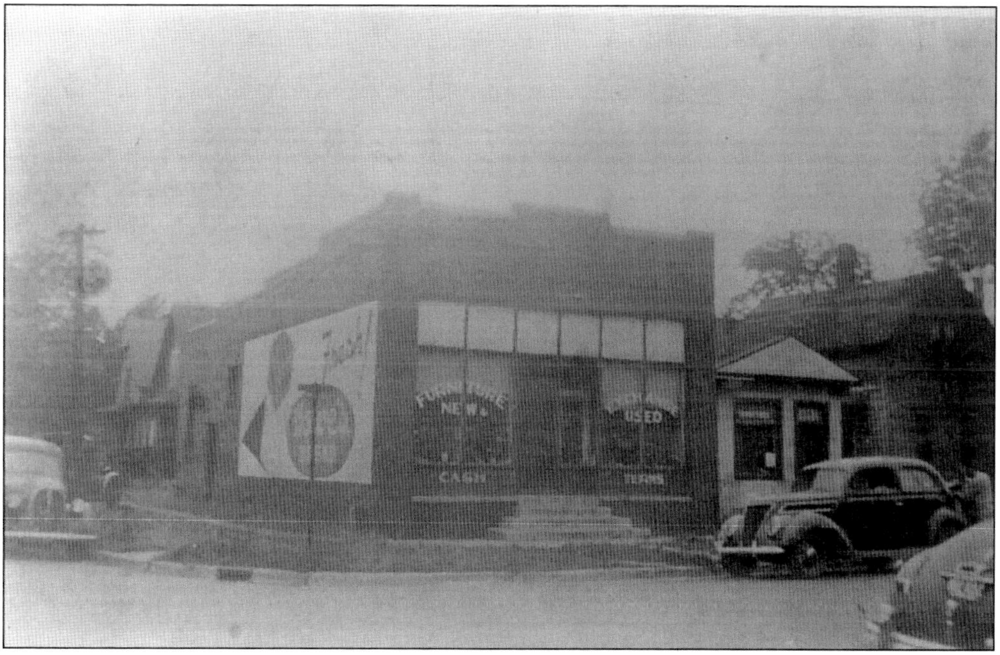

Pictured above is the first known African-American community center in west central Illinois. The temporary U.S.O. Service Center (and formerly the Mary Bethune Day Nursery), July 1, 1943 through February 11, 1944, of Galesburg, Illinois. (Courtesy of Steve Abrams Personal Collection, Galesburg, Illinois.)

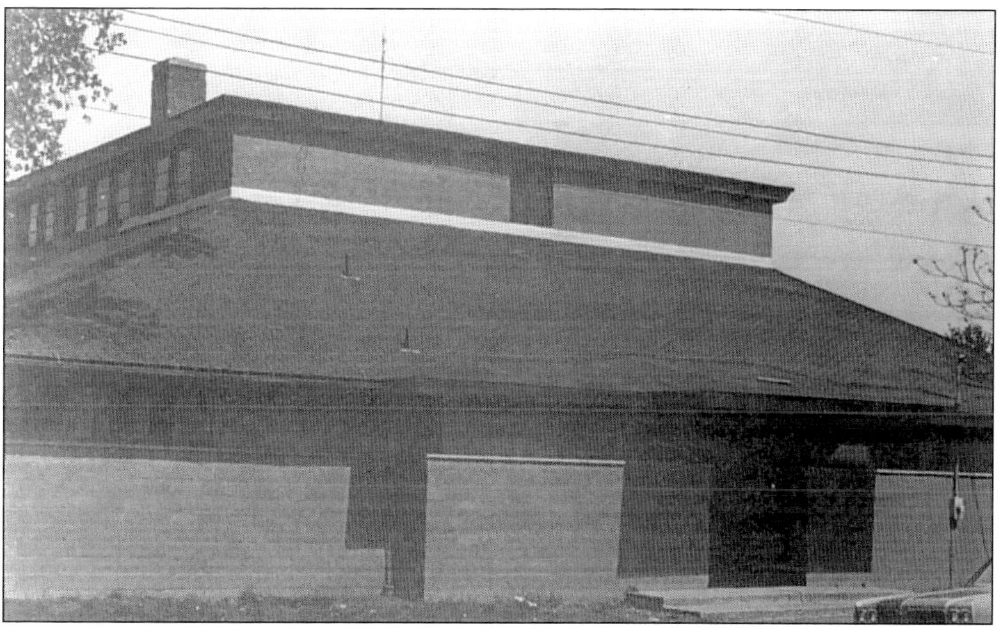

By February 12, 1944, the black community of Galesburg had constructed a permanent site for a new home to house its community center. It has since been known as the George Washington Carver Community Center. (Courtesy of Steve Abrams Personal Collection, Galesburg, Illinois.)

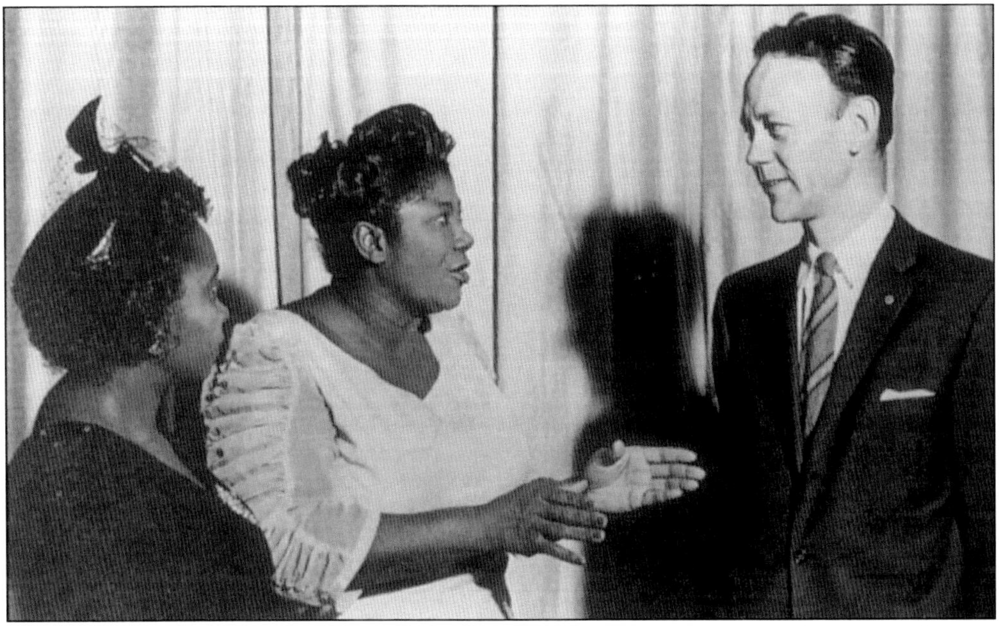

When gospel diva Mahalia Jackson came to the town of Galesburg in 1960, she paid a visit to the Carver Center. Here, Mrs. Willa Bell H. Williams, executive director of the center, and Mayor Cabeen of Galesburg, flanked Ms. Jackson. (Courtesy of Steve Abrams Personal Collection, Galesburg, Illinois.)

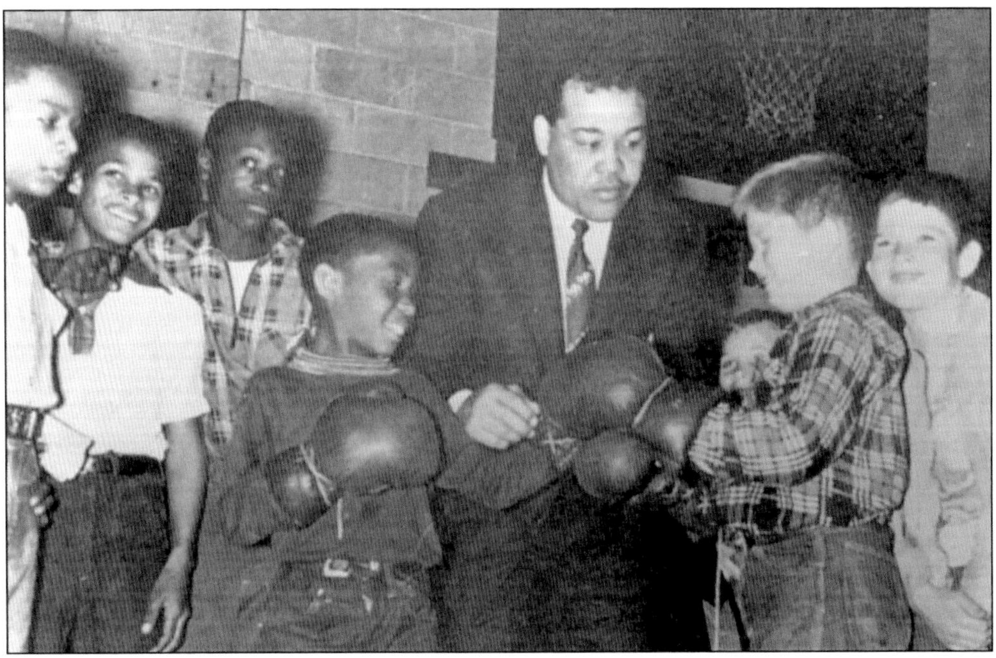

Early in its history, the Carver Center played host to local black and white children of the community, particularly when someone such as Boxer Joe Louis (The Brown Bomber) came to town. Joe Louis visited Galesburg during the late 1940s or 1950s. (Courtesy of Steve Abrams Personal Collection, Galesburg, Illinois.)

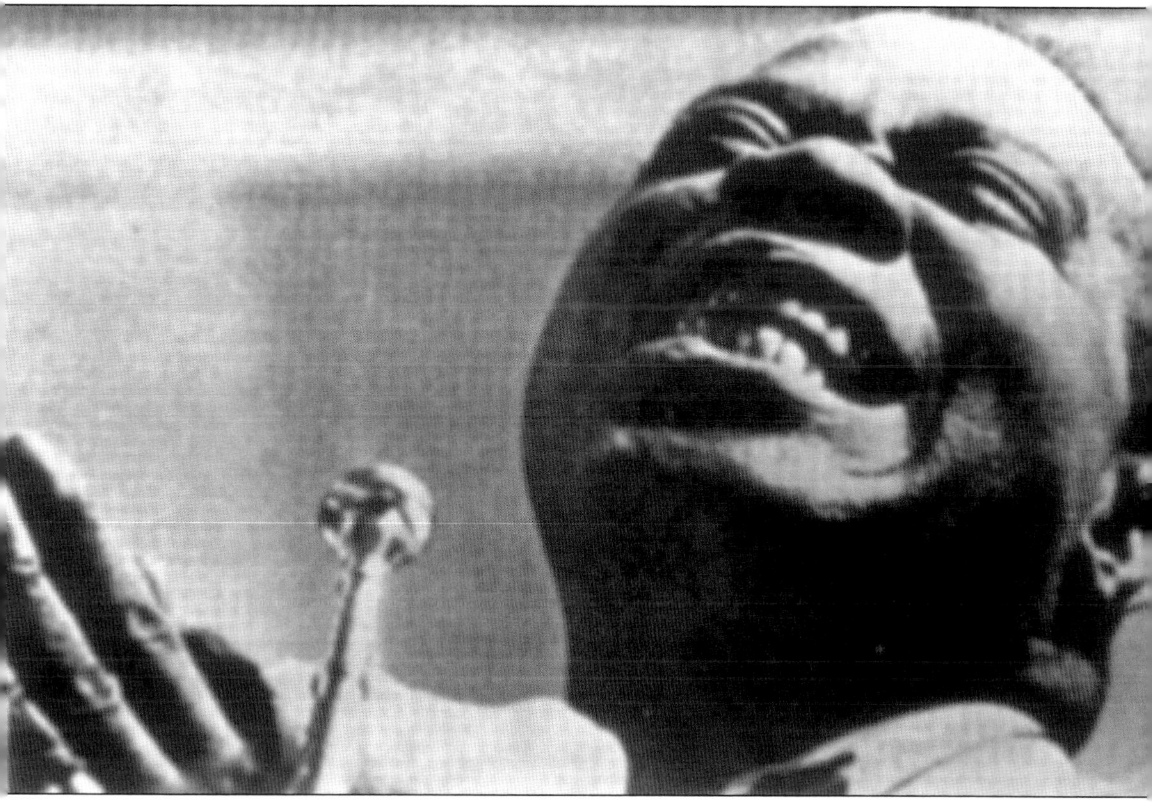

The George Washington Carver Center of Galesburg welcomed such well-known and legendary performers as Louis Armstrong. This photograph was taken of Armstrong during his performance at the Carver Center. (Courtesy of Steve Abrams Personal Collection, Galesburg, Illinois.)

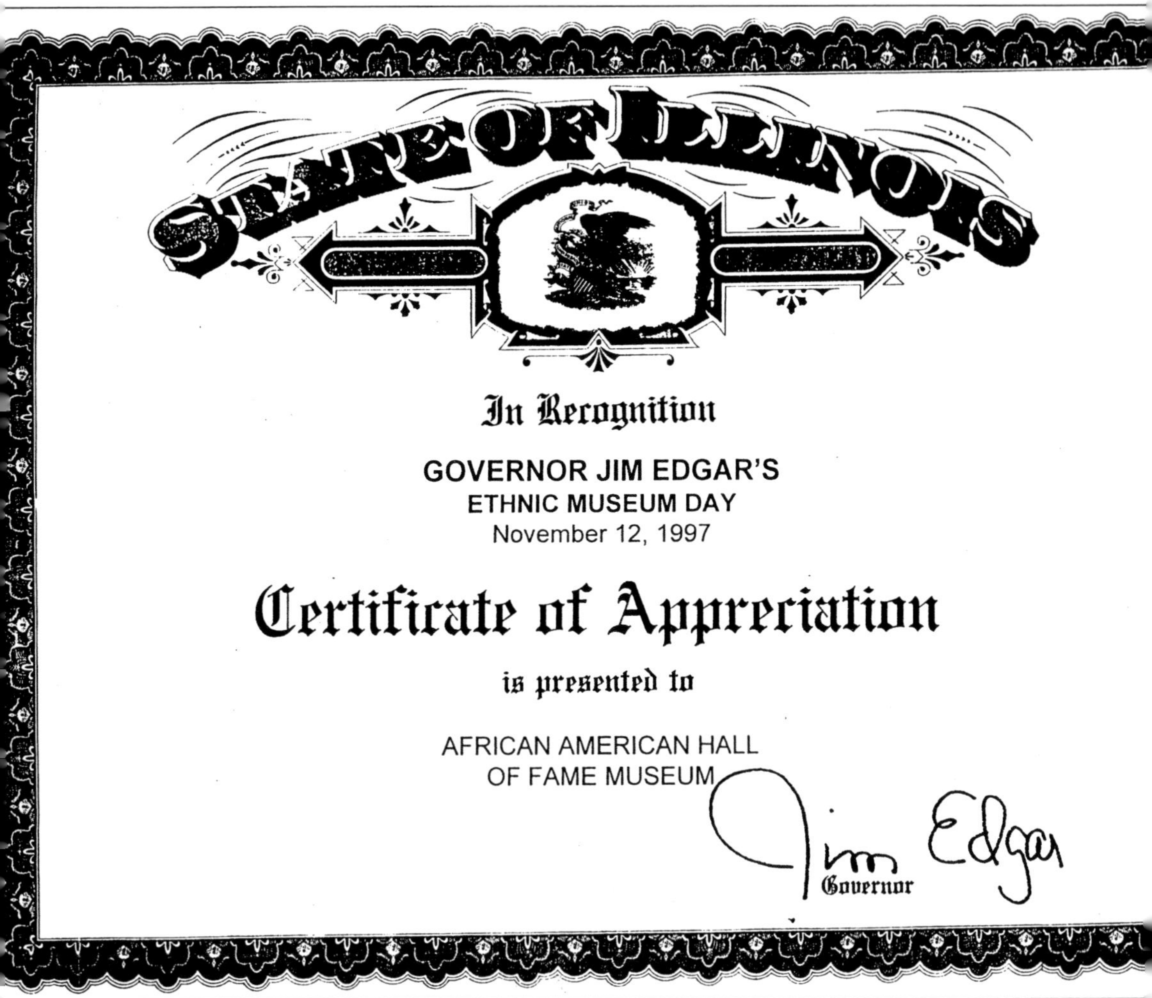
State of Illinois

In Recognition

GOVERNOR JIM EDGAR'S
ETHNIC MUSEUM DAY
November 12, 1997

Certificate of Appreciation

is presented to

AFRICAN AMERICAN HALL
OF FAME MUSEUM

Jim Edgar
Governor

In 1997, the African American Hall of Fame Museum in Peoria, Illinois, received Governor Jim Edgar's Ethnic Museum Day Certificate of Appreciation. (Courtesy of the Garrett Collection, Peoria, Illinois.)

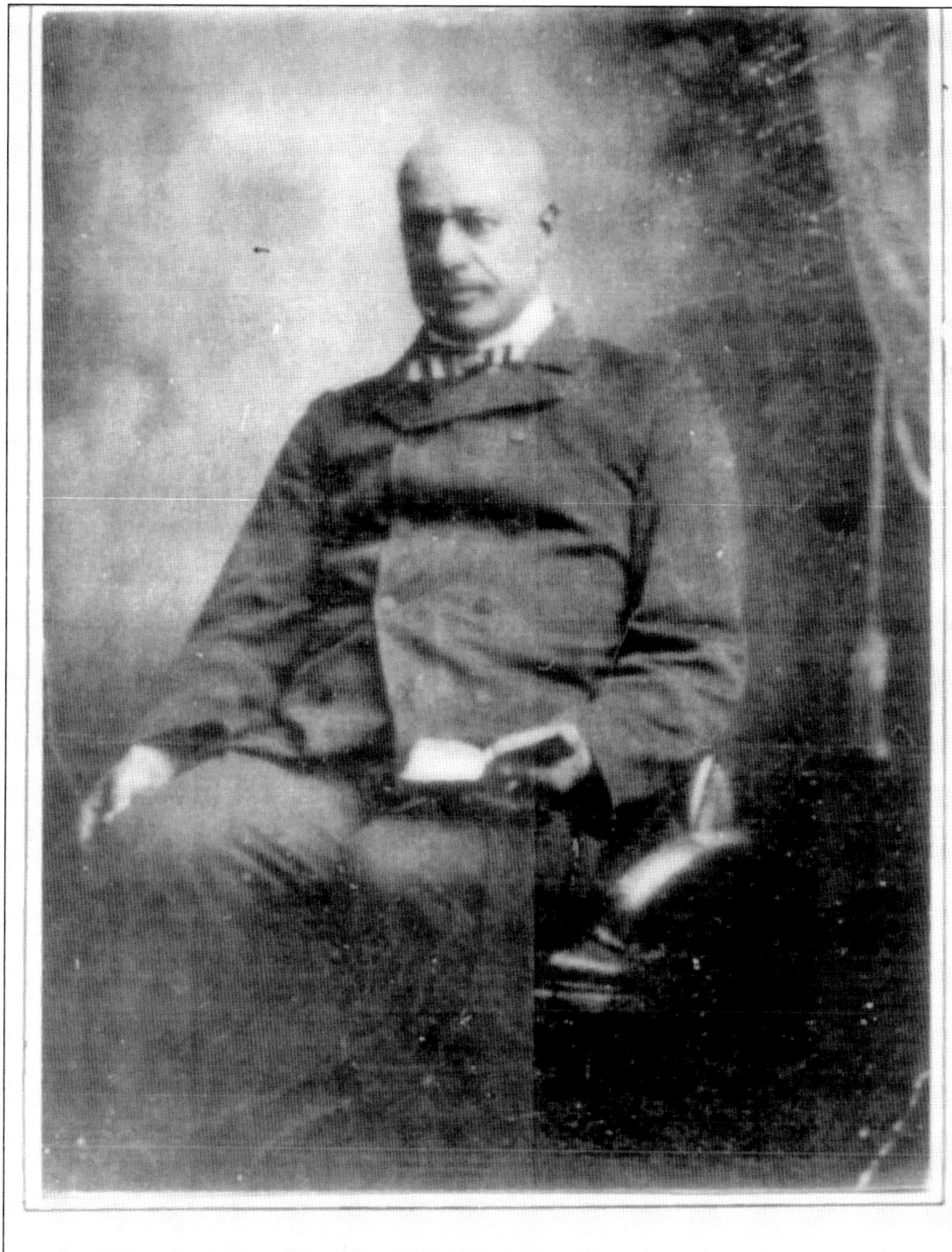

African Americans from west central Illinois have served the United States at home and abroad when it comes to its military efforts. Private James Gardiner served in the 36th U.S. Colored troops during the Civil War. He received the Congressional Medal of Honor for his actions in the Battle of New Market Heights. He lived out the rest of his life after the war in Peoria. (Courtesy of the Garrett Collection, Peoria, Illinois.)

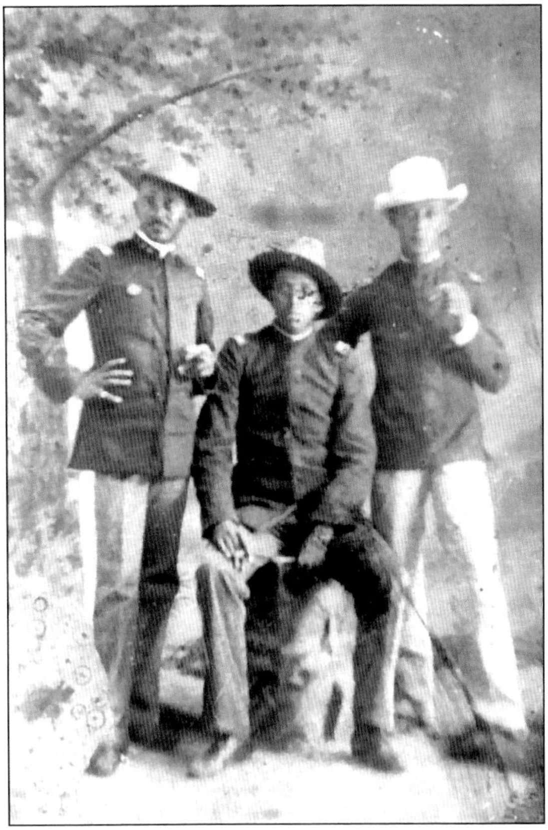

Here three returning soldiers pose for this photograph after their service in the United States military. It is not certain whether they were returning from the Civil War or the Spanish American War of 1898. (Courtesy of Knox College Archives, Galesburg, Illinois.)

During World War II, Galesburg served as a host site for African-American soldiers. The Carver Center became the center of much activity by 1944. United States Officers of Post Number 2 pose for a group shot. (Courtesy of Steve Abrams Personal Collection.)

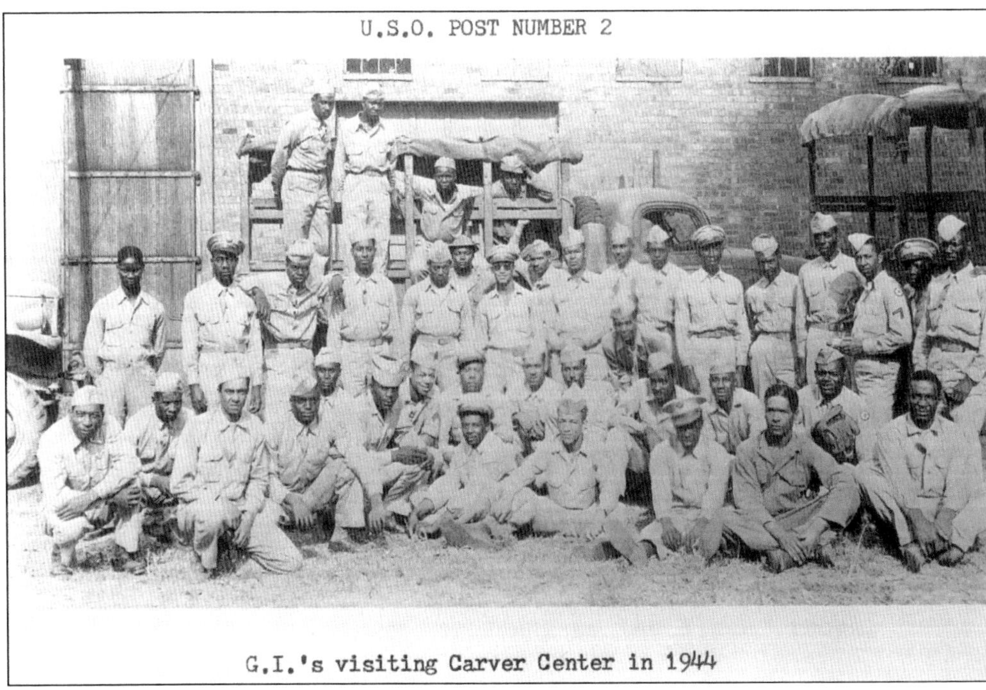

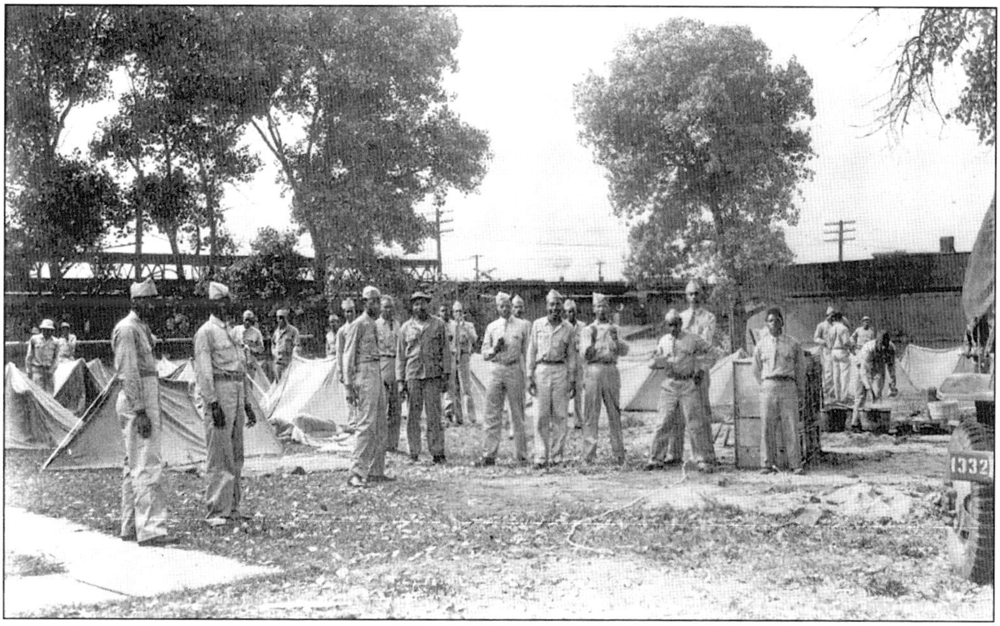

Here the soldiers set up camp on the grounds of the Carver Center in 1944. (Courtesy of Steve Abrams Personal Collection.)

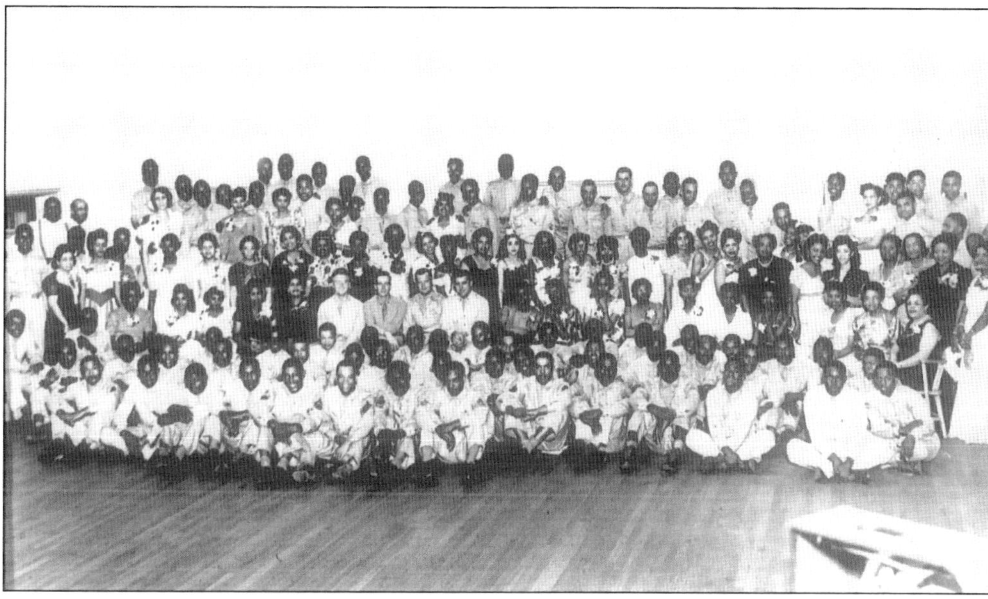

It is reported that some of the soldiers pictured here found the girl of their dreams in the town of Galesburg during World War II—ultimately making it home. It is also true that a couple of the young women left Galesburg after the war to make their homes with their new husbands. This gathering of soldiers, junior hostesses, and adult volunteers at a Service Center social event in 1944 would have provided just such an opportunity. If one observes the photograph closely, the four commanding officers at the center of the photograph were white. It speaks to the United States' history of racism in the military. (Courtesy of Steve Abrams Personal Collection.)

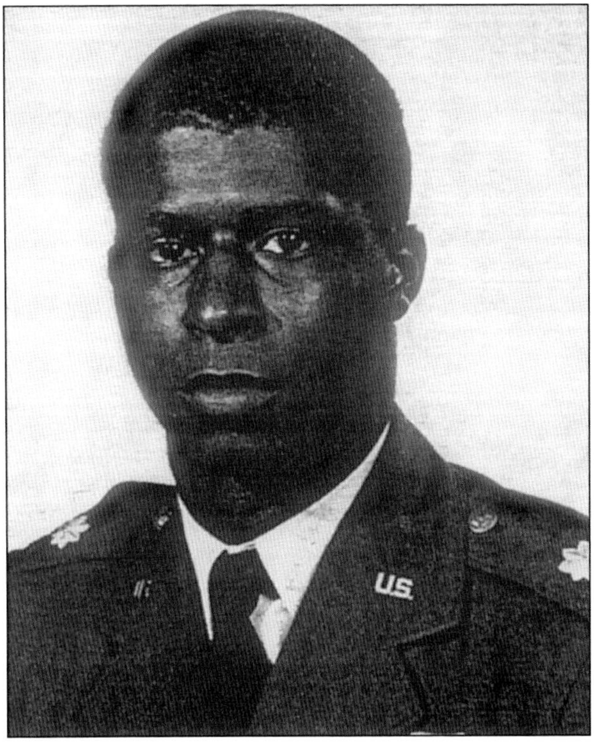

Air Force Major Robert H. Lawrence, a 1956 graduate of Bradley University, died tragically during a routine test of an F-104 Starfighter at Edwards Air Force Base in California in December 1967. Lawrence had also earned a Ph.D. in physical chemistry from Ohio State University, and in June of 1967, he became the first African American selected as an astronaut through the United States military. (Courtesy of Garrett Collection, Peoria, Illinois.)

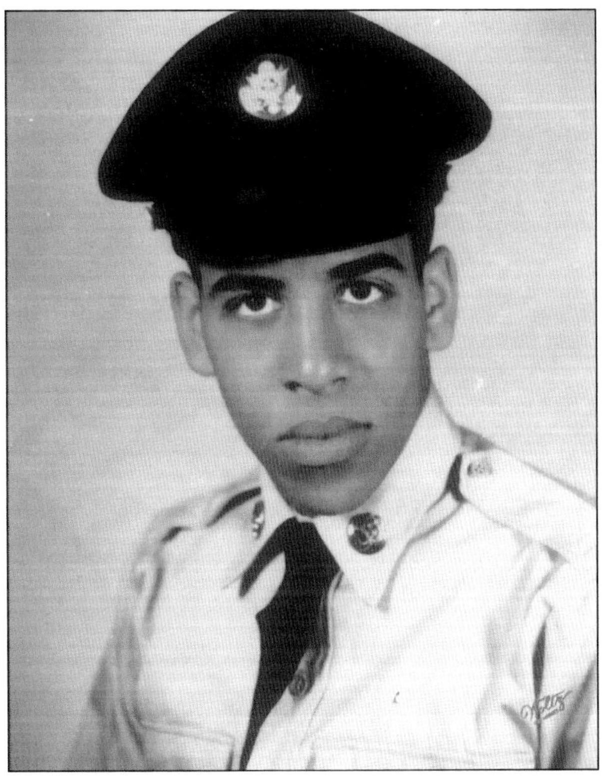

Wayman Thorpe, a member of one of Macomb's first and long-standing black families, served during World War II. (Courtesy of the Archives and Special Collections, Western Illinois University Library.)

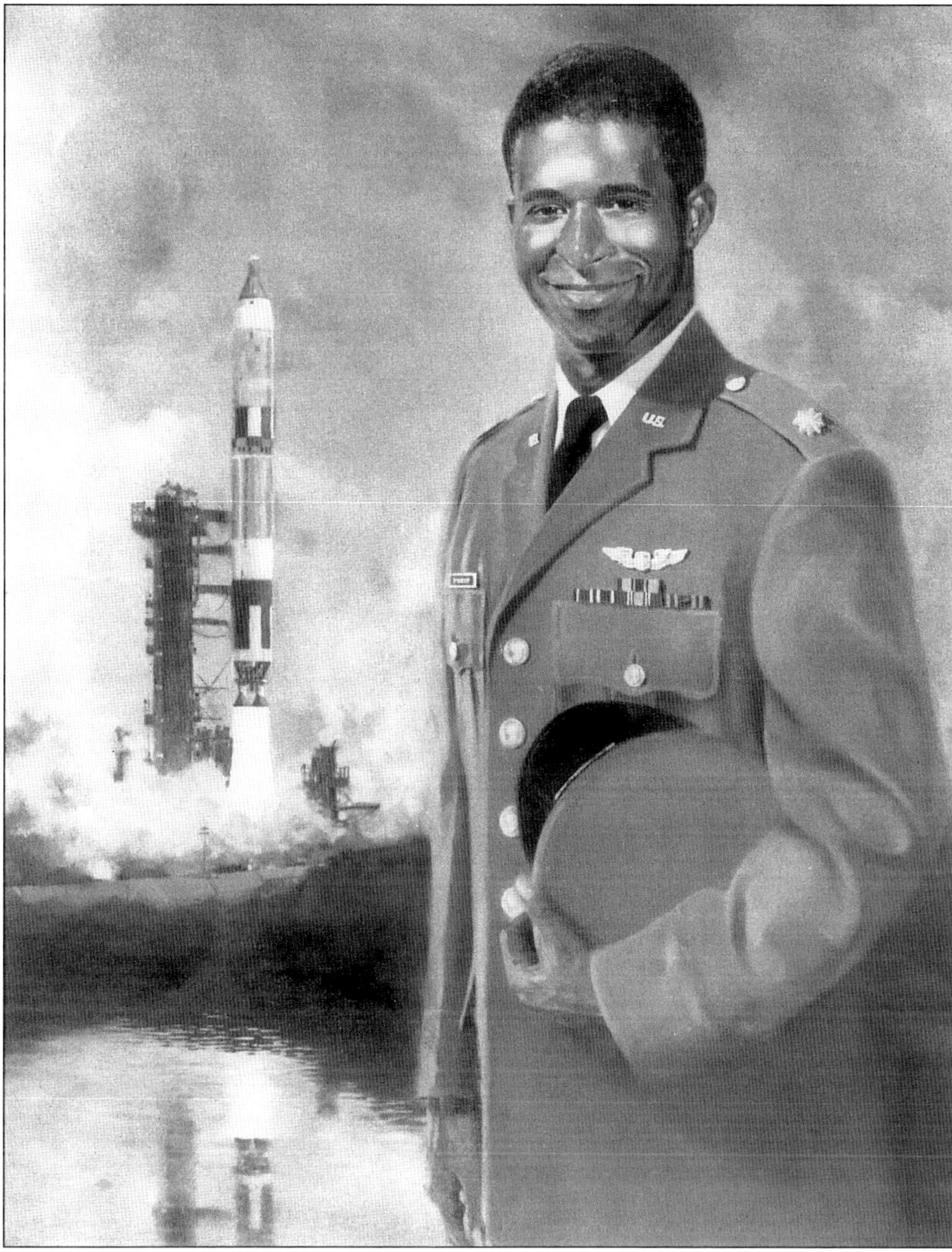

This painting of Major Lawrence can now be seen at the African American Hall of Fame Museum in Peoria. (Courtesy of Garrett Collection, Peoria, Illinois.)

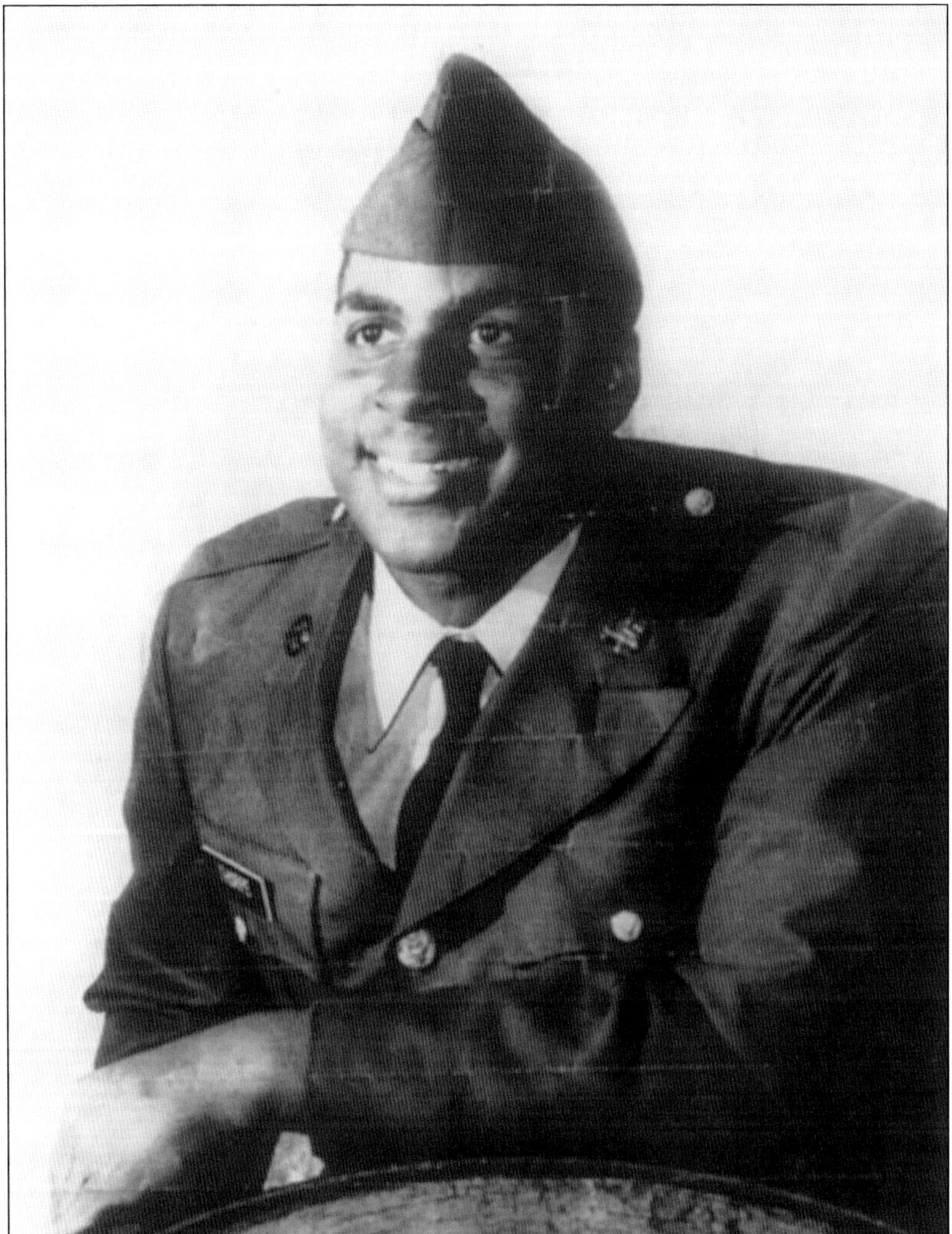

Without question, the Thorpes have offered their services to the good of the country. Shawn Thorpe of Macomb served the United States military cause during the Vietnam War. (Courtesy of the Archives and Special Collections, Western Illinois University Library.)

Three

Religion and Church(es)

St. William Church
Perry, Missouri 63462

January 25, 1974

Dear Fr. Jenosky,

Fr. Dick Hunkins called me this morning inquiring about a baptismal certificate for Augustine Tolten. I found this record and I am mailing it to you. Note that the parents names are NOT in the record.

Hoping this record will be of help to you,

I am,

Yours in Christ,

P. J. McMyler

Fr. Patrick J. McKyler

P.S. Augustine was probably baptized at St. Paul Church near Perry. This Church is now closed and the parishioners who belonged there now belong in St. William Parish, Perry. St. William Church was formerly called Immaculate Conception.

This 1974 record discussed the fact that Father Tolton's parents' names were not listed with his baptismal record, which was apparent with all the enslaved persons. Instead, the owners' names were listed. (Courtesy of Quincy University Library and Archives.)

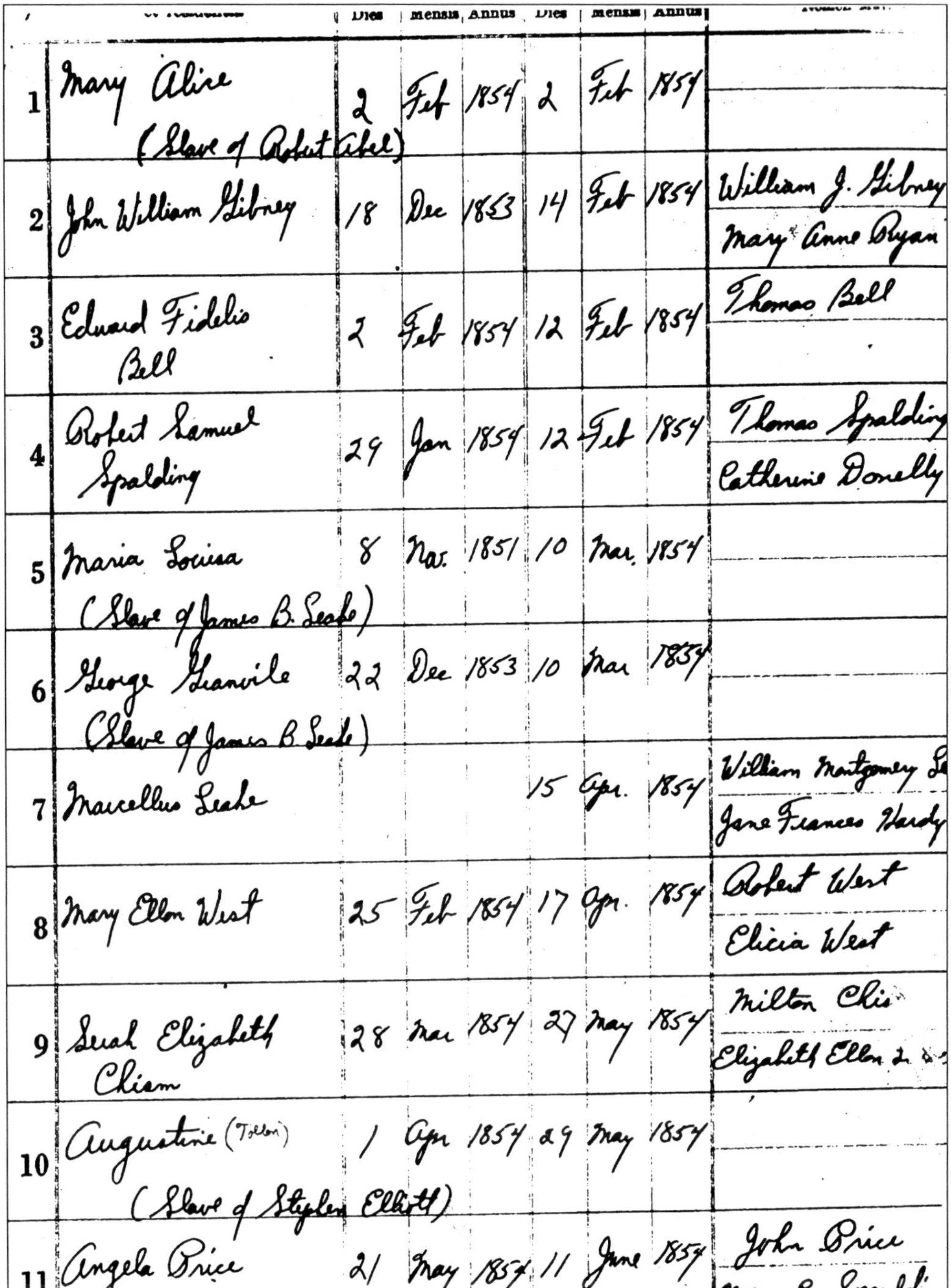

		Dies	mensis	Annus	Dies	mensis	Annus	
1	Mary Alice (Slave of Robert Abel)	2	Feb	1854	2	Feb	1854	
2	John William Gibney	18	Dec	1853	14	Feb	1854	William J. Gibney Mary Anne Ryan
3	Edward Fidelis Bell	2	Feb	1854	12	Feb	1854	Thomas Bell
4	Robert Samuel Spalding	29	Jan	1854	12	Feb	1854	Thomas Spalding Catherine Donelly
5	Maria Louisa (Slave of James B. Seale)	8	Nov.	1851	10	Mar.	1854	
6	George Granvile (Slave of James B. Seale)	22	Dec	1853	10	Mar	1854	
7	Marcellus Leake				15	Apr.	1854	William Montgomery Le[illegible] Jane Frances Hardy
8	Mary Ellen West	25	Feb	1854	17	Apr.	1854	Robert West Elicia West
9	Sarah Elizabeth Chism	28	Mar	1854	27	May	1854	Milton Chi[illegible] Elizabeth Ellen [illegible]
10	Augustine (Tolton) (Slave of Stephen Elliott)	1	Apr	1854	29	May	1854	
11	Angela Price	21	May	1854	11	June	1854	John Price Mary E. Spauld[illegible]

This is the baptismal record of Augustine Tolton of Quincy, the first black priest in the United States. He was born enslaved at Brush Creek, Missouri, in 1854. A Stephen Elliott enslaved him. (Courtesy of Quincy University Library and Archives.)

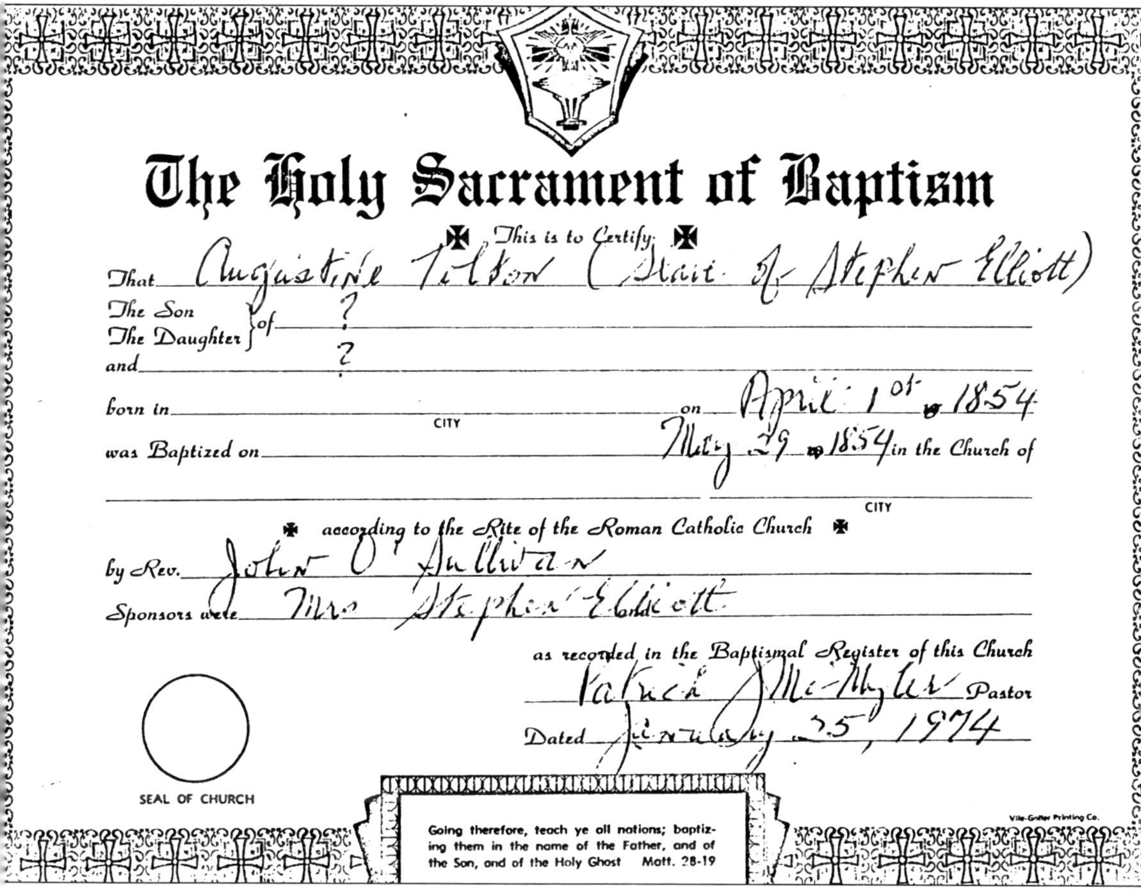

The Holy Sacrament of Baptism

This is to Certify:

That Augustine Tolton (Slave of Stephen Elliott)

The Son / The Daughter of ?

and ?

born in ______ CITY on April 1st 1854

was Baptized on May 29 1854 in the Church of ______ CITY

according to the Rite of the Roman Catholic Church

by Rev. John O'Sullivan

Sponsors were Mrs Stephen Elliott

as recorded in the Baptismal Register of this Church

Patrick McMyler Pastor

Dated January 25, 1974

SEAL OF CHURCH

Going therefore, teach ye all nations; baptizing them in the name of the Father, and of the Son, and of the Holy Ghost Matt. 28-19

Vile-Goller Printing Co.

Unfortunately, the records of enslaved persons did not list the names of birth parents for official purposes. It was more important in the state of Missouri in the 1850s that the slaveholder's name be listed. (Courtesy of Quincy University Library and Archives.)

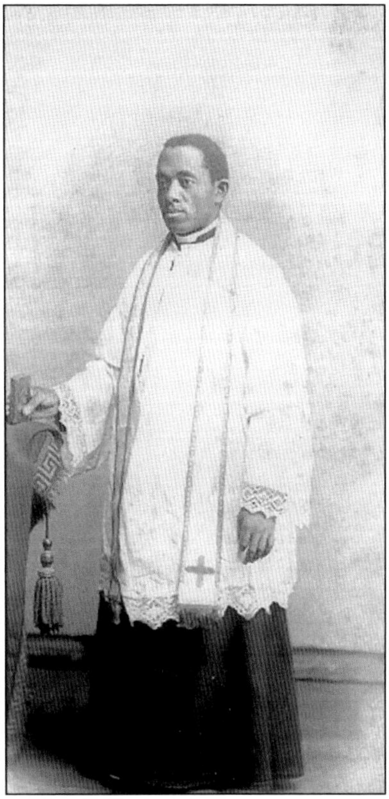

Father Augustine Tolton, the first African-American priest in the United States, is pictured after his ordination in Rome, Italy, in 1886. (Courtesy of Quincy University Library and Archives.)

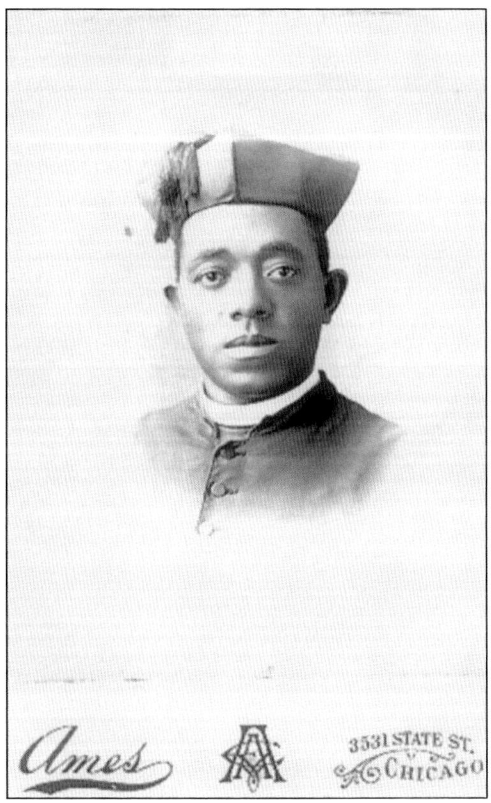

Father Tolton is shown wearing the cap that indicated that he had studied at the highest level of Catholicism in Rome. (Courtesy of Quincy University Library and Archives.)

This is the earliest photograph of St. Joseph Negro Church, which stood at the corner of 7th and Jersey Streets in Quincy. This was the first church that Father Tolton pastored at upon returning from Rome. (Courtesy of Quincy University Library and Archives.)

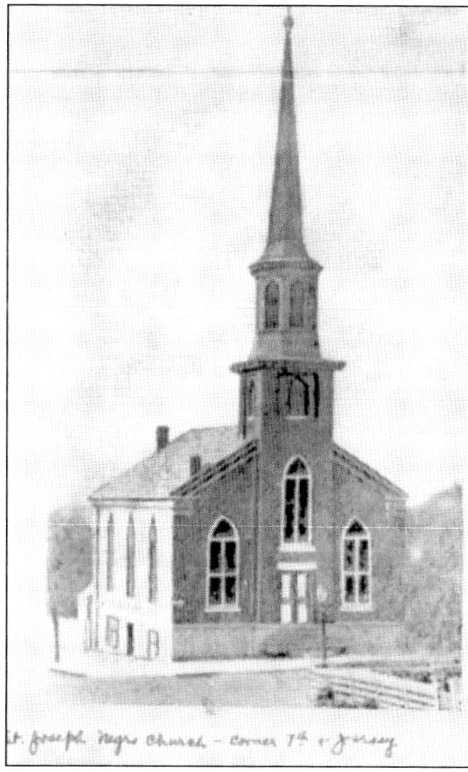

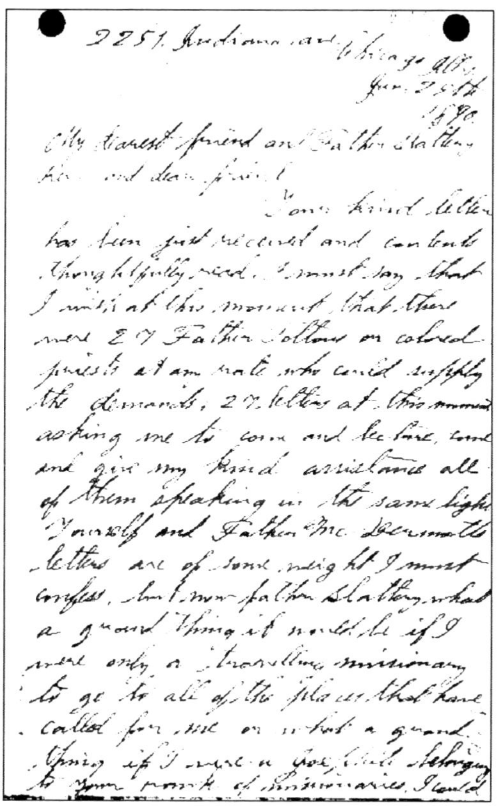

2251 Indiana ave, Chicago Ill, Jan. 29th 1890.

My dearest friend and Father Slattery [illegible] and dear friend

Your kind letter has been just received and contents thoughtfully read. I must say that I wish at this moment that there were 27 Father Toltons or colored priests at any rate who could supply the demands. 27 letters at this moment asking me to come and lecture, come and give my kind assistance all of them speaking in the same light. Yourself and Father Mc Dermott's letters are of some weight I must confess. But now Father Slattery what a grand thing it would be if I were only a travelling missionary to go to all of the places that have called for me or what a grand thing if I were a [illegible] belonging to your [illegible] of missionaries. I could

By 1890, Father Tolton had moved from Quincy to Chicago to establish St. Monica's Church. In this letter that he wrote to his friend in Quincy, Father Tolton discussed with him how he wished "that there were 27 Father Toltons or colored priests at any rate who could supply the demands," of the African-American community of Chicago. (Courtesy of Quincy University Library and Archives.)

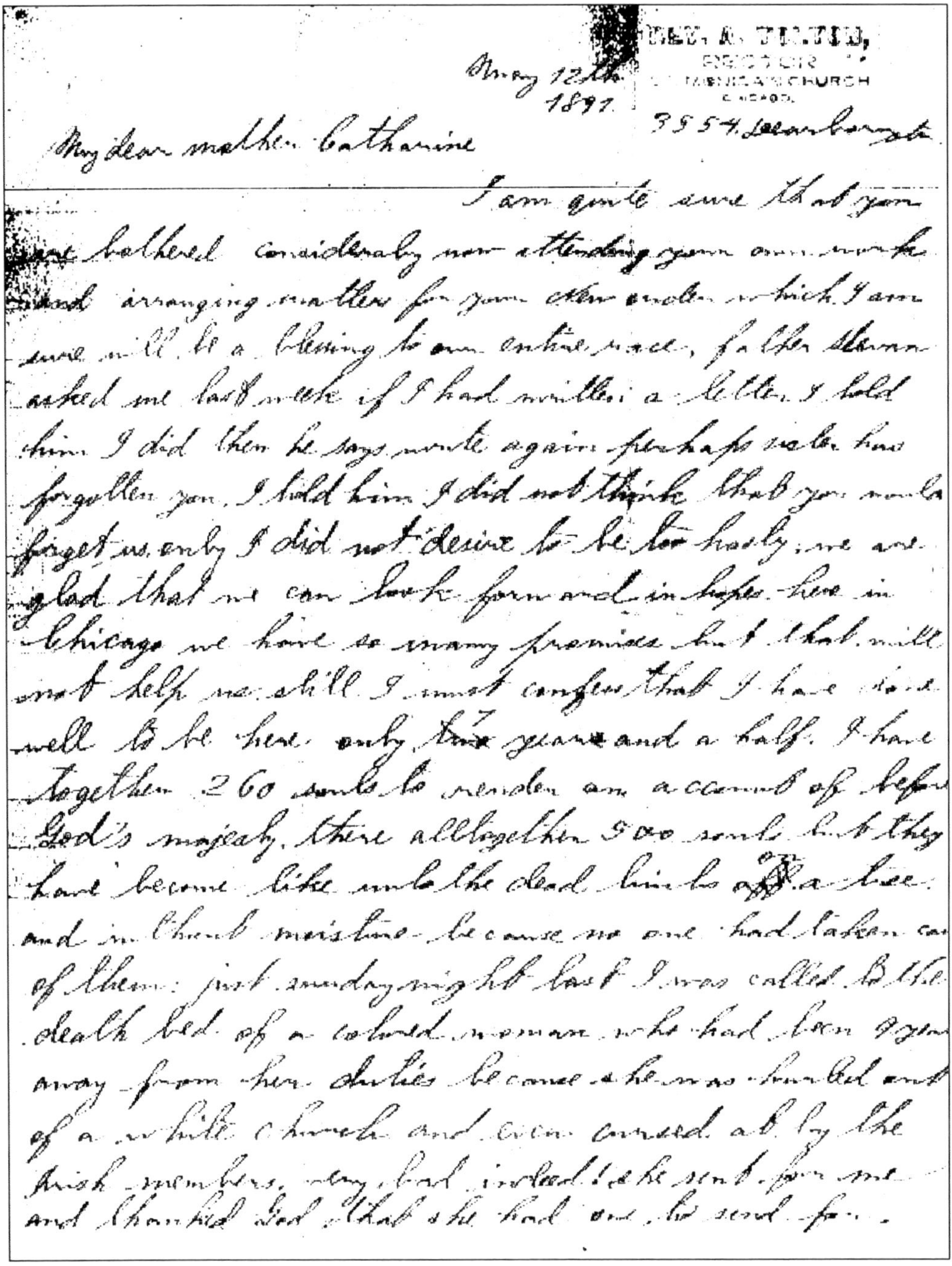

REV. A. TOLTON, RECTOR ST. MONICA'S CHURCH CHICAGO.

May 12th 1897

3354 Dearborn st.

My dear mother Catharine

I am quite sure that you are bothered considerably now attending your own work and arranging matters for your other order which I am sure will be a blessing to our entire race, father Stern asked me last week if I had written a letter. I told him I did then he says write again perhaps she has forgotten you. I told him I did not think that you would forget us, only I did not desire to be too hasty, we are glad that we can look forward in hopes. here in Chicago we have so many promises but that will not help us. still I must confess that I have done well to be here only two years and a half. I have together 260 souls to render an account of before God's majesty. there altogether 900 souls but they have become like unto the dead limbs on a tree. and in that mission because no one had taken care of them; just sunday night last I was called to the death bed of a colored woman who had been 9 years away from her duties because she was hurled out of a white church and even cursed at by the Irish members, very bad indeed! she sent for me and thanked God that she had one to send for.

Father Tolton wrote to his mother Catharine in May of 1897, telling her about his work in the city of Chicago. (Courtesy of Quincy University Library and Archives.)

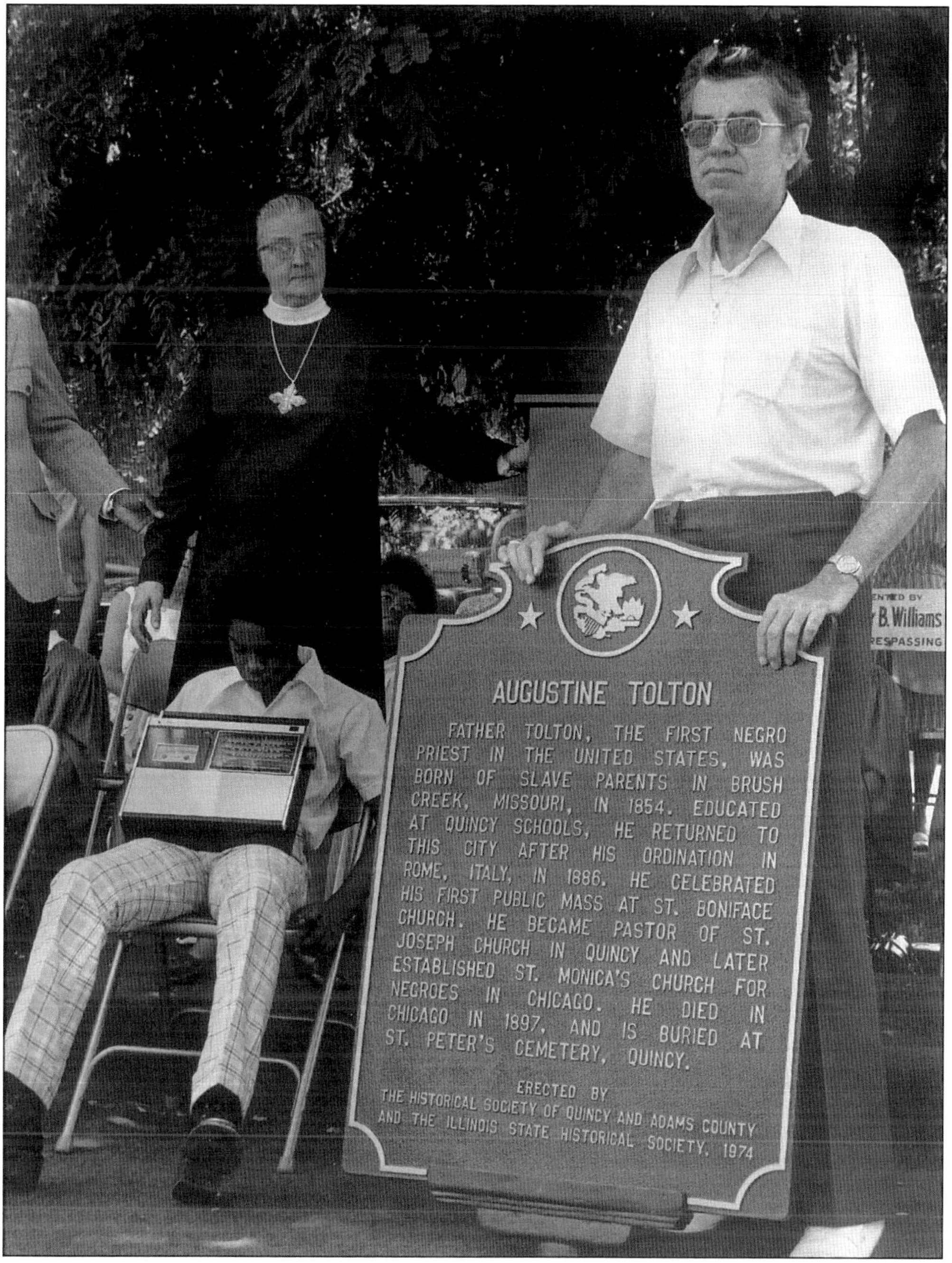

In 1974, the City of Quincy erected this official historical marker of the state near Father Tolton's grave at St. Peter's cemetery in Quincy. Father Augustine Tolton died in the city of Chicago in 1897. (Courtesy of the Quincy University Library and Archives.)

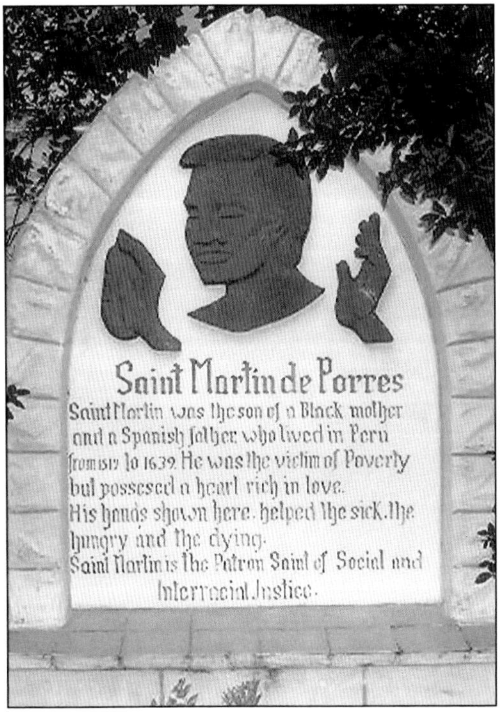

Saint Martin de Porres, the Patron Saint of Social and Interracial Justice of Peru, is the first black to reach sainthood in west central Illinois in 1975 in Peoria. (Courtesy of the author.)

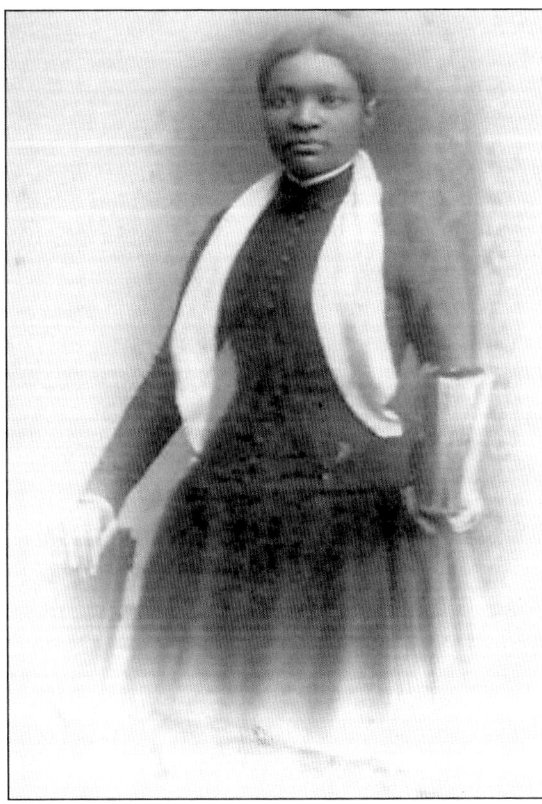

The first reported black woman to minister the Christian Gospel in west central Illinois was Emma Brewington. (Courtesy of Schuyler County Historical Society.)

This is the wedding photograph of Henry and Emma Brewington, taken around the 1910s. (Courtesy of Schuyler County Historical Society.)

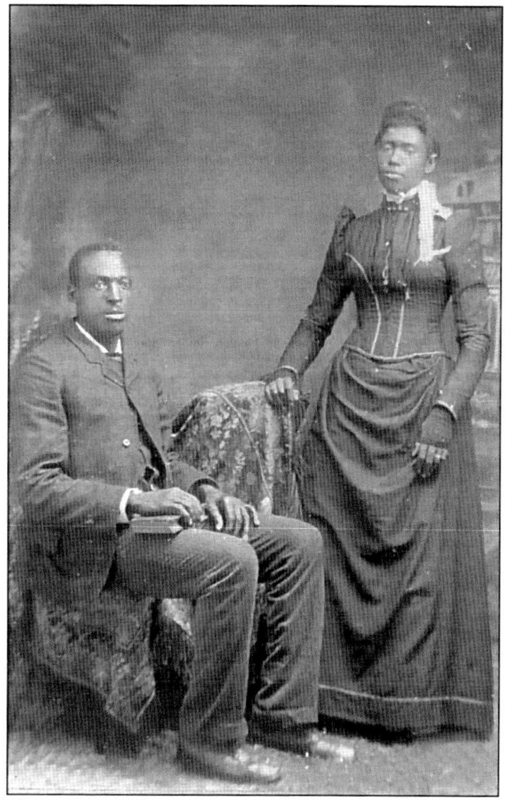

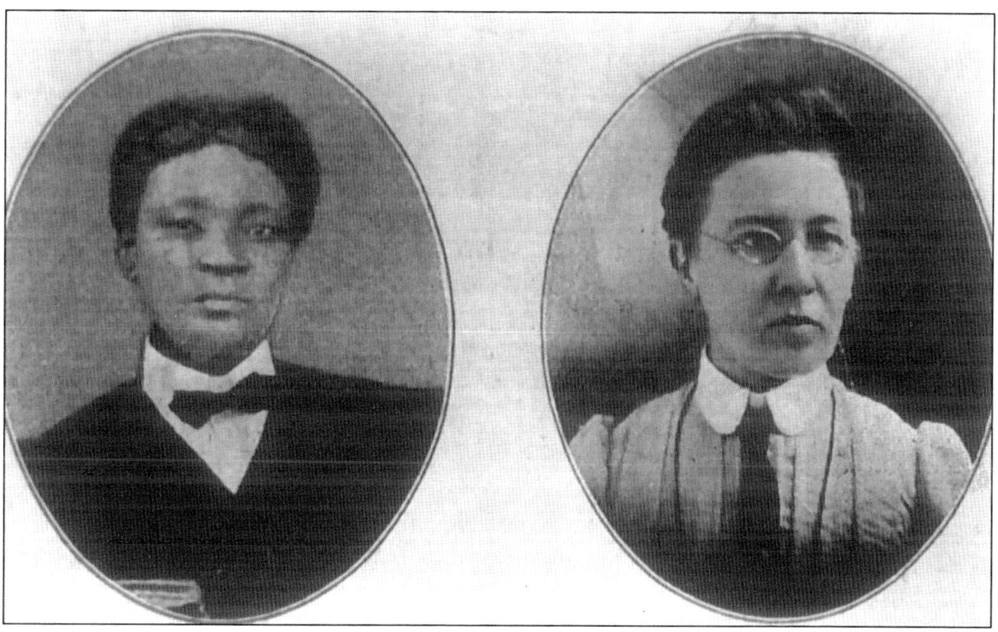

Given that Brewington preached often to white congregates, she usually had a white female traveling companion. This is the business card that was given out, which pictured her traveling companion, Miss Jessie Bessell. (Courtesy of Schuyler County Historical Society.)

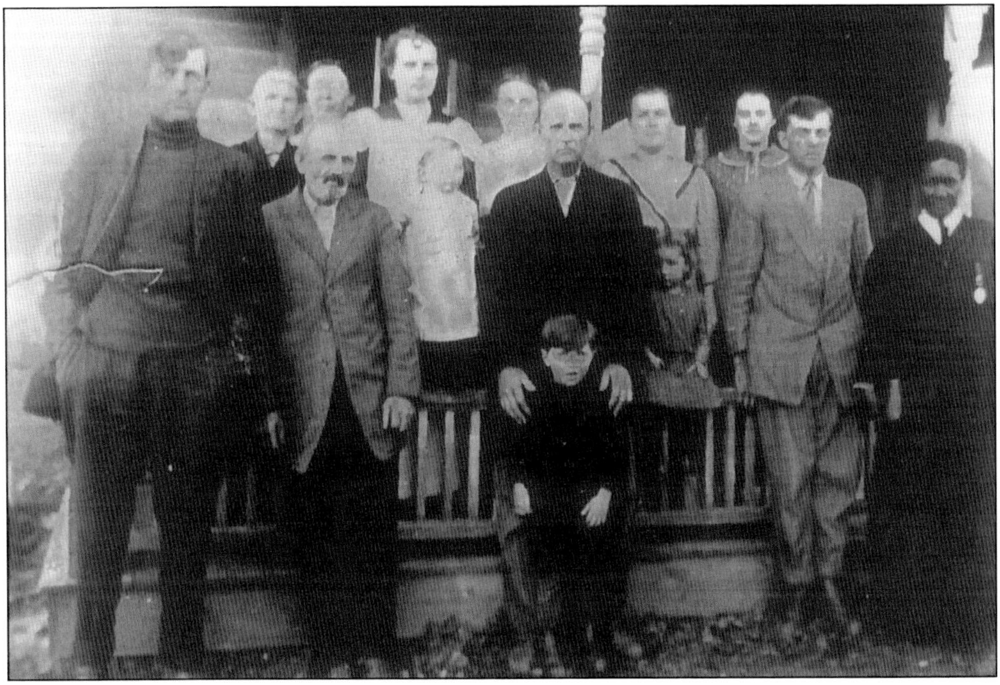

Sister Brewington is shown at a home prayer meeting in Rushville. (Courtesy of Schuyler County Historical Society.)

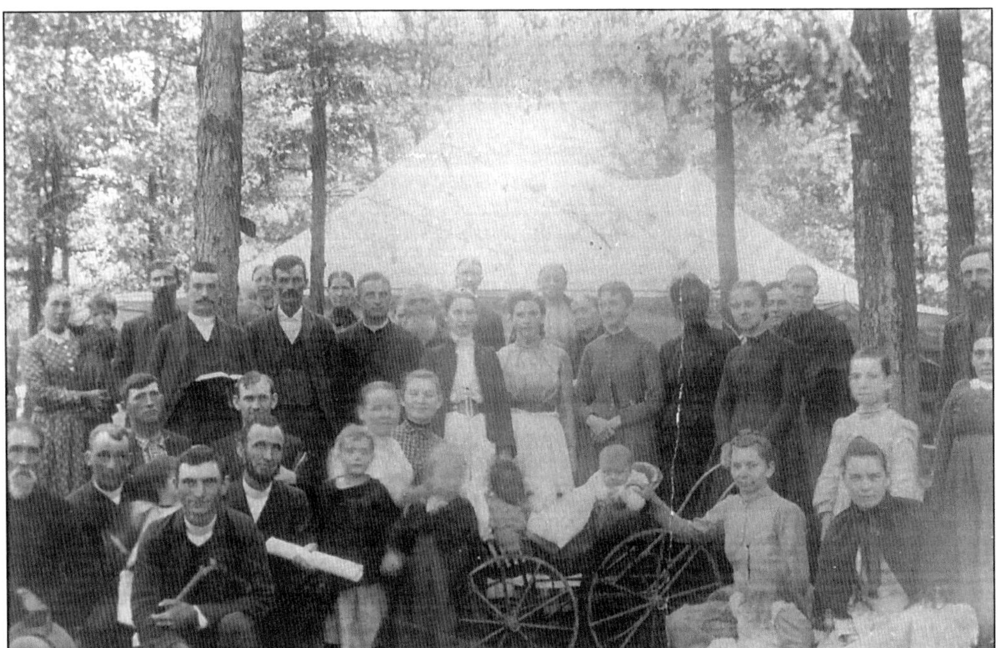

Sister Brewington, as she was referred to by the locals, is pictured at a camp meeting at Rushville. Her son, Paul Brewington, is seated at the left end of the carriage, along with a white baby at the right end. (Courtesy of Schuyler County Historical Society.)

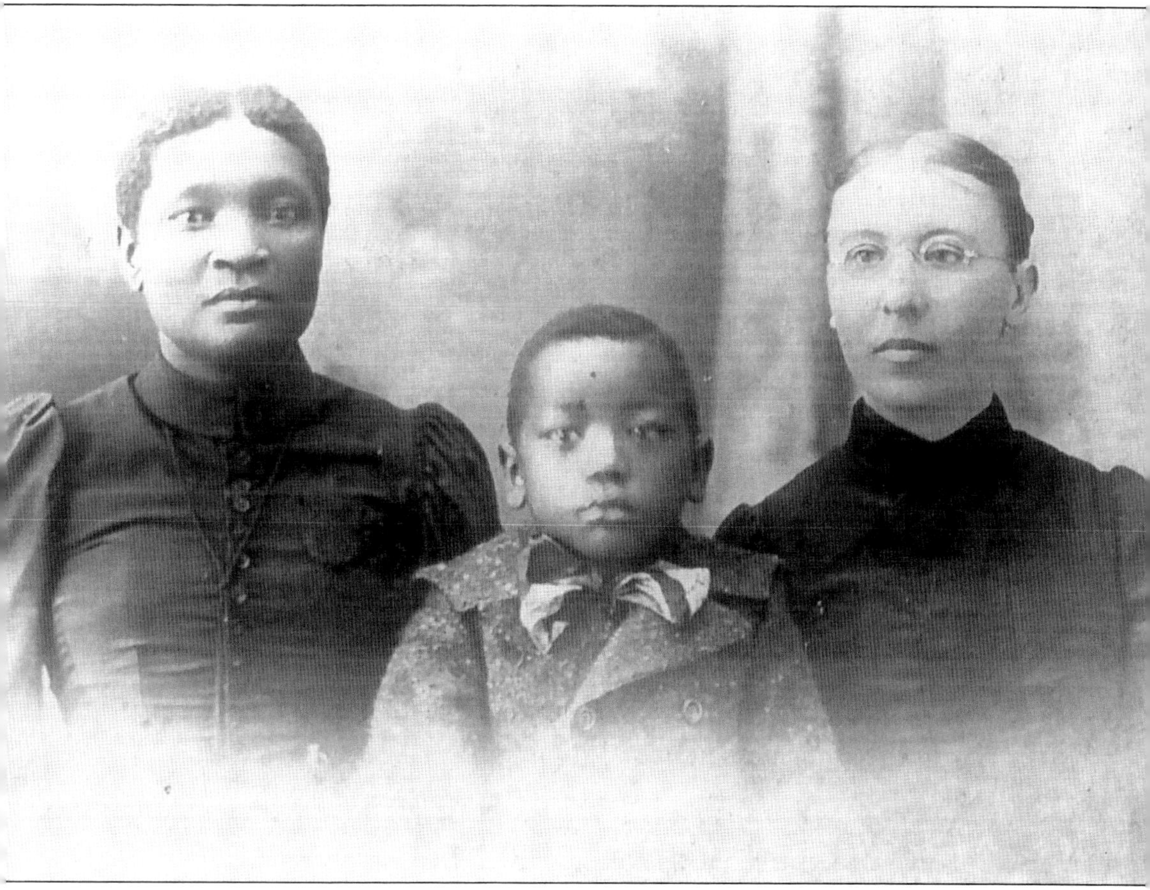

This is a photograph of Sister Brewington, her son Paul, and traveling companion, Jessie Bessell. (Courtesy of Schuyler County Historical Society.)

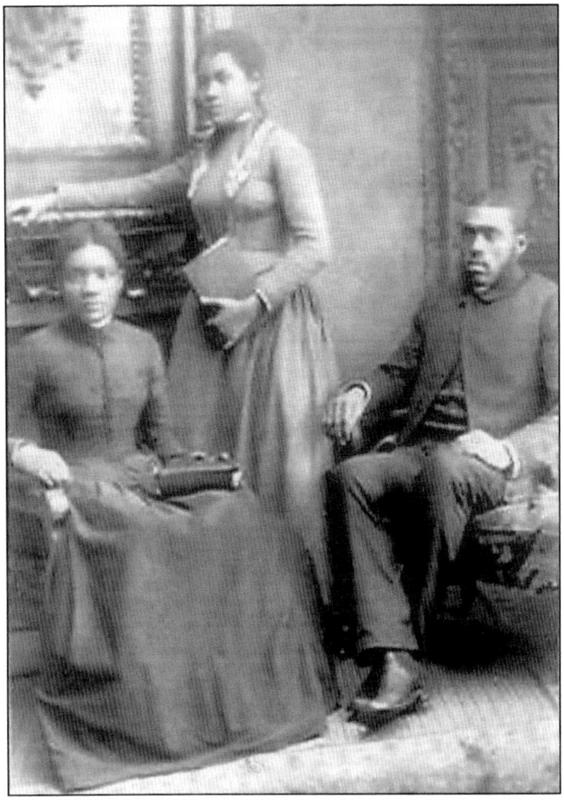

This photograph is of Sister Brewington, her husband Henry, and an unknown black woman. (Courtesy of the Schuyler County Historical Society.)

This photograph of Sister Brewington was taken much later in life, as she continued to travel throughout west central Illinois administering the Gospel to all who listened. She is shown with some of her old faithfuls in Rushville, Illinois. (Courtesy of Schuyler County Historical Society.)

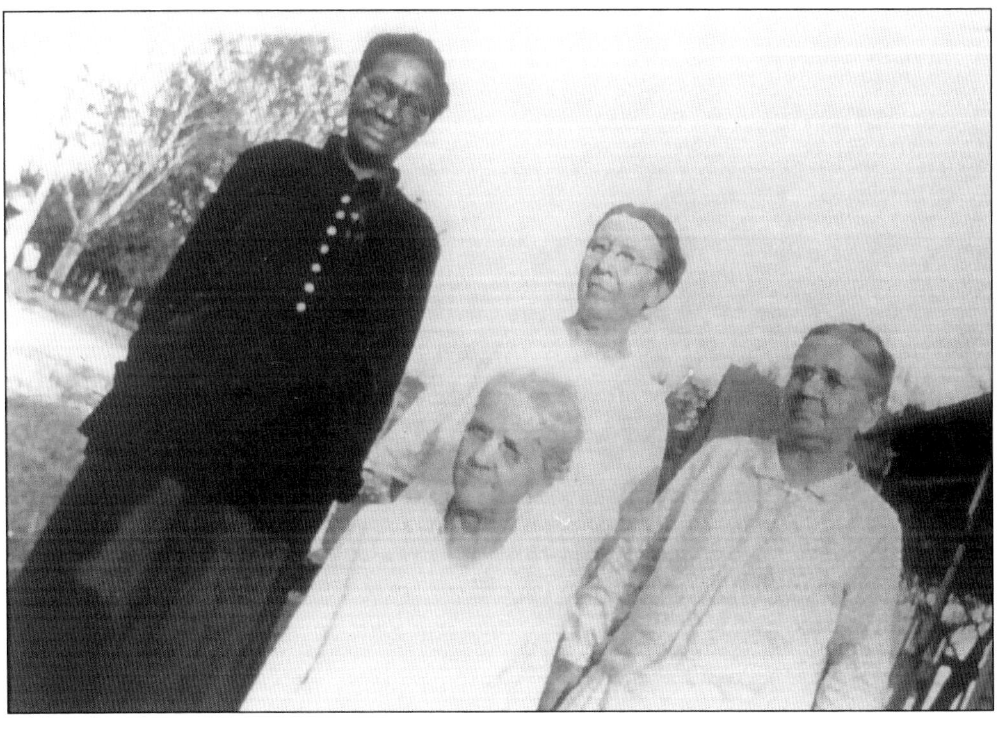

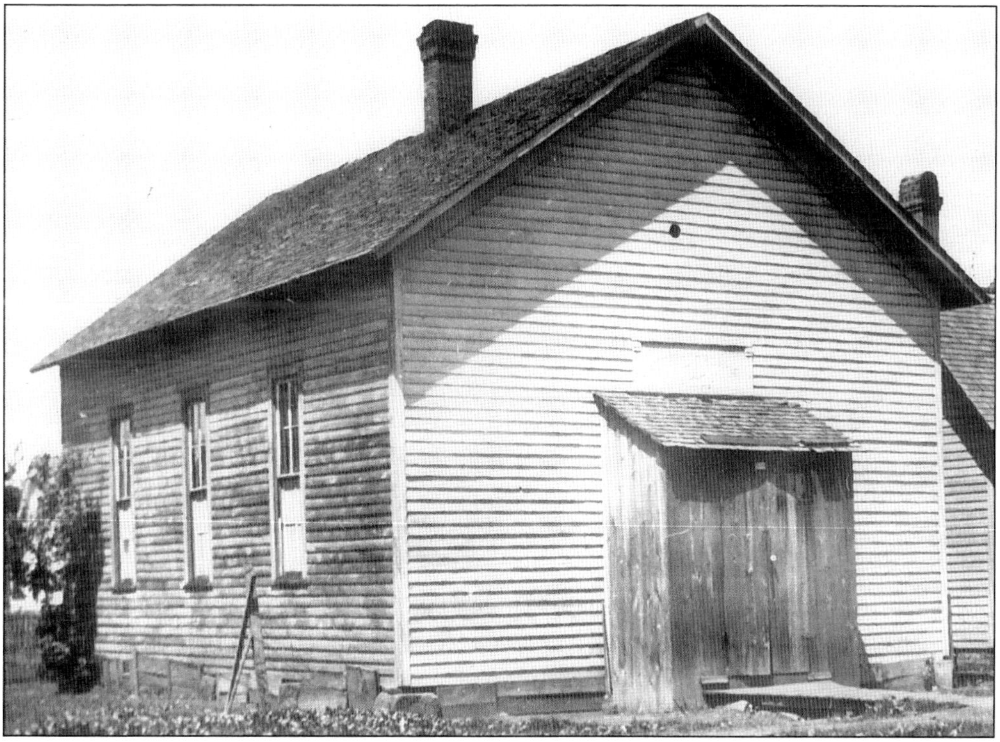

This is the first known black church structure in Macomb, Illinois. It was named Brown's Chapel. (Courtesy of the Archives and Special Collections, Western Illinois University Library.)

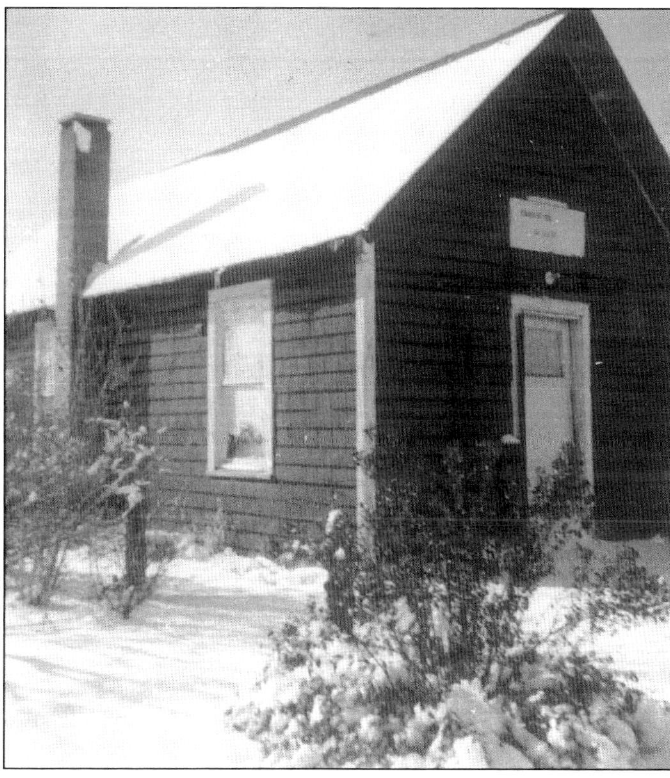

Brown's Chapel served the black community of Macomb until well into the twentieth century. Mount Calvary Church of God in Christ has remained the only surviving black church in Macomb. This structure was the place of worship of Macomb's black community in the 1970s. (Courtesy of the Archives and Special Collections, Western Illinois University Library.)

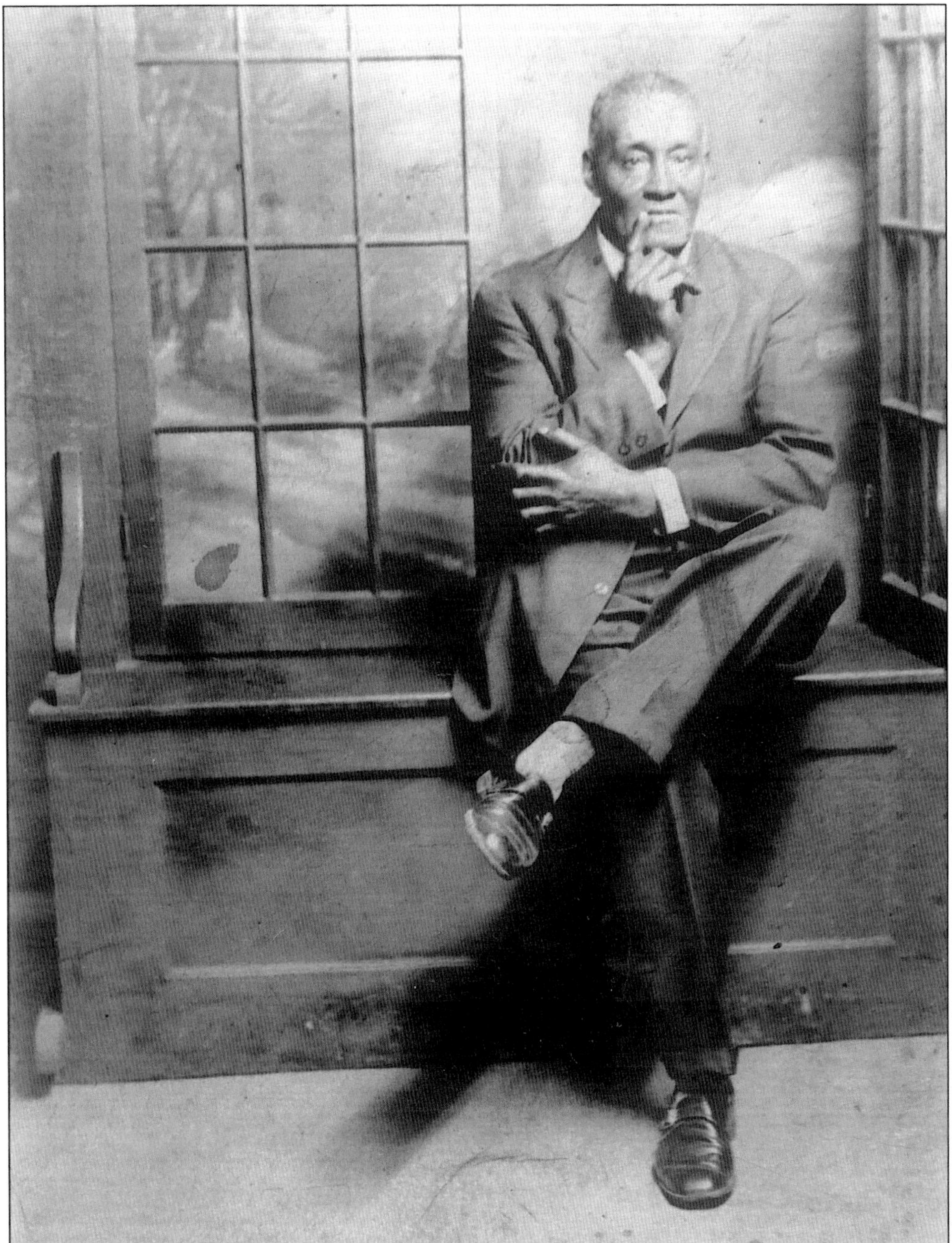

Reverend Oscar Clark was the founder of Macomb's Church of God in Christ. (Courtesy of the Archives and Special Collections, Western Illinois University Library.)

Ward Chapel

African Methodist Episcopal Church
511 N. Elliott Street
Peoria, Illinois 61605

Pastor Larry James Bell

Church Office
309-676-1348

Parsonage
309-693-0835

AFRICAN AMERICAN HALL OF
FAME MUSEUM BOARD OF
DIRECTORS
Mrs. Millie Hall,
President

October 16, 1996

Ward Chapel A.M.E. Church will celebrate it's 150th. Anniversary Celebration with a Banquet which will be held at the church, 511 N. Elliott St, on Saturday, November 16, at 6:30 P.M.

The Speaker will be Mr. Andrae Bohannon, Ist District Councilman, City of Peoria. The donation for each ticket is $15.50. The donation for a table of ten persons is $155.00.

We are asking for your participation in this Event, by purchasing a table. Our contact person is Mrs. Virgie Collins.

Thank you for your consideration of this letter.

Yours in Christ,
Bessie Mitchell,
Church Secretary,

Rev. Larry James Bell
Pastor (By Sec't.)

Rev. Larry James Bell, Pastor
Ward Chapel A.M.E. Church
511 North Elliott Street
Peoria, Illinois 61605
(309) 676-1348

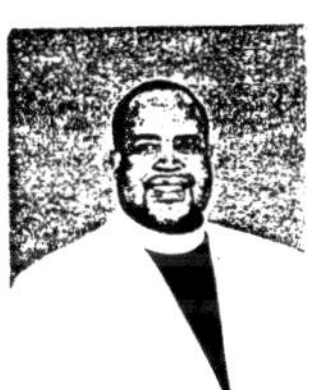

Rev. Larry James Bell, Pastor
Ward Chapel A.M.E. Church
511 North Elliott Street
Peoria, Illinois 61605
(309) 676-1348

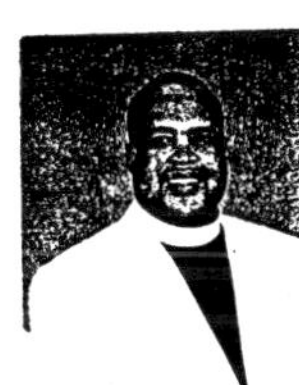

The African Methodist Episcopal Church has had a long-standing existence in west central Illinois. There are congregations at practically every locale of black visibility within west central Illinois. This 1996 celebration of Ward Chapel marked the churches 150th anniversary in the city of Peoria. Therefore, Ward Chapel was established at Peoria in 1846, giving every indication that blacks were established in portions of west central Illinois. (Courtesy of the African American Hall of Fame Museum, Peoria, Illinois.)

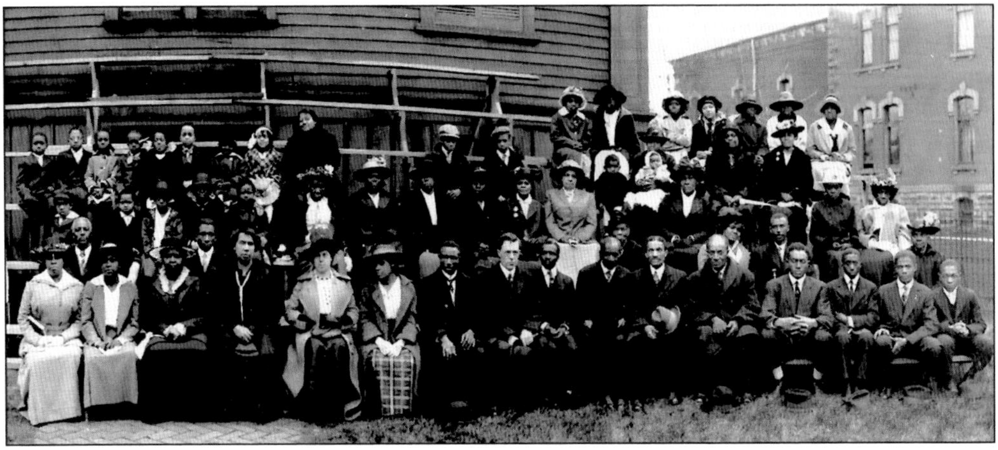

This is a congregational photograph of the Second Baptist Church of Galesburg. This photo was taken early in the twentieth century. (Courtesy of Knox College Archives.)

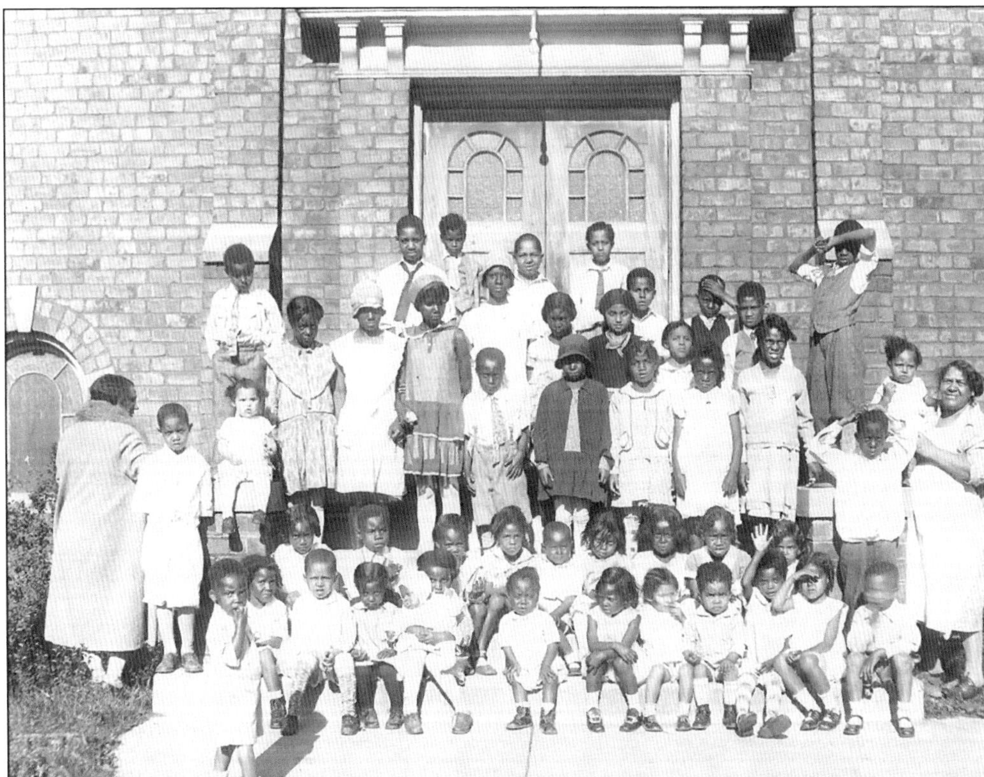

Second Baptist Church and the children's program are depicted here during the mid-twentieth century. Children factored into the mission of most black churches at all times. (Courtesy of Knox College Archives.)

Four

EDUCATIONAL LEGACIES

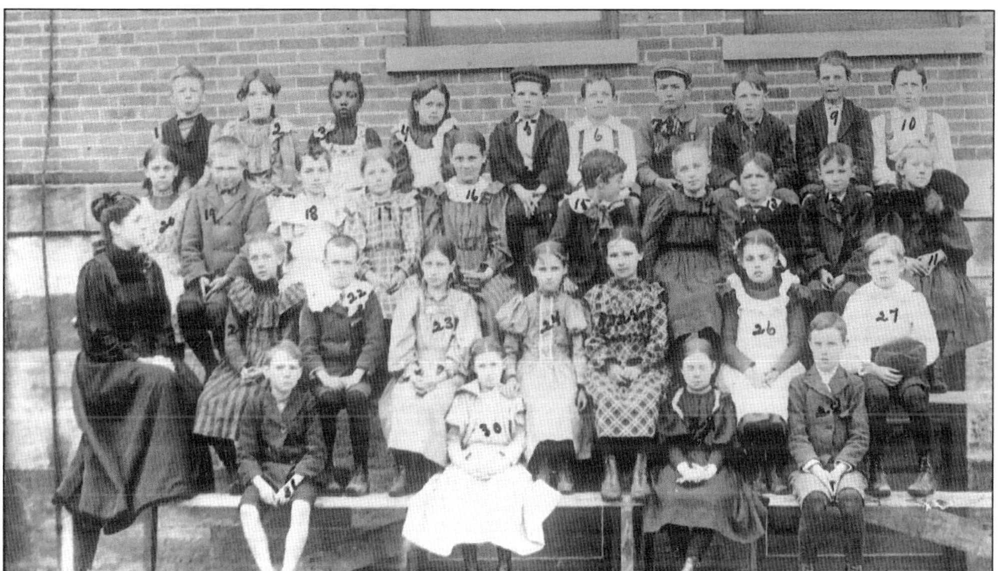

The following photographs depict some of the earliest African-American children in the schools of Macomb, Illinois. Often they were the only children in the schools and/or in their classes. (Courtesy of the Archives and Special Collections, Western Illinois University Library.)

The Rubicon Crossed

Last Monday, for the first time, a few colored children in this city went and took their places in our public schools. In spite of this "degradation of white children," the bell rings as clearly in calling school as it did when only Anglo-Saxon juveniles obeyed its summons; business is just as brisk at our stores and saloons, and Crooked Creek still runs unvexed to the sea.

At last the problem of what colored children in town are to do for an education is solved and in a manner creditable to the good sense of the citizens of a sensible city. We learn that a few rascally boys on Monday succeeded in frightening one little colored boy from the school and driving him home; but the teacher immediately had the little fellow returned and gave him all the protection necessary.

We hope the colored "bugaboo" question, as far as Macomb is concerned, is now settled for all time. The colored man has a right to walk our streets, a free man, has a right to work and acquire property, a right to use the elective franchise in reference to the laws under which he lives, and his children have free access to the schools which he pays his portion of tax to support.

The advent of this era, instead of being accepted grudgingly, should be hailed with delight by a people who, casting prejudice to the winds, should feel proud that justice and equal privilege is meted out to all, alike.

—*Macomb Journal,* September 5, 1872.

In 1872, the town of Macomb ran this piece in its local newspaper, the *Macomb Journal*. It was the first time that African-American children began attending the public schools of McDonough County. (Courtesy of the Archives and Special Collections, Western Illinois University Library.)

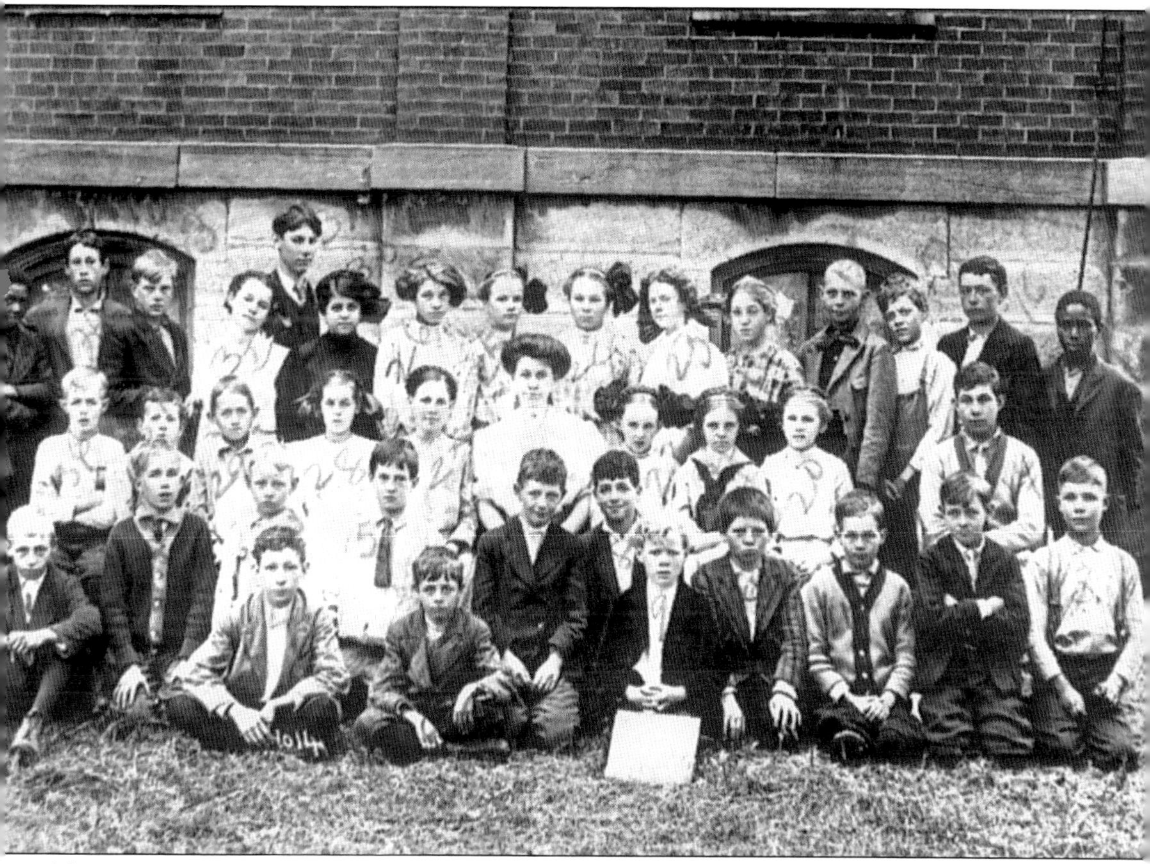

These two young boys are believed to have been brothers in the Macomb School. (Courtesy of the Archives and Special Collections, Western Illinois University Library.)

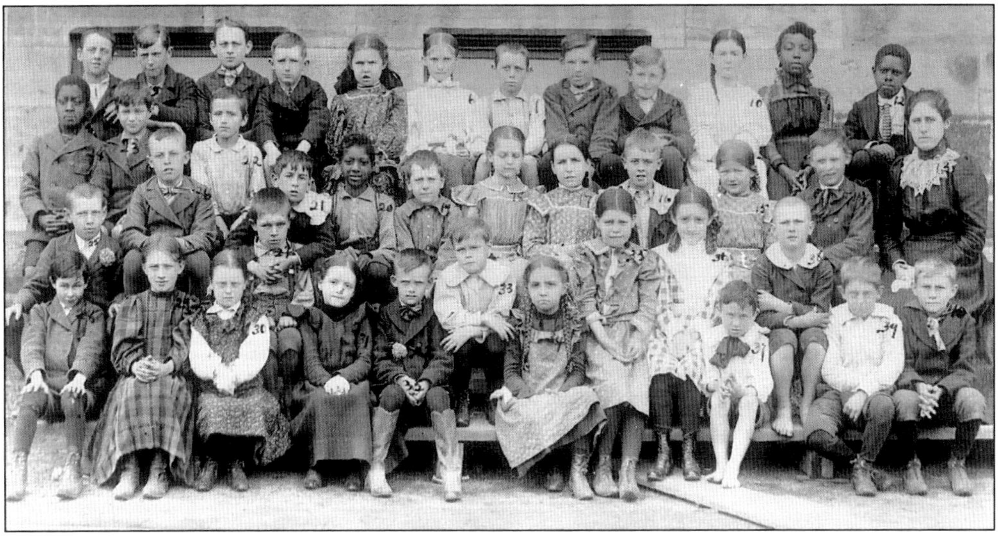

The African-American children depicted here would have been a rare encouter, with at least four of them obviously of African-American descent in the same classroom. (Courtesy of the Archives and Special Collections Western Illinois University Library.)

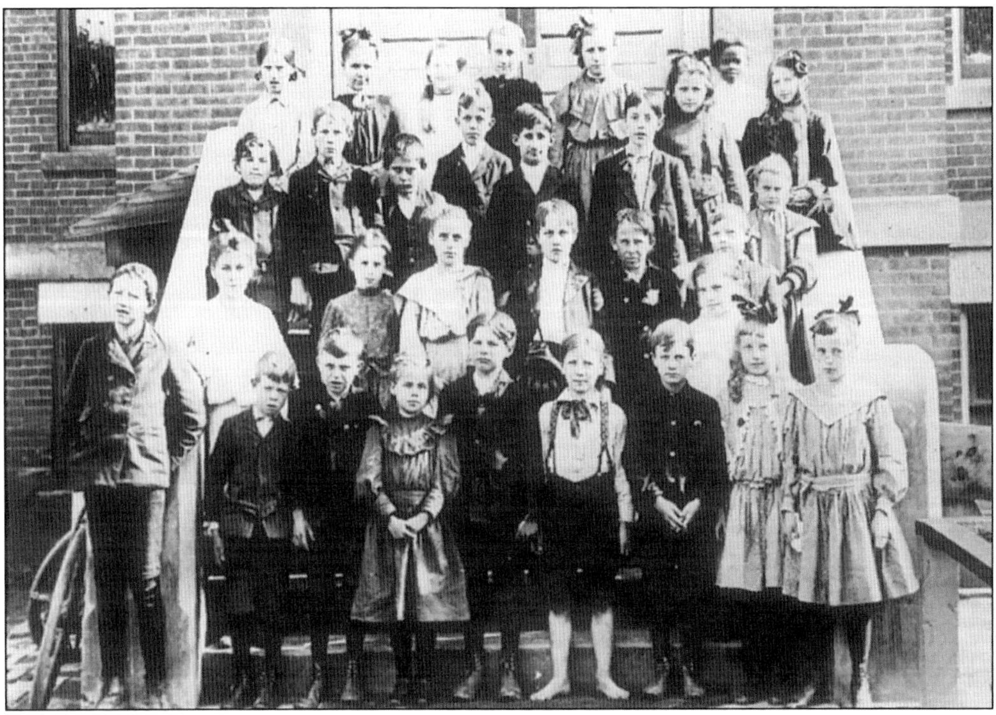

This photograph depicts the solitude that African-American children have often endured in the public schools throughout much of west central Illinois. Here is a late nineteenth century classroom in Macomb with one of the African-American children from one of Macomb's early prominent black families. Garnet McGruder served as the matriarch of the McGruder family well into the twentieth century. (Courtesy of the Archives and Special Collections, Western Illinois University Library.)

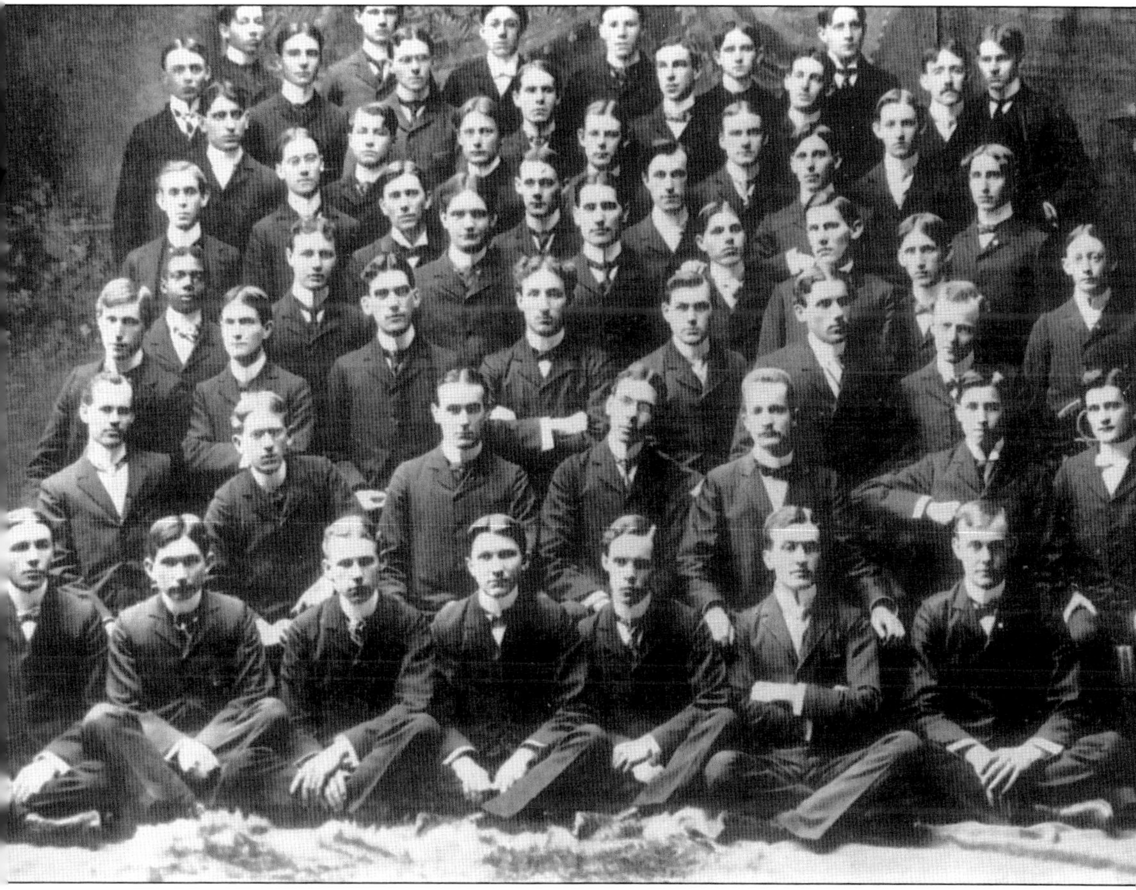

Not only did grade school children endure isolation, but also college students throughout west central Illinois often had a similar fate. Here is a class of young men from Monmouth College, which depicts a single young African-American male in 1900. (Courtesy of Monmouth College Library and Archives.)

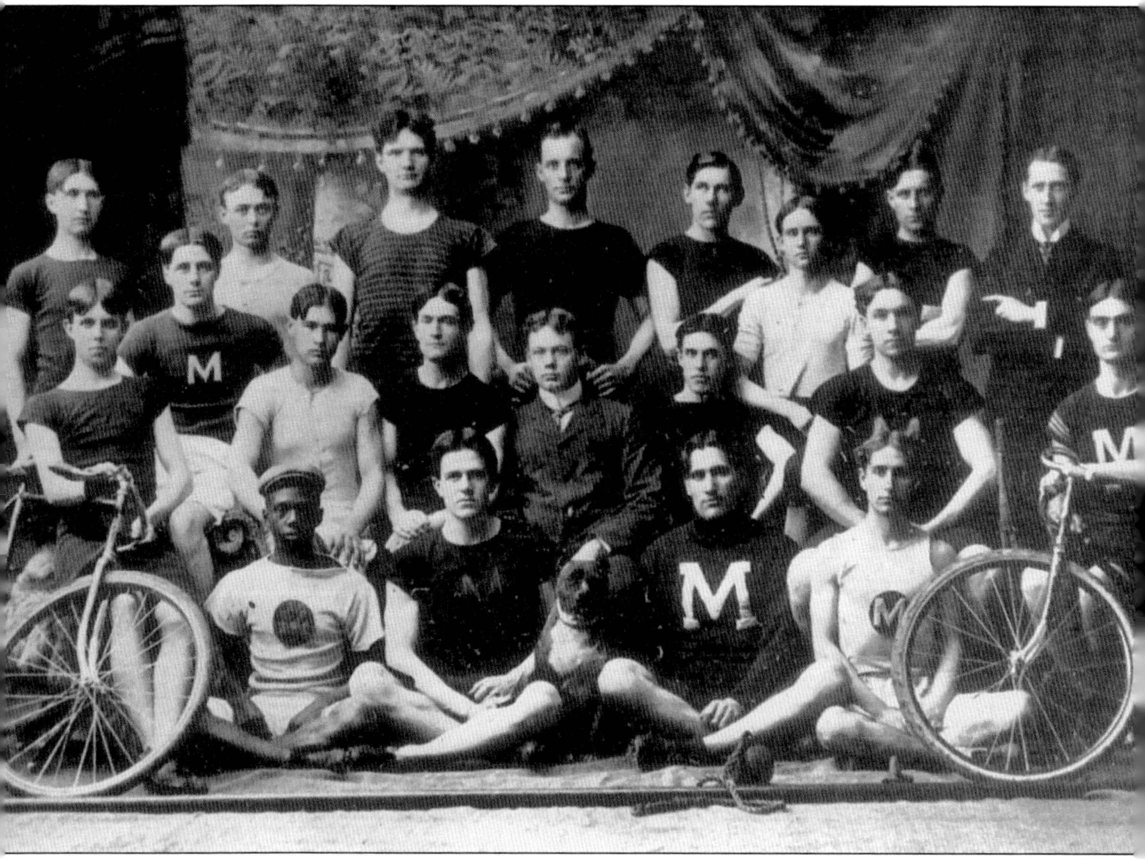

In all likelihood, the same young man participated in college sports at Monmouth College. (Courtesy of Monmouth College Library and Archives.)

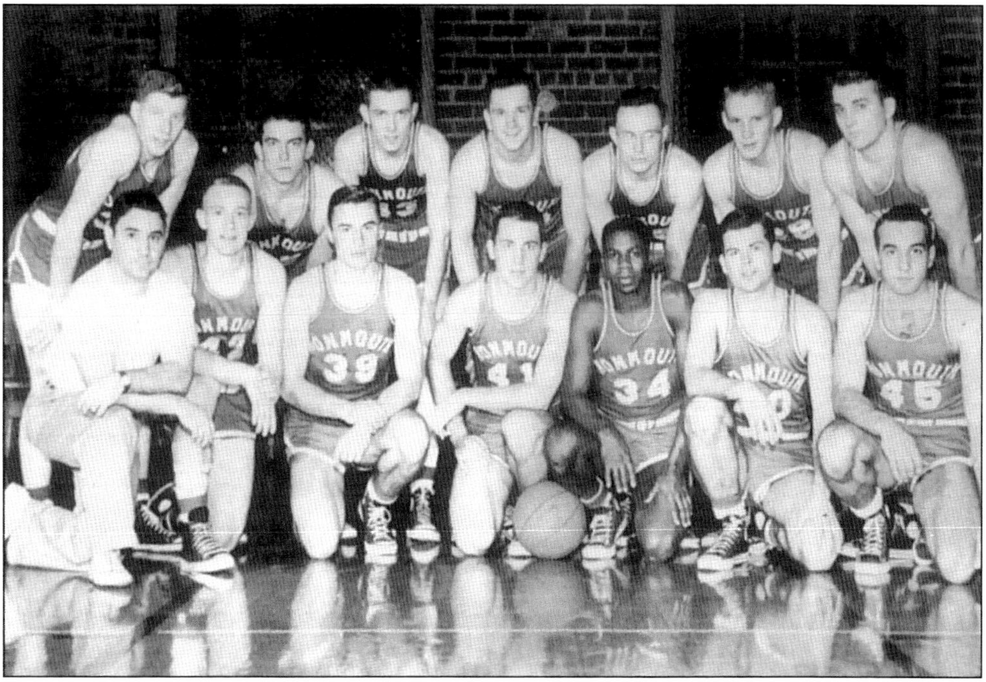

By the 1950s, African-American students often still found themselves without other African-American peers on college campuses throughout west central Illinois. Ray Brooks of Monmouth, Illinois, endured in the early 1950s at Monmouth College and was perhaps one of the college's most noted athletes. In 1953, he graduated from Monmouth College as an all-around athlete. (Courtesy of Monmouth College Library and Archives.)

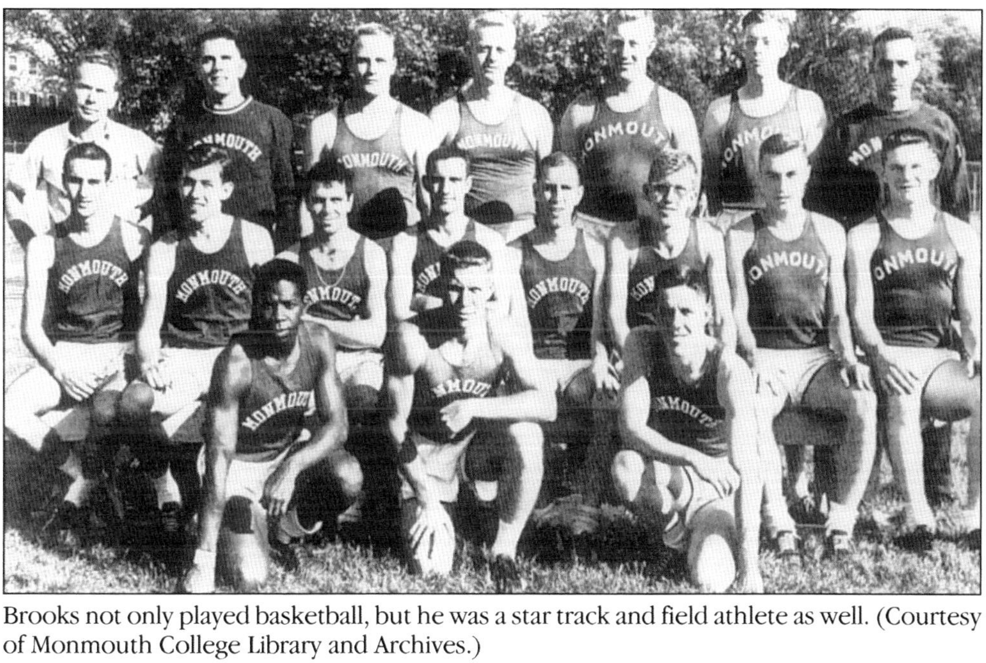

Brooks not only played basketball, but he was a star track and field athlete as well. (Courtesy of Monmouth College Library and Archives.)

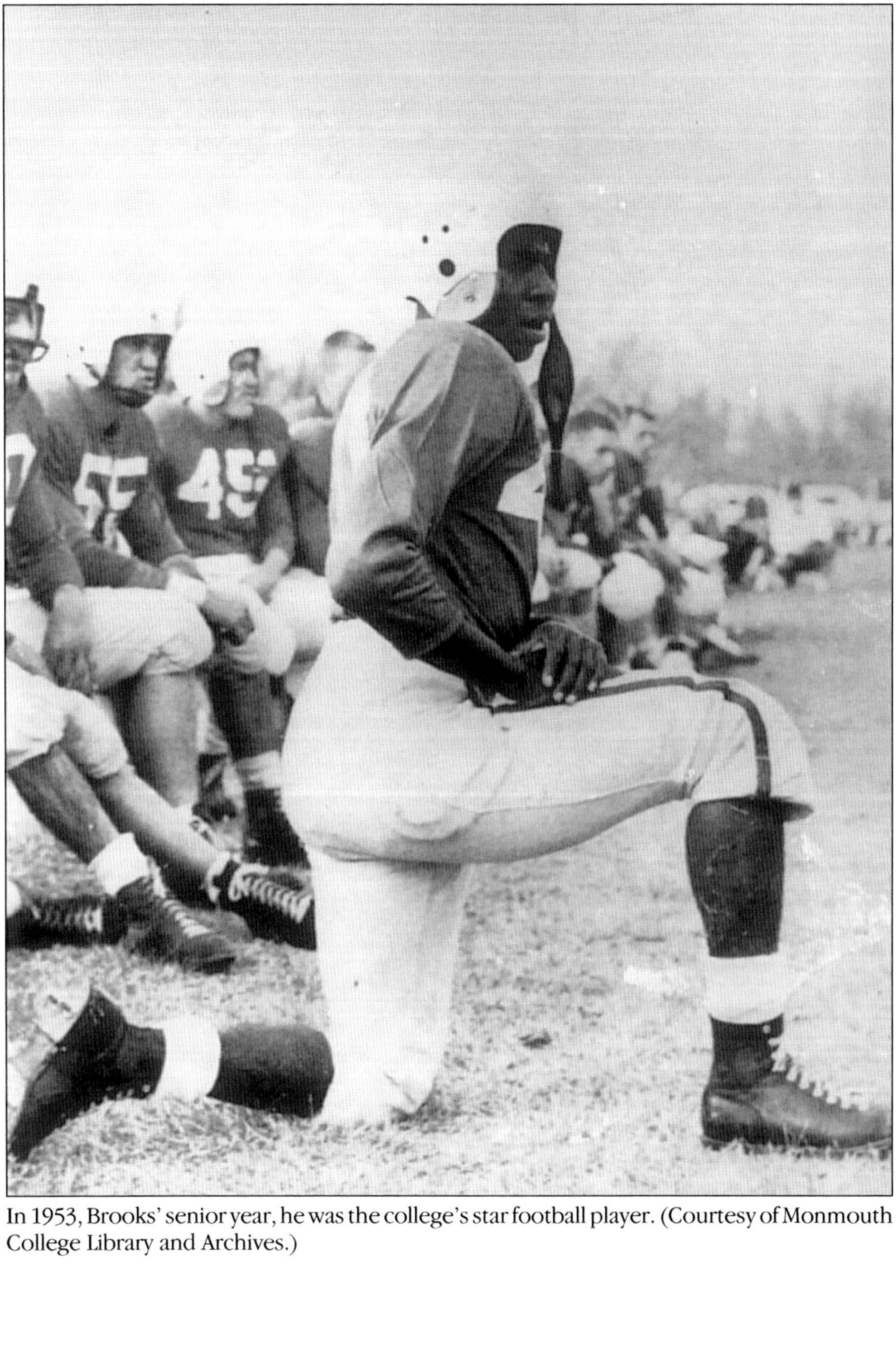

In 1953, Brooks' senior year, he was the college's star football player. (Courtesy of Monmouth College Library and Archives.)

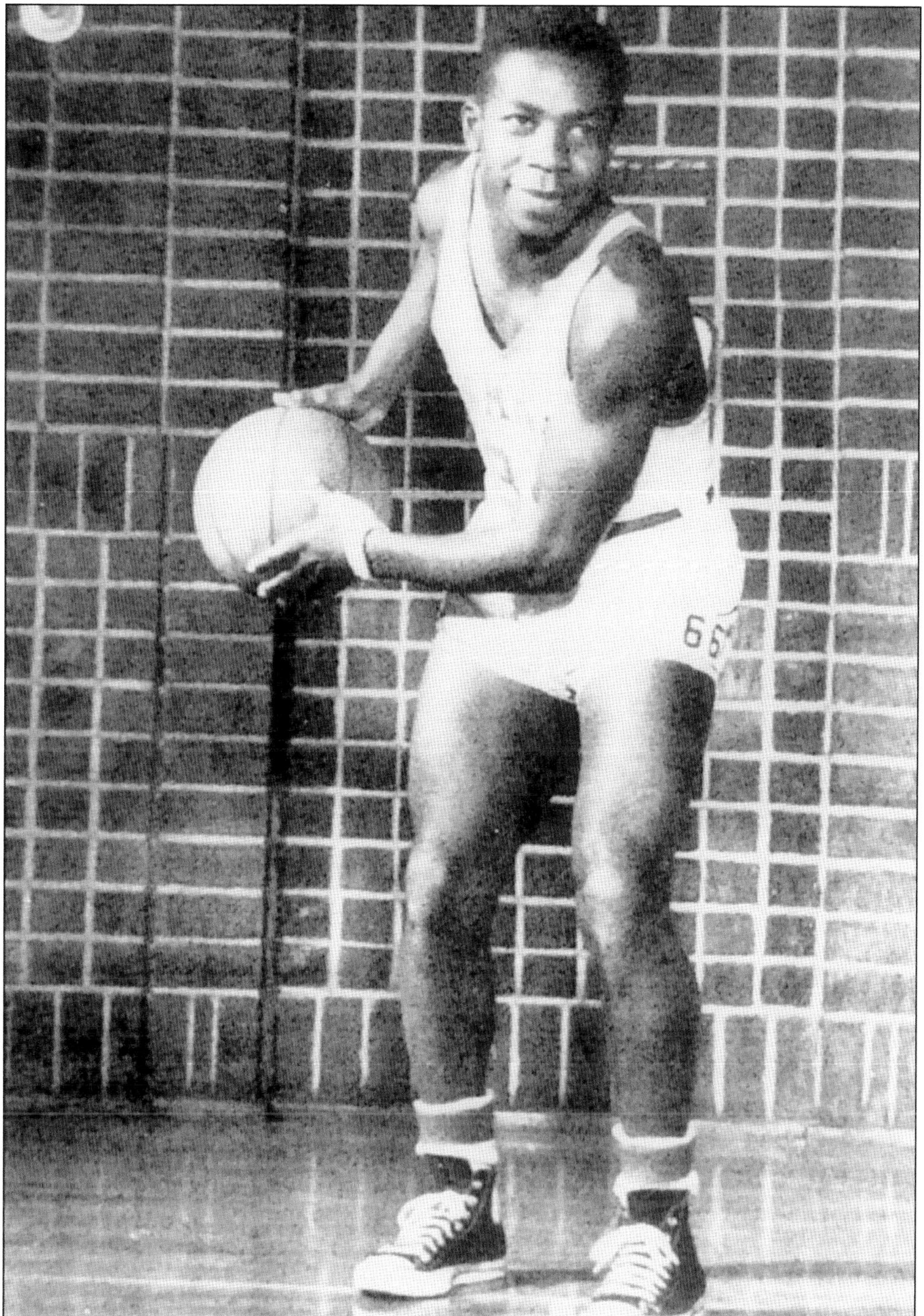

Brooks was an early example of what it meant to be young, gifted, and black—a true scholar athlete. Here he posed for the 1953 college yearbook in his basketball uniform. (Courtesy of Monmouth College Library and Archives.)

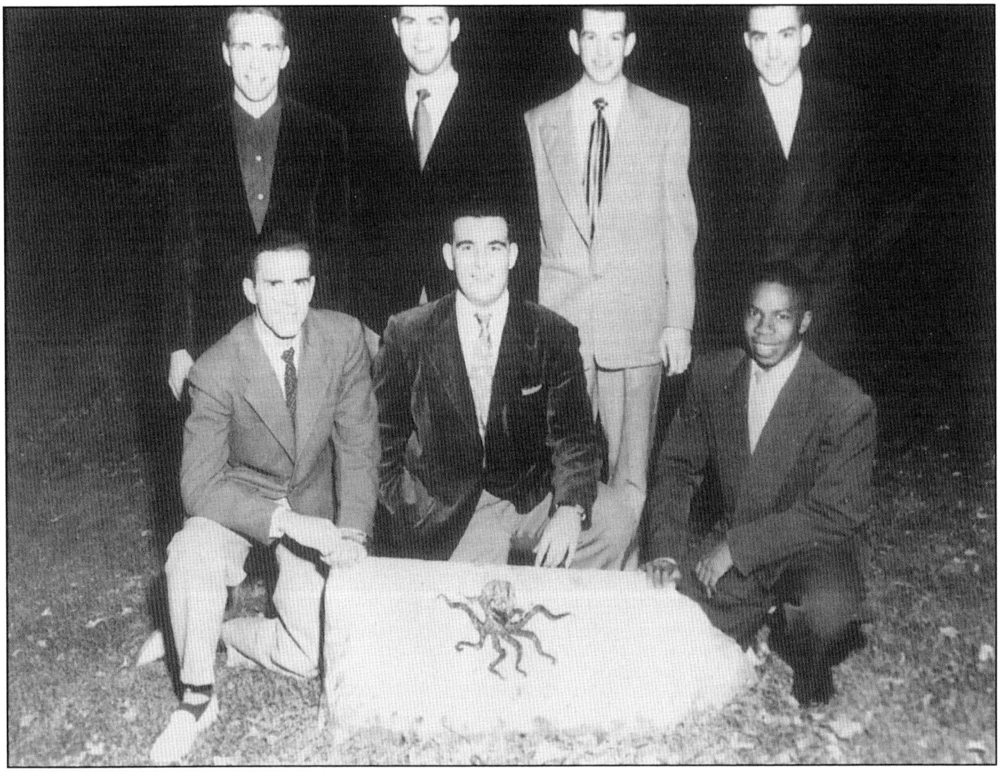

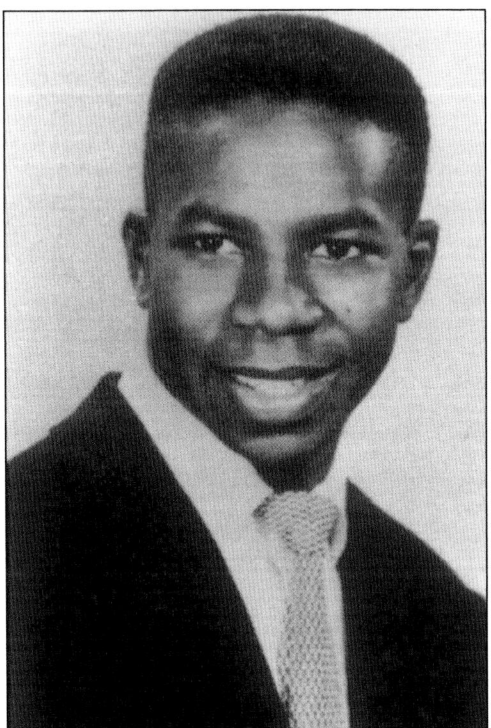

Brooks graduated as a noted senior in the class of 1953 from Monmouth College. (Courtesy of Monmouth College Library and Archives.)

The Brooks family is one of Monmouth's most noted black families. Ray Brooks remains a tough act to follow, despite the racial adversity that he endured. (Courtesy of Monmouth College Library and Archives.)

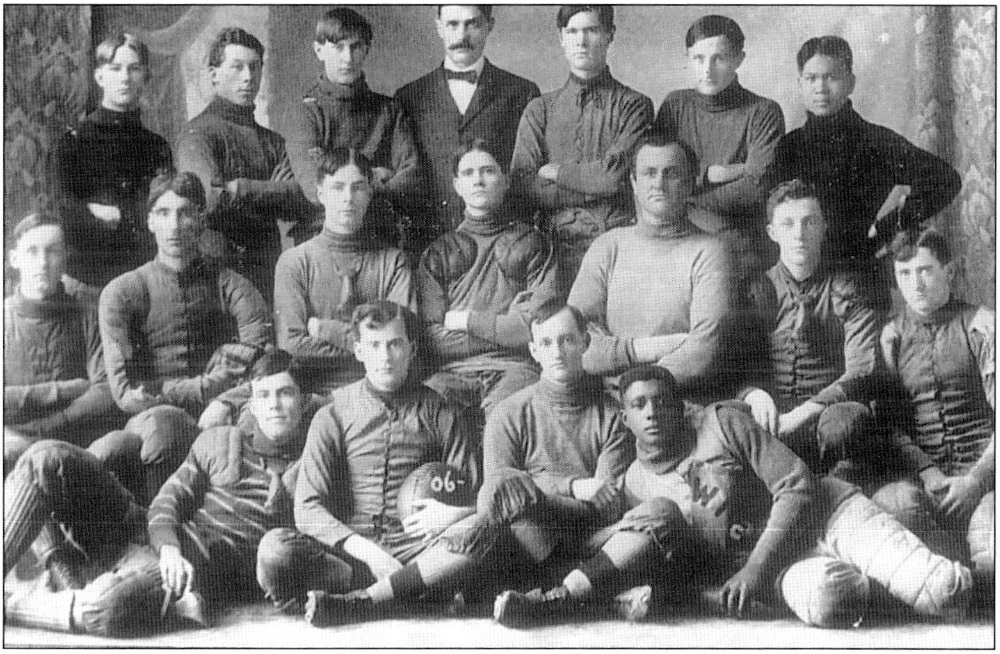

Western Illinois University's early history was not unlike that of other colleges throughout west central Illinois. Alonzo Thorpe belonged to one of Macomb's earliest black families to settle in the area. Here Thorpe is seen in an early football team photograph. Thorpe never attended the college; he was enrolled in the preparatory school in 1906. (Courtesy of the Archives and Special Collections, Western Illinois University Library.)

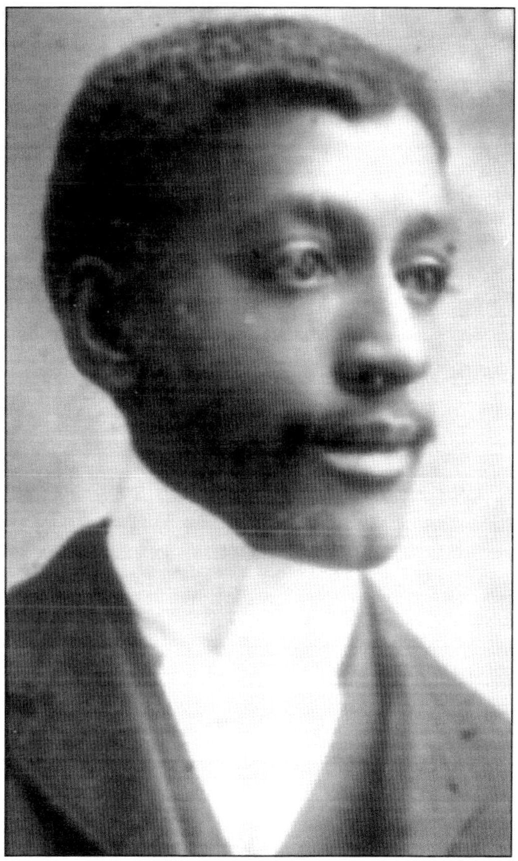

Thorpe posed for this strikingly handsome photograph later in life. The Thorpes remain another one of Macomb's long standing black families. (Courtesy of the Archives and Special Collections, Western Illinois University Library.)

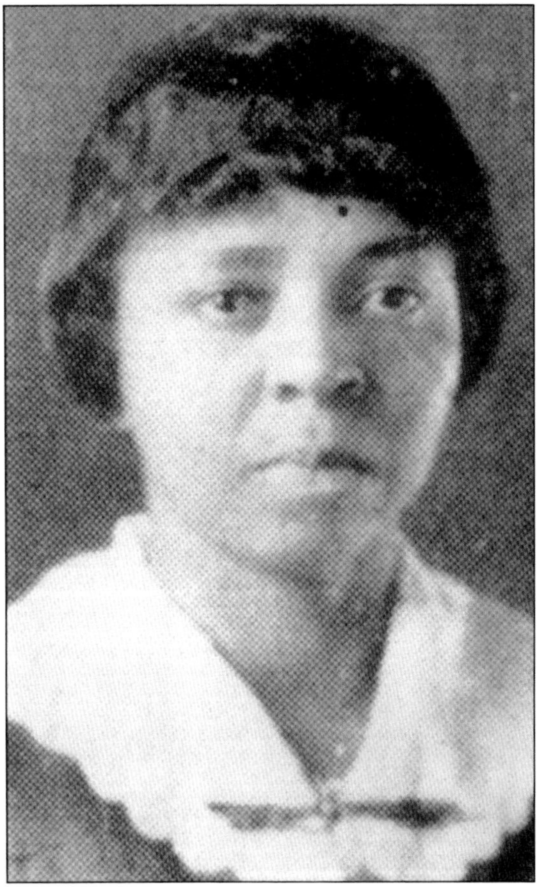

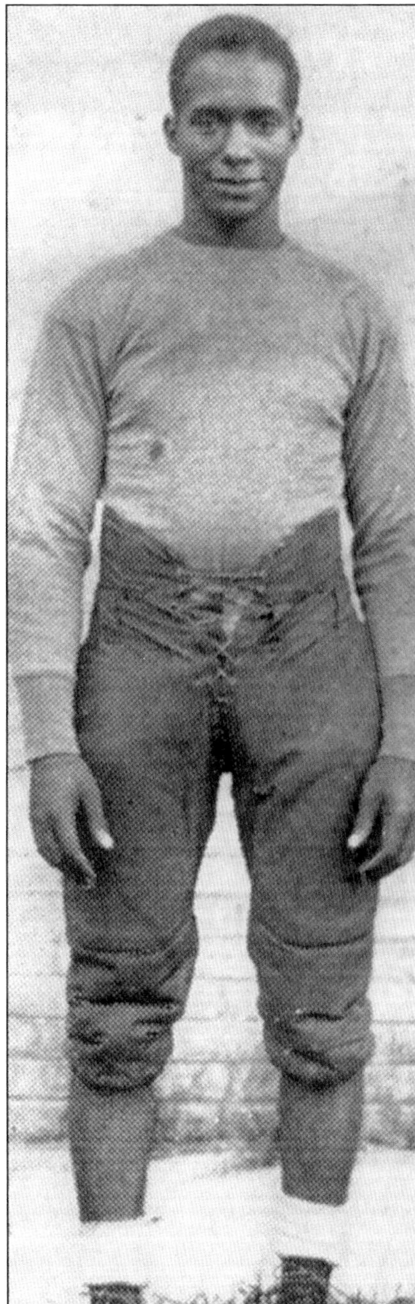

ABOVE: In the fall of 1921, a young woman from Quincy enrolled in the teacher-training program at Western Illinois State Teachers College (WIU). Leala Burnett, a non-traditional student from Quincy, graduated from Western in the class of 1923. She is the first African-American graduate of the institution. (Courtesy of the Archives and Special Collections, Western Illinois University Library.)

RIGHT: Ernest Page of Peoria was one of Western Illinois State Teachers College's (WIU) first African-American student athletes. He made the school's all-star team by the time of his senior year in college. Here he is ready for the gridiron. (Courtesy of the Archives and Special Collections, Western Illinois University Library.)

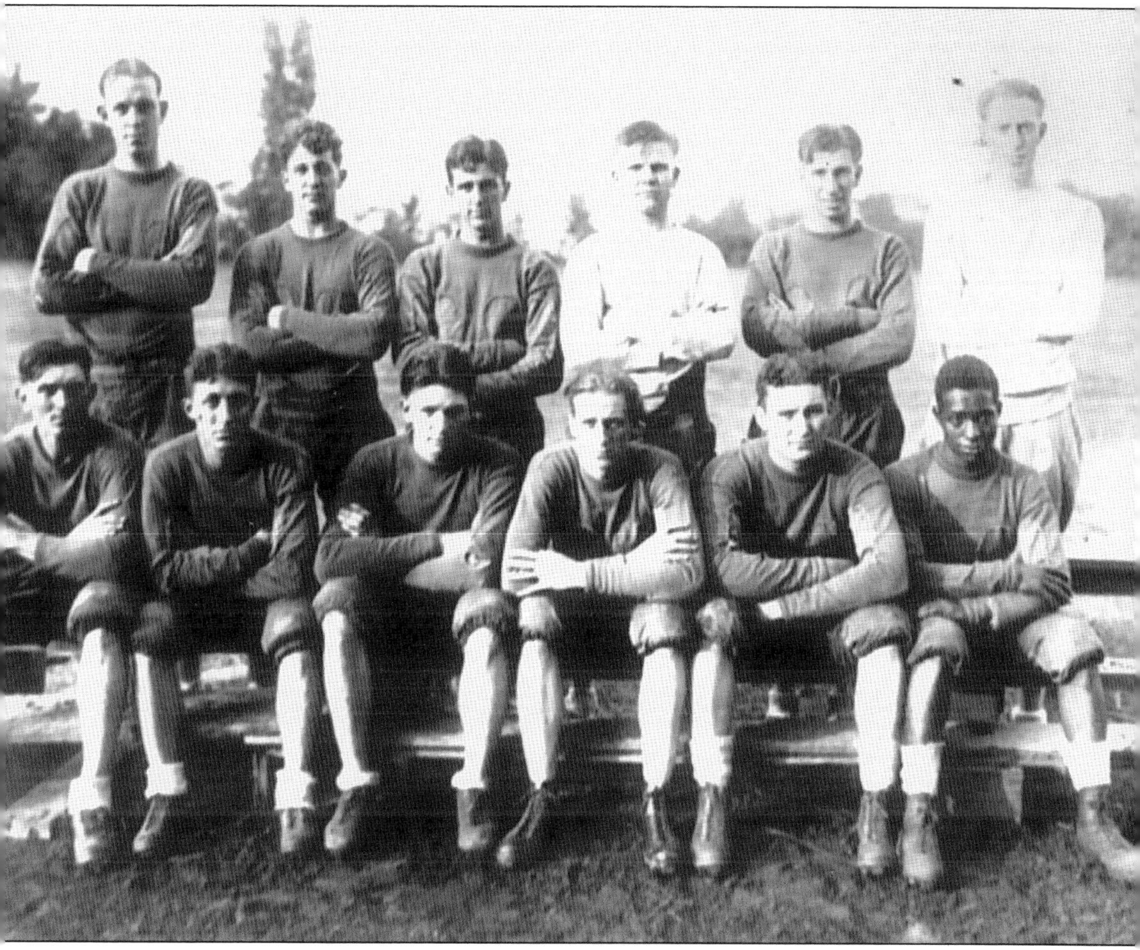

Page also endured as the only African-American student and athlete at Western Illinois State Teachers College (WIU) at the time. (Courtesy of the Archives and Special Collections, Western Illinois University Library.)

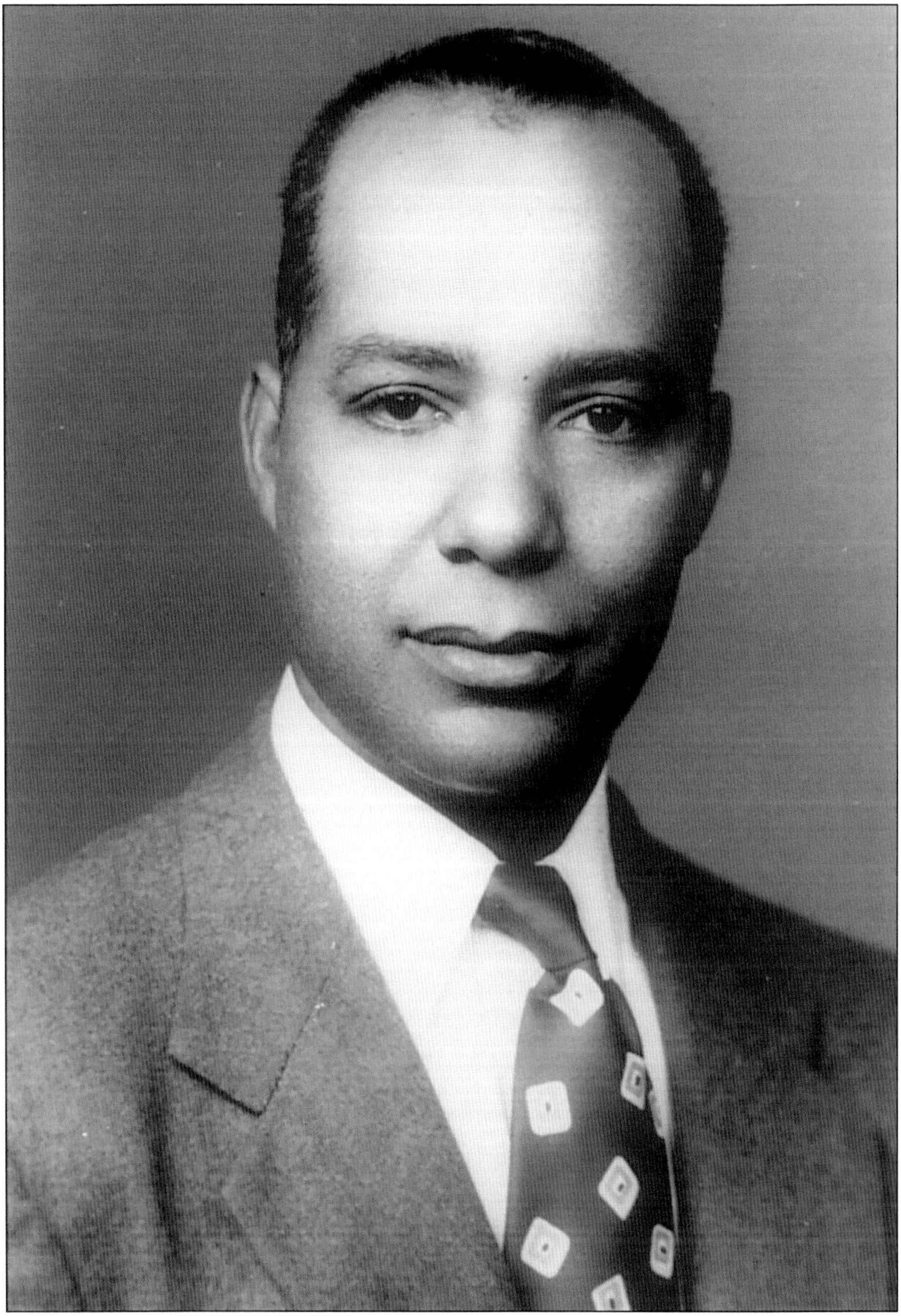

Ernest Page posed for this photograph later in life. He remains one of the institution's most honorable African-American graduates. (Courtesy of the Archives and Special Collections, Western Illinois University Library.)

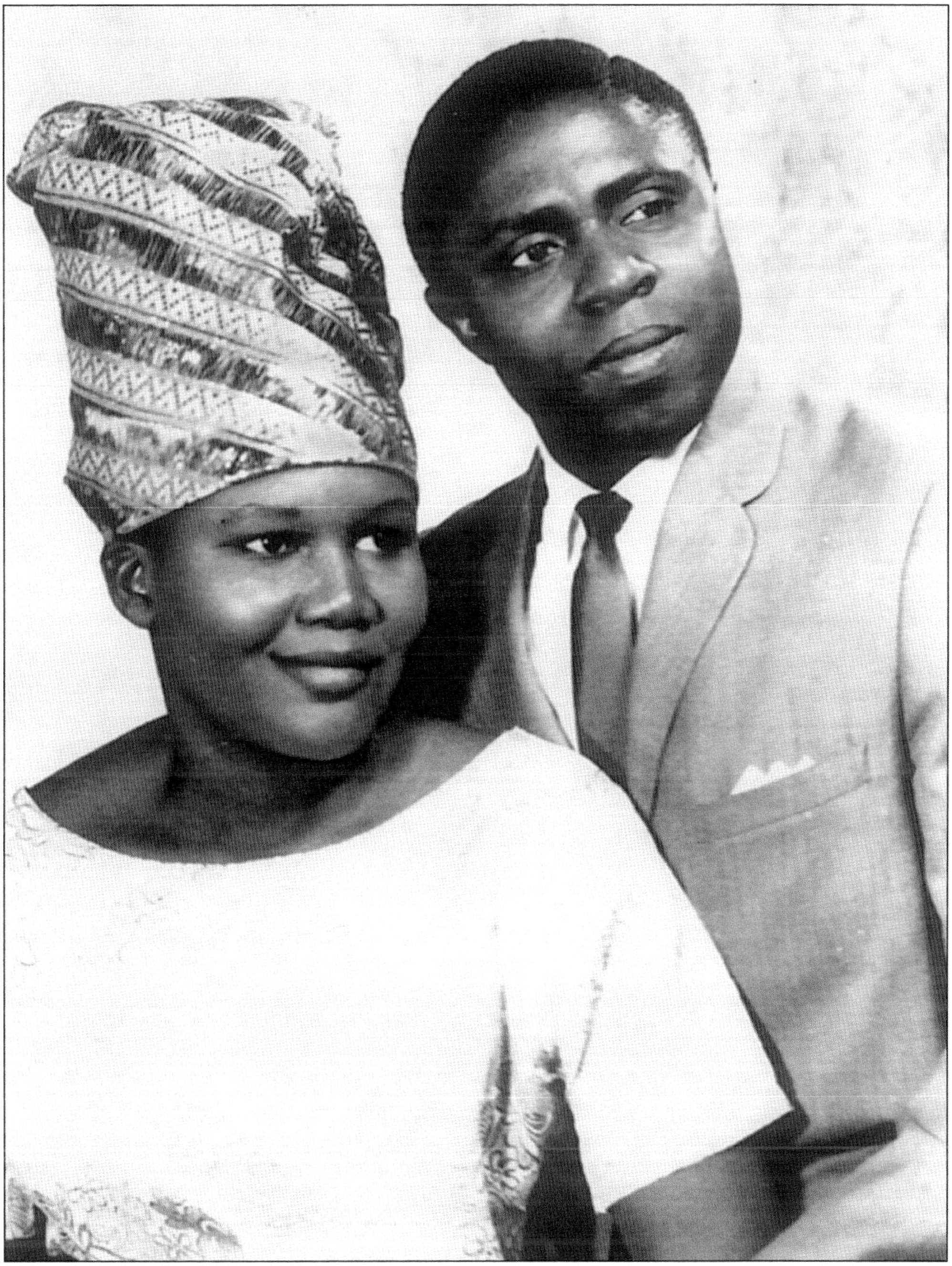

African-American students often endured without cultural and ethnic peers at most colleges throughout west central Illinois. Rarely were there any African-American instructors early in the history of west central Illinois educational institutions. Western Illinois University did not hire its first black instructor until 1965. Igolima Amachree was the first black professor to join the faculty of Western Illinois University. He remains on the faculty today in the department of Sociology and Anthropology. (Courtesy of the Archives and Special Collections, Western Illinois University Library.)

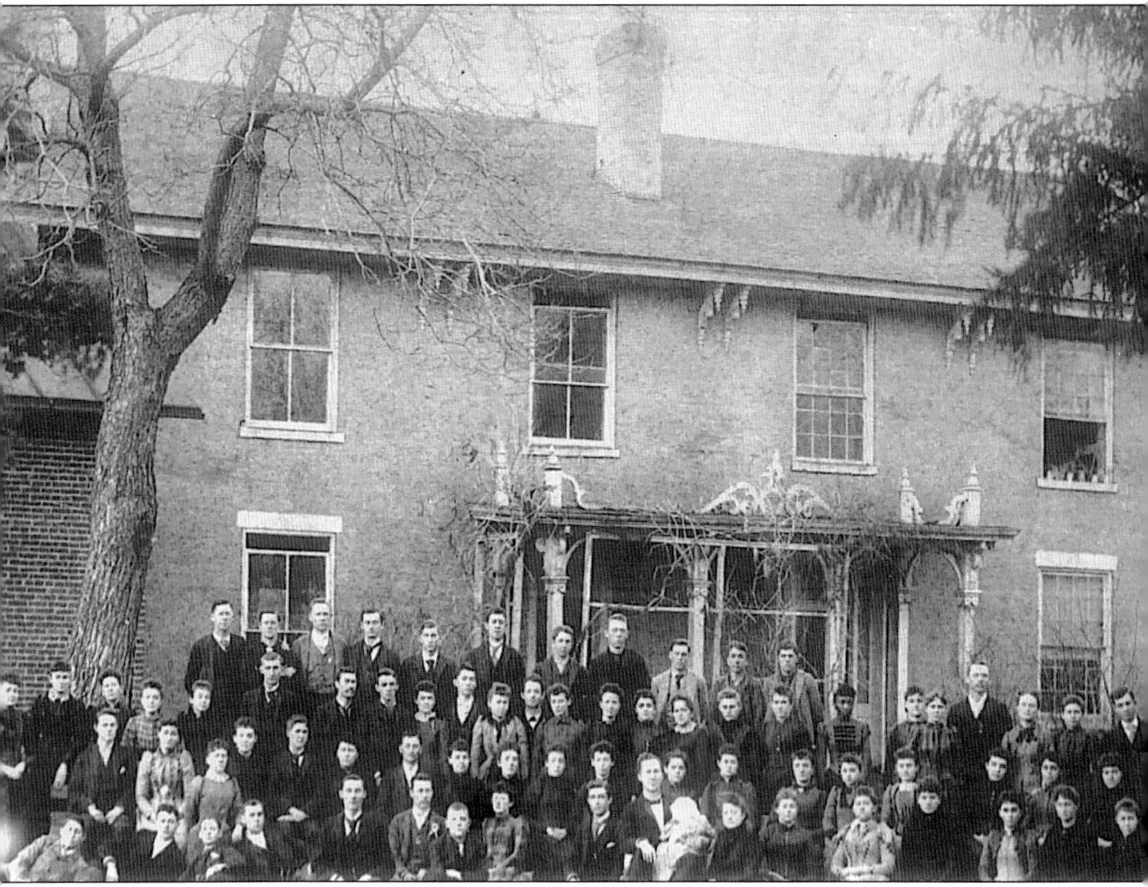

McDonough College existed in McDonough County in the mid-to-late 1800s. Again, one lone African-American female can be seen in the photograph. (Courtesy of the Archives and Special Collections, Western Illinois University Library.)

During the late 1920s, Jesse Routte continually made the local news. Routte was a conservatory student at Augustana College in Rock Island. (Courtesy of Augustana College Archives.)

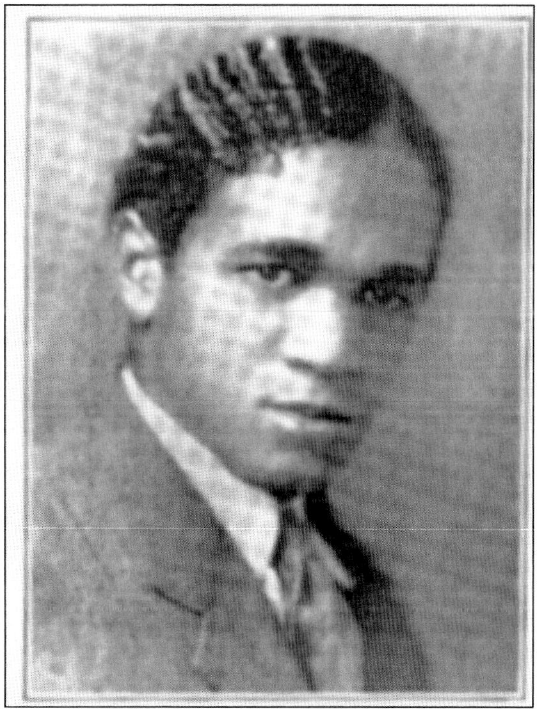

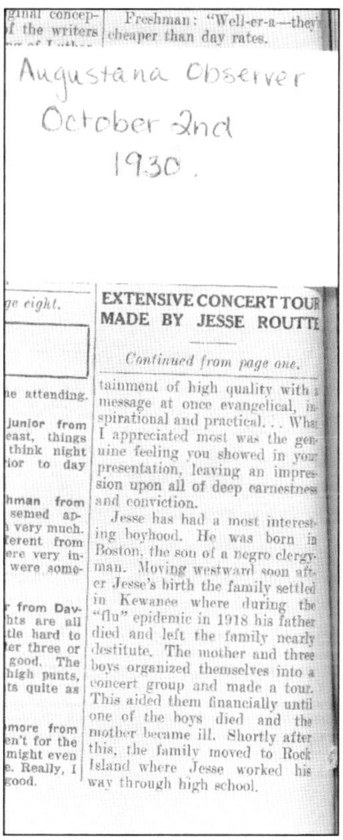

Augustana Observer
October 2nd
1930.

EXTENSIVE CONCERT TOUR MADE BY JESSE ROUTTE

Continued from page one.

tainment of high quality with a message at once evangelical, inspirational and practical. . . What I appreciated most was the genuine feeling you showed in your presentation, leaving an impression upon all of deep earnestness and conviction.

Jesse has had a most interesting boyhood. He was born in Boston, the son of a negro clergyman. Moving westward soon after Jesse's birth the family settled in Kewanee where during the "flu" epidemic in 1918 his father died and left the family nearly destitute. The mother and three boys organized themselves into a concert group and made a tour. This aided them financially until one of the boys died and the mother became ill. Shortly after this, the family moved to Rock Island where Jesse worked his way through high school.

LEFT: The *Augustana Observer* profiled the interesting manner in which Routte was financing his college education. (Courtesy of Augustana College Archives.)

RIGHT: Aside from giving recitals, Routte also gave public lectures as this news article detailed from November 22, 1928. (Courtesy of Augustana College Archives.)

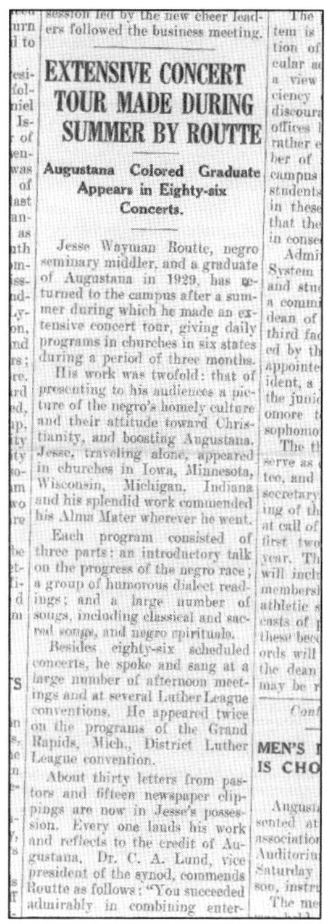

EXTENSIVE CONCERT TOUR MADE DURING SUMMER BY ROUTTE

Augustana Colored Graduate Appears in Eighty-six Concerts.

Jesse Wayman Routte, negro seminary middler, and a graduate of Augustana in 1929, has returned to the campus after a summer during which he made an extensive concert tour, giving daily programs in churches in six states during a period of three months.

His work was twofold: that of presenting to his audiences a picture of the negro's homely culture and their attitude toward Christianity, and boosting Augustana. Jesse, traveling alone, appeared in churches in Iowa, Minnesota, Wisconsin, Michigan, Indiana and his splendid work commended his Alma Mater wherever he went.

Each program consisted of three parts: an introductory talk on the progress of the negro race; a group of humorous dialect readings; and a large number of songs, including classical and sacred songs, and negro spirituals.

Besides eighty-six scheduled concerts, he spoke and sang at a large number of afternoon meetings and at several Luther League conventions. He appeared twice on the programs of the Grand Rapids, Mich., District Luther League convention.

About thirty letters from pastors and fifteen newspaper clippings are now in Jesse's possession. Every one lauds his work and reflects to the credit of Augustana. Dr. C. A. Lund, vice president of the synod, commends Routte as follows: "You succeeded admirably in combining enter-

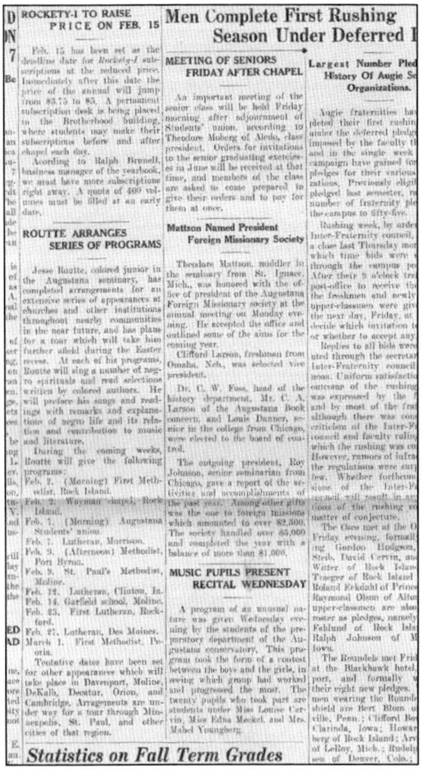

Men Complete First Rushing Season Under Deferred

ROCKETY-I TO RAISE PRICE ON FEB. 15

Feb. 15 has been set as the deadline date for *Rockety-I* subscriptions at the reduced price. Immediately after this date the price of the annual will jump from $3.75 to $5. A permanent subscription desk is being placed in the Brotherhood building, where students may make their subscriptions before and after chapel each day.

Acording to Ralph Brunell, business manager of the yearbook, we must have more subscriptions right away. A quota of 400 volumes must be filled at an early date.

ROUTTE ARRANGES SERIES OF PROGRAMS

Jesse Routte, colored junior in the Augustana seminary, has completed arrangements for an extensive series of appearances at churches and other institutions throughout nearby communities in the near future, and has plans for a tour which will take him further afield during the Easter recess. At each of his programs, Routte will sing a number of negro spirituals and read selections written by colored authors. He will preface his songs and readings with remarks and explanations of negro life and its relation and contribution to music and literature.

During the coming weeks, Routte will give the following programs:

Feb. 2. (Morning) First Methodist, Rock Island.
Feb. 2. Wayman chapel, Rock Island.
Feb. 7. (Morning) Augustana Students' union.
Feb. 7. Lutheran, Morrison.
Feb. 9. (Afternoon) Methodist, Port Byron.
Feb. 9. St. Paul's Methodist, Moline.
Feb. 12. Lutheran, Clinton, Ia.
Feb. 14. Garfield school, Moline.
Feb. 23. First Lutheran, Rockford.
Feb. 27. Lutheran, Des Moines.
March 1. First Methodist, Peoria.

Tentative dates have been set for other appearances which will take place in Davenport, Moline, DeKalb, Decatur, Orion, and Cambridge. Arragements are under way for a tour through Minneapolis, St. Paul, and other cities of that region.

MEETING OF SENIORS FRIDAY AFTER CHAPEL

An important meeting of the senior class will be held Friday morning after adjournment of Students' union, according to Theodore Moberg of Aledo, class president. Orders for invitations to the senior graduating exercieses in June will be received at that time, and members of the class are asked to come prepared to give their orders and to pay for them at once.

Mattson Named President Foreign Missionary Society

Theodore Mattson, middler in the seminary from St. Ignace, Mich., was honored with the office of president of the Augustana Foreign Missionary society at the annual meeting on Monday evening. He accepted the office and outlined some of the aims for the coming year.

Clifford Larson, freshman from Omaha, Neb., was selected vice president.

Dr. C. W. Foss, head of the history department, Mr. C. A. Larson of the Augustana Book concern, and Louis Danner, senior in the college from Chicago, were elected to the board of control.

The outgoing president, Roy Johnson, senior seminarian from Chicago, gave a report of the activities and accomplishments of the past year. Among other gifts was the one to foreign missions which amounted to over $2,500. The society handled over $5,000 and completed the year with a balance of more than $1,000.

MUSIC PUPILS PRESENT RECITAL WEDNESDAY

A program of an unusual nature was given Wednesday evening by the students of the preparatory department of the Augustana conservatory. This program took the form of a contest between the boys and the girls, in seeing which group had worked and progressed the most. The twenty pupils who took part are students under Miss Louise Cervin, Miss Edna Meckel, and Mrs. Mabel Youngberg.

Statistics on Fall Term Grades

Routte continually made appearances throughout the region, as he was noted for his renditions of Negro Spirituals. The paper noted that "he will preface his songs and readings with remarks and explanation of Negro life and its relation and contribution to music and literature." (Courtesy of Augustana College Archives.)

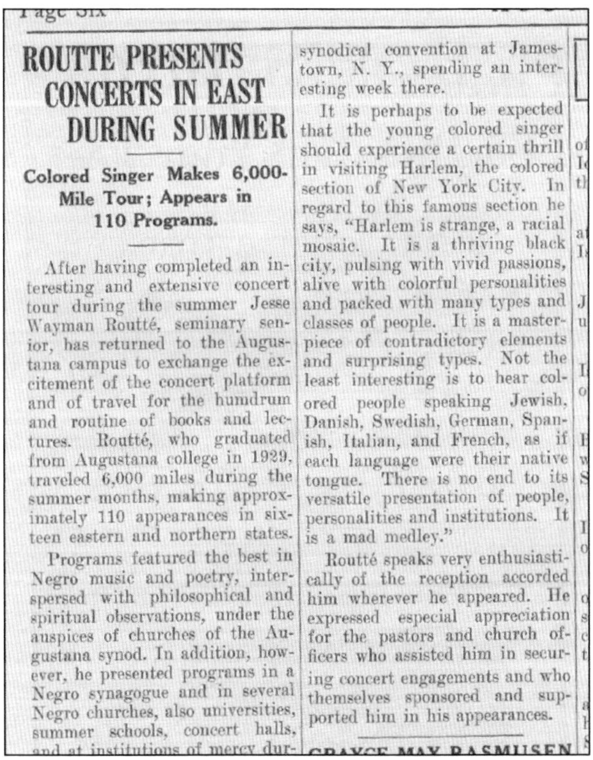

ROUTTE PRESENTS CONCERTS IN EAST DURING SUMMER

Colored Singer Makes 6,000-Mile Tour; Appears in 110 Programs.

After having completed an interesting and extensive concert tour during the summer Jesse Wayman Routté, seminary senior, has returned to the Augustana campus to exchange the excitement of the concert platform and of travel for the humdrum and routine of books and lectures. Routté, who graduated from Augustana college in 1929, traveled 6,000 miles during the summer months, making approximately 110 appearances in sixteen eastern and northern states.

Programs featured the best in Negro music and poetry, interspersed with philosophical and spiritual observations, under the auspices of churches of the Augustana synod. In addition, however, he presented programs in a Negro synagogue and in several Negro churches, also universities, summer schools, concert halls, synodical convention at Jamestown, N. Y., spending an interesting week there.

It is perhaps to be expected that the young colored singer should experience a certain thrill in visiting Harlem, the colored section of New York City. In regard to this famous section he says, "Harlem is strange, a racial mosaic. It is a thriving black city, pulsing with vivid passions, alive with colorful personalities and packed with many types and classes of people. It is a masterpiece of contradictory elements and surprising types. Not the least interesting is to hear colored people speaking Jewish, Danish, Swedish, German, Spanish, Italian, and French, as if each language were their native tongue. There is no end to its versatile presentation of people, personalities and institutions. It is a mad medley."

Routté speaks very enthusiastically of the reception accorded him wherever he appeared. He expressed especial appreciation for the pastors and church officers who assisted him in securing concert engagements and who themselves sponsored and supported him in his appearances.

As late as 1931, Routte was still hailed as one of the college's most noteworthy alumni. In 1931, the college welcomed him back to the campus after his rather extensive summer schedule. (Courtesy of Augustana College Archives.)

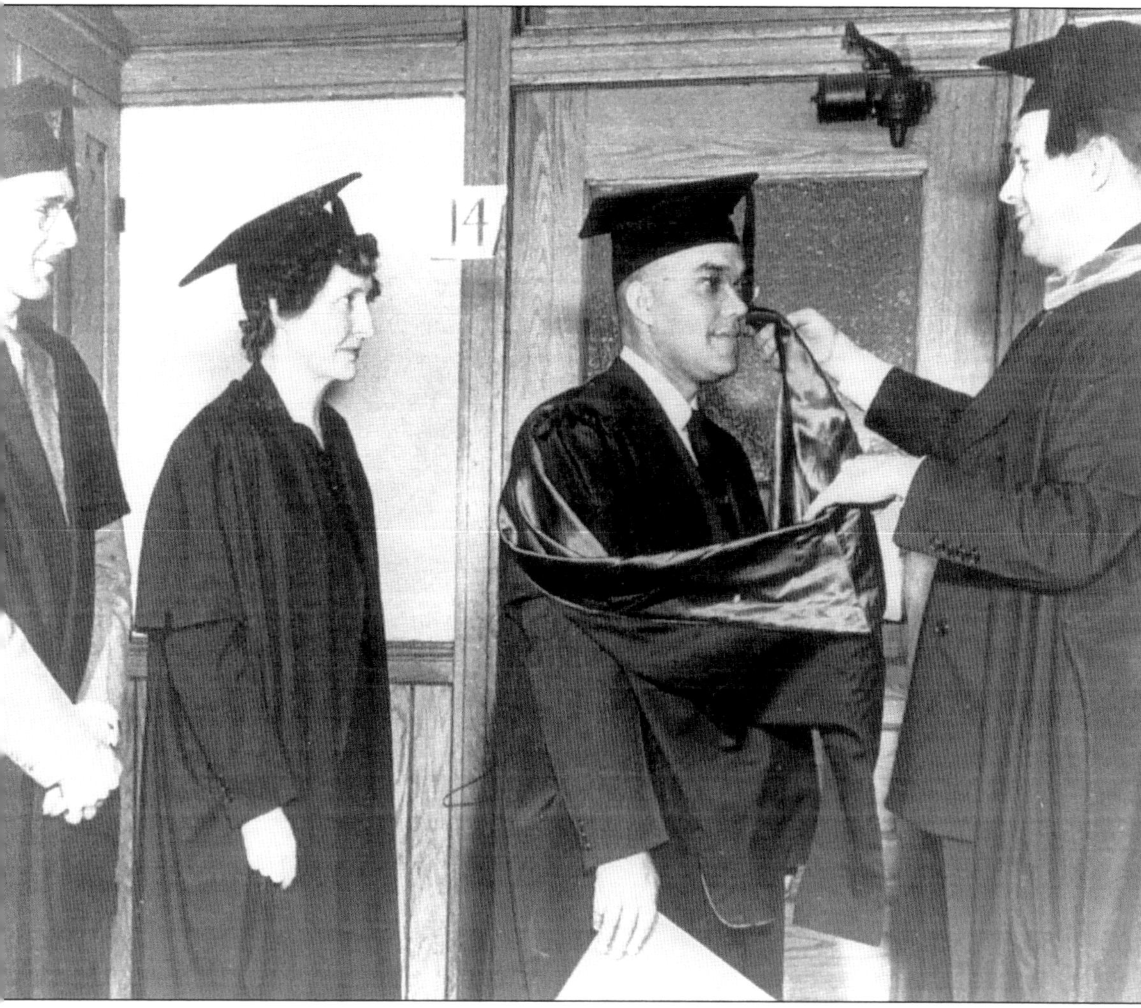

Romeo B. Garrett was the first African-American student to receive a master's degree in any field from Bradley University in Peoria, Illinois. (Courtesy of the Garrett Collection.)

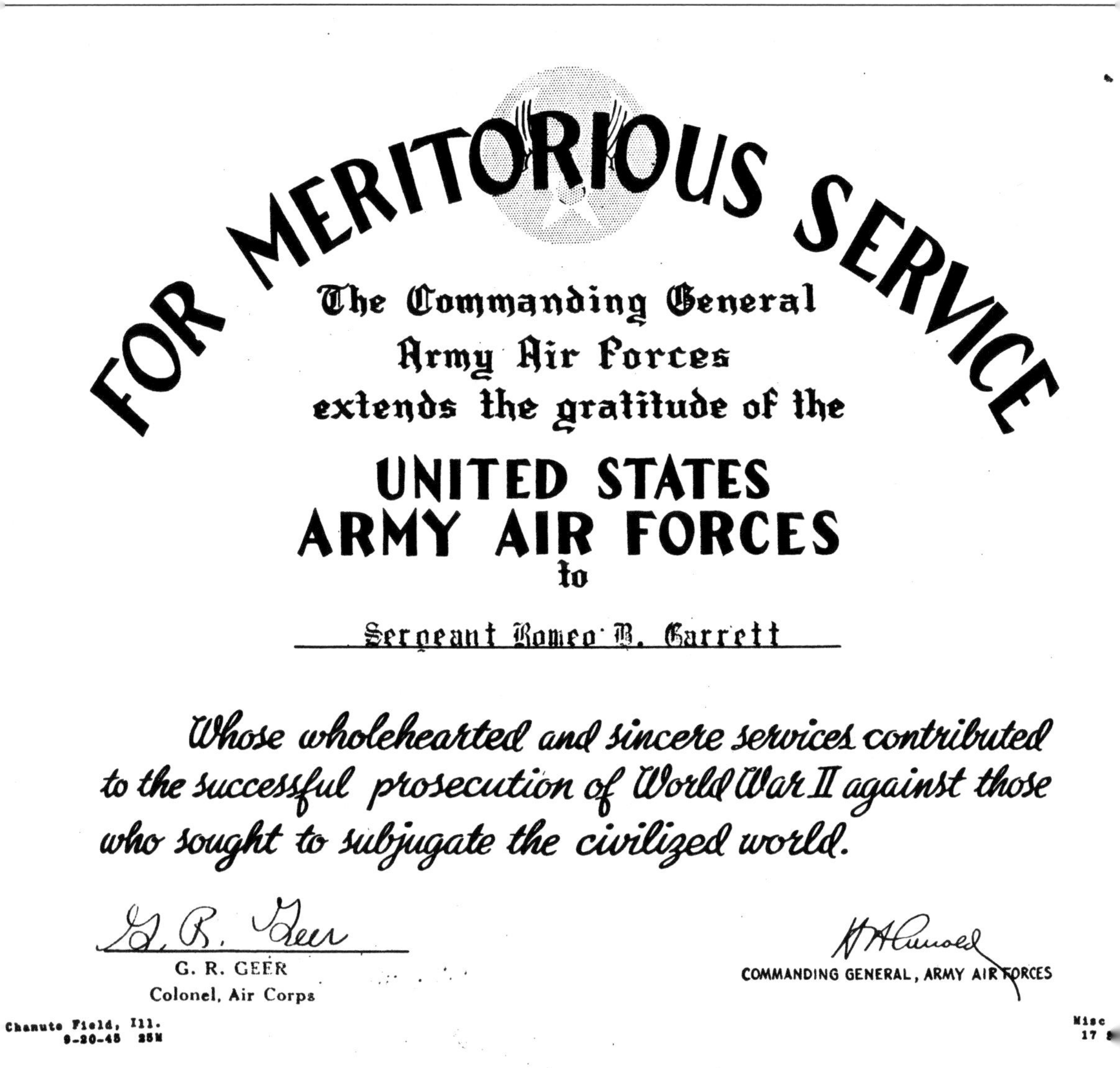

FOR MERITORIOUS SERVICE

The Commanding General
Army Air Forces
extends the gratitude of the

UNITED STATES
ARMY AIR FORCES
to

Sergeant Romeo B. Garrett

Whose wholehearted and sincere services contributed to the successful prosecution of World War II against those who sought to subjugate the civilized world.

G. R. Geer
G. R. GEER
Colonel, Air Corps

H. H. Arnold
COMMANDING GENERAL, ARMY AIR FORCES

Chanute Field, Ill.
9-20-45 25M

Misc
17

Garrett served the nation with much grace and honor, as he was granted this certificate for Meritorious Service after his service in the United States Army during World War II. (Courtesy of the Garrett Collection.)

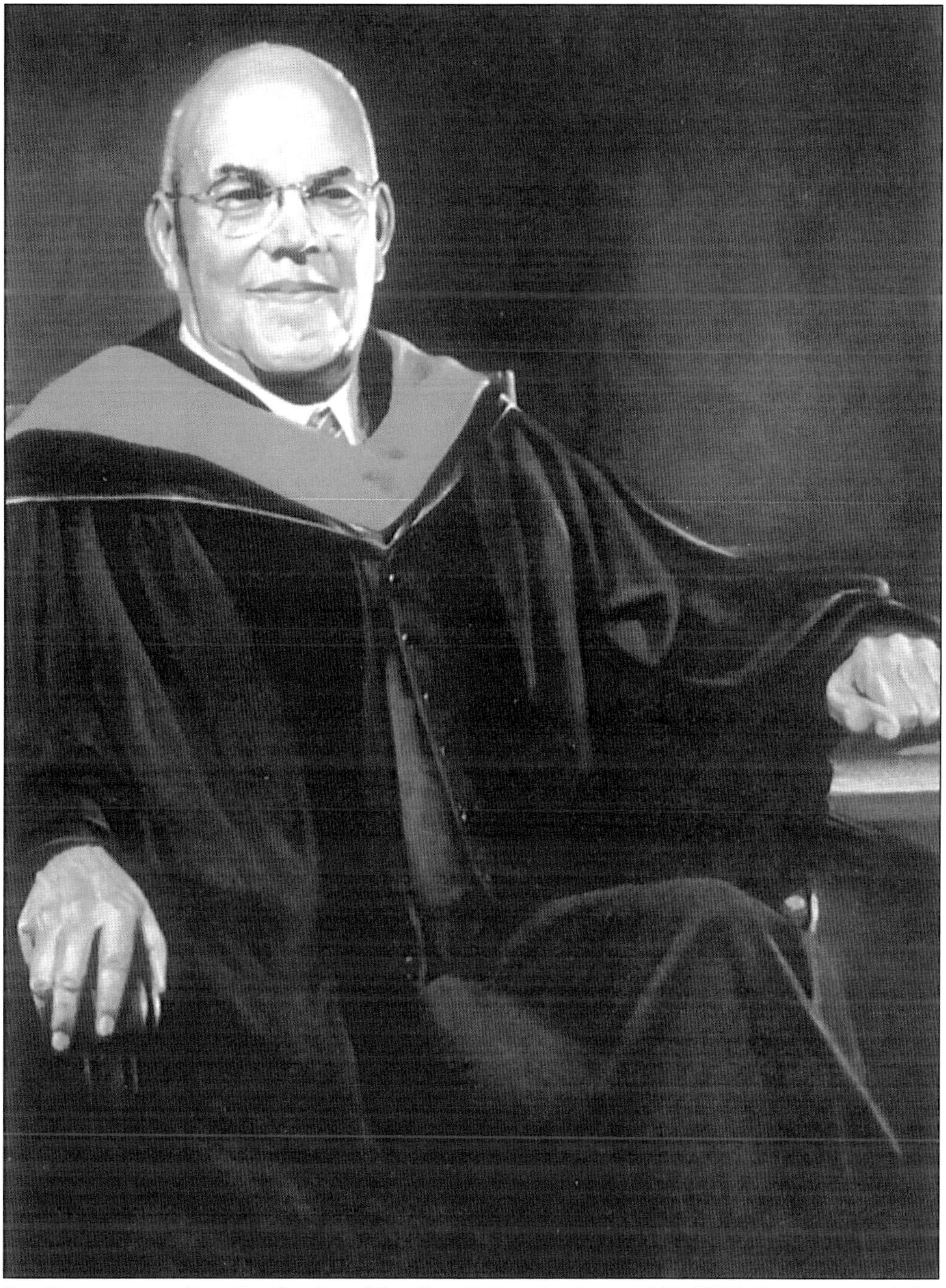

Dr. Garrett served on the faculty of Bradley University from 1947–1976. Garrett joined the faculty of Bradley University at a time when most black scholars could not find employment at white educational institutions. Dr. Garrett wrote most of the early histories of black life in Peoria. (Courtesy of the Garrett Collection.)

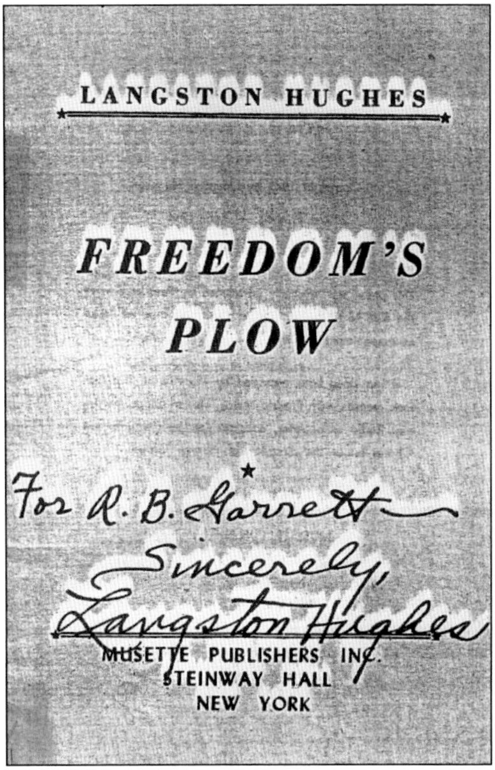
LANGSTON HUGHES

FREEDOM'S PLOW

For R. B. Garrett—
Sincerely,
Langston Hughes

MUSETTE PUBLISHERS INC.
STEINWAY HALL
NEW YORK

Dr. Garrett is said to have lived by many of the words of Langston Hughes, the great American poet and poet laureate of the Harlem Renaissance. In the Garrett Collection, the book *Freedom's Plow*, which was autographed by Hughes to Garrett is among the numerous items belonging to Peoria's most noted African-American scholar. (Courtesy of the Garrett Collection.)

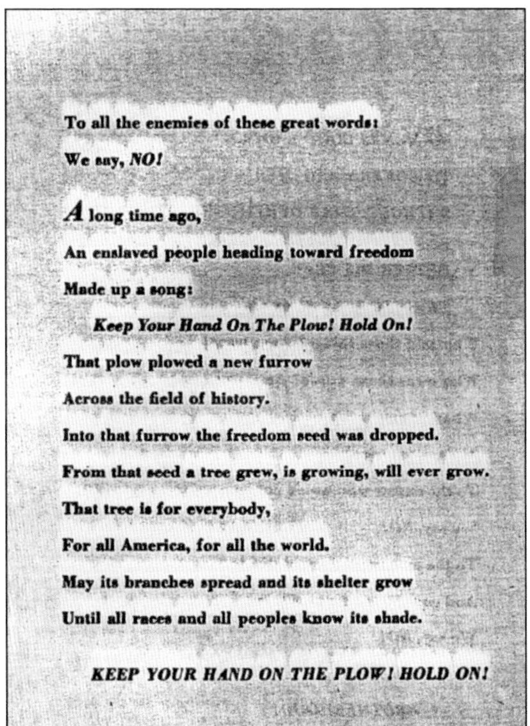
To all the enemies of these great words:
We say, *NO!*

A long time ago,
An enslaved people heading toward freedom
Made up a song:
Keep Your Hand On The Plow! Hold On!
That plow plowed a new furrow
Across the field of history.
Into that furrow the freedom seed was dropped.
From that seed a tree grew, is growing, will ever grow.
That tree is for everybody,
For all America, for all the world.
May its branches spread and its shelter grow
Until all races and all peoples know its shade.

KEEP YOUR HAND ON THE PLOW! HOLD ON!

Here Hughes' poem, "Keep Your Hand on the Plow! Hold On!" summons up the life and commitment to black history that Dr. Romeo Garrett exemplified. (Courtesy of the Garrett Collection.)

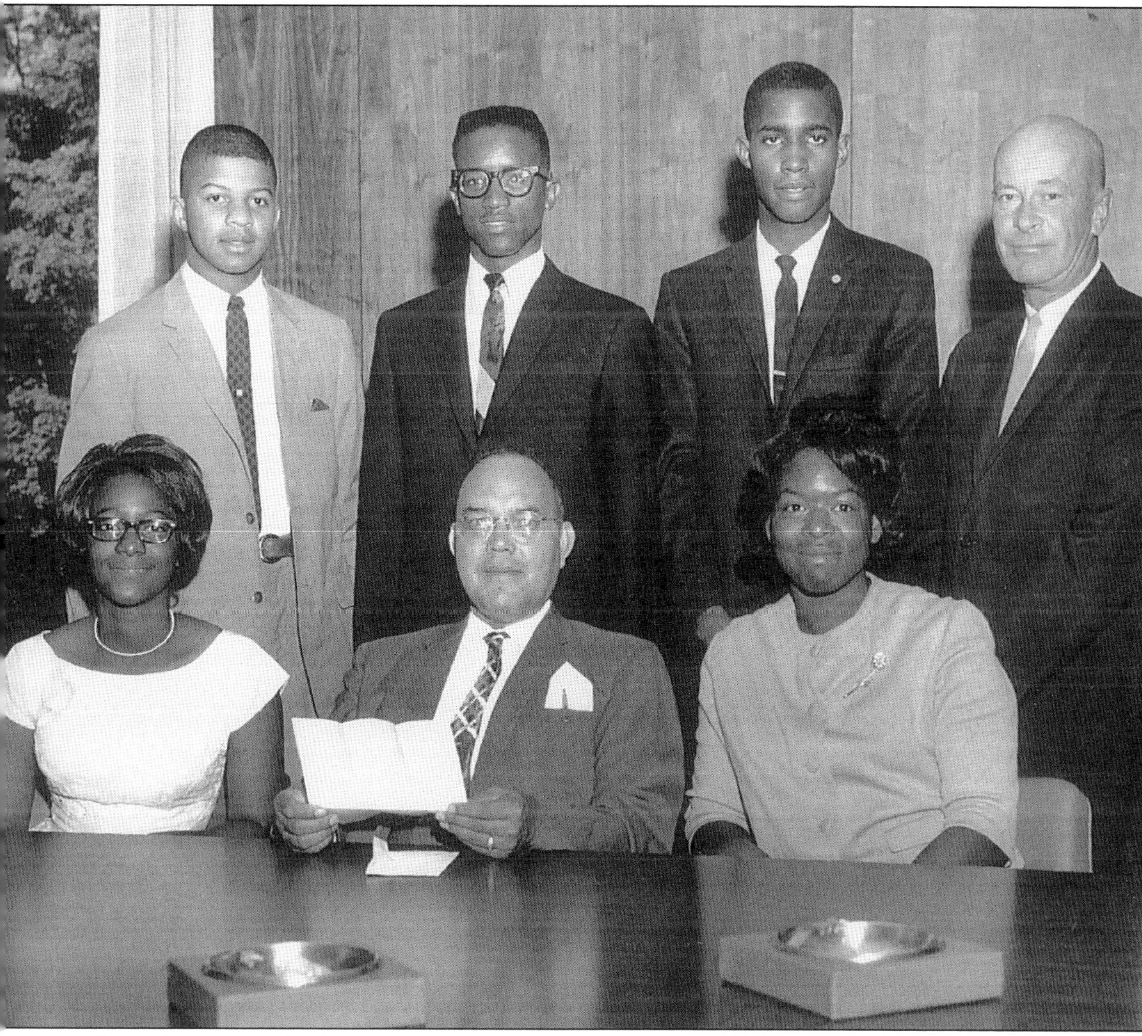

By the 1960s, Garrett had convinced Bradley University and their Board of Trustees to endow financial assistance to promising young African-American students who attended Bradley University. Dr. Garrett, seated at the center with a group of Garrett Scholars in 1965, along with the president of the college, is shown here. (Courtesy of the Garrett Collection.)

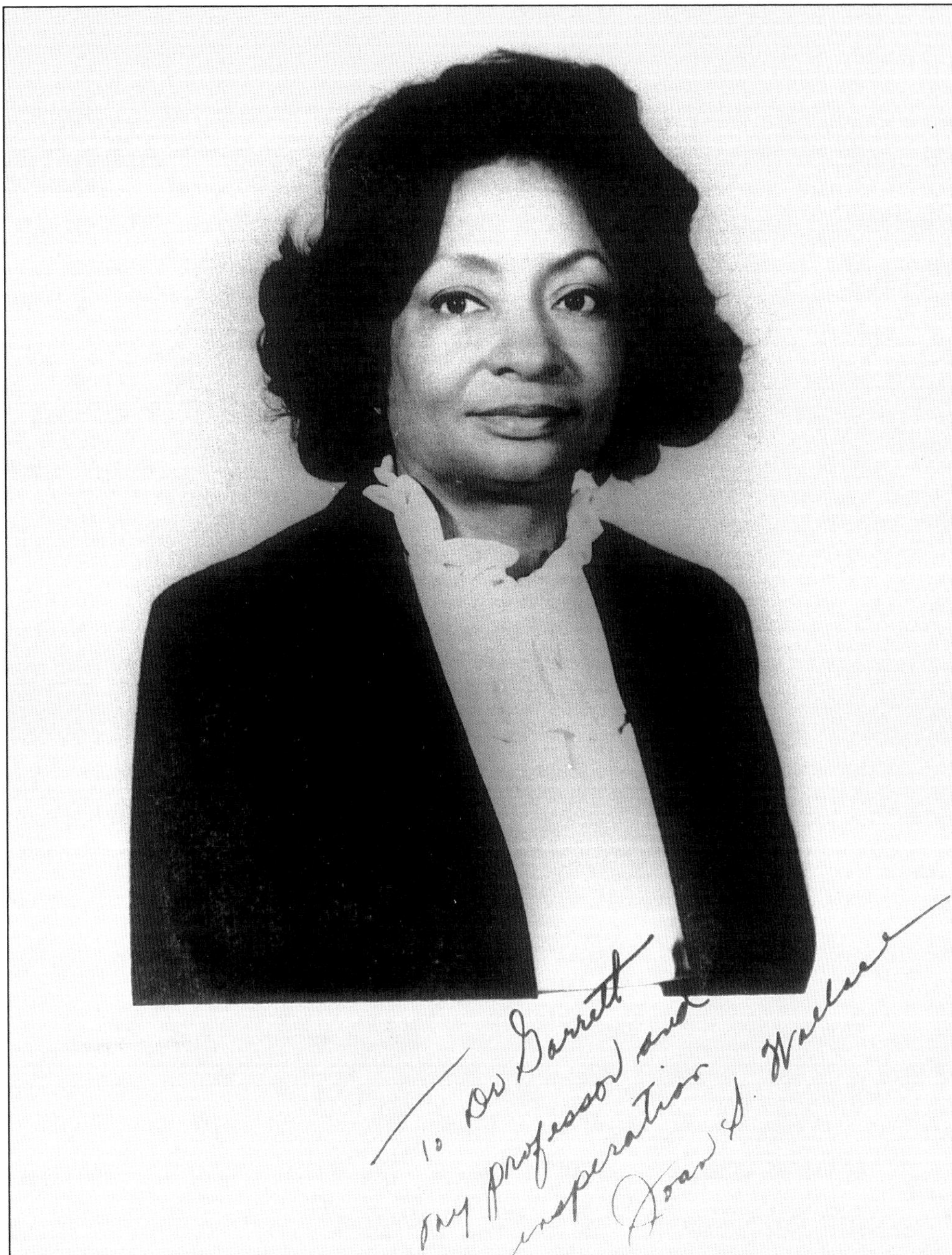

The Garrett Scholars have proven their worth time and time again throughout the country and abroad. Joan Scott Wallace, who was a student of Dr. Garrett's, gave him this autographed copy of a photograph that announced her diplomatic involvement in Trinidad and Tobago. She was a 1978 graduate of Bradley University. (Courtesy of the Garrett Collection.)

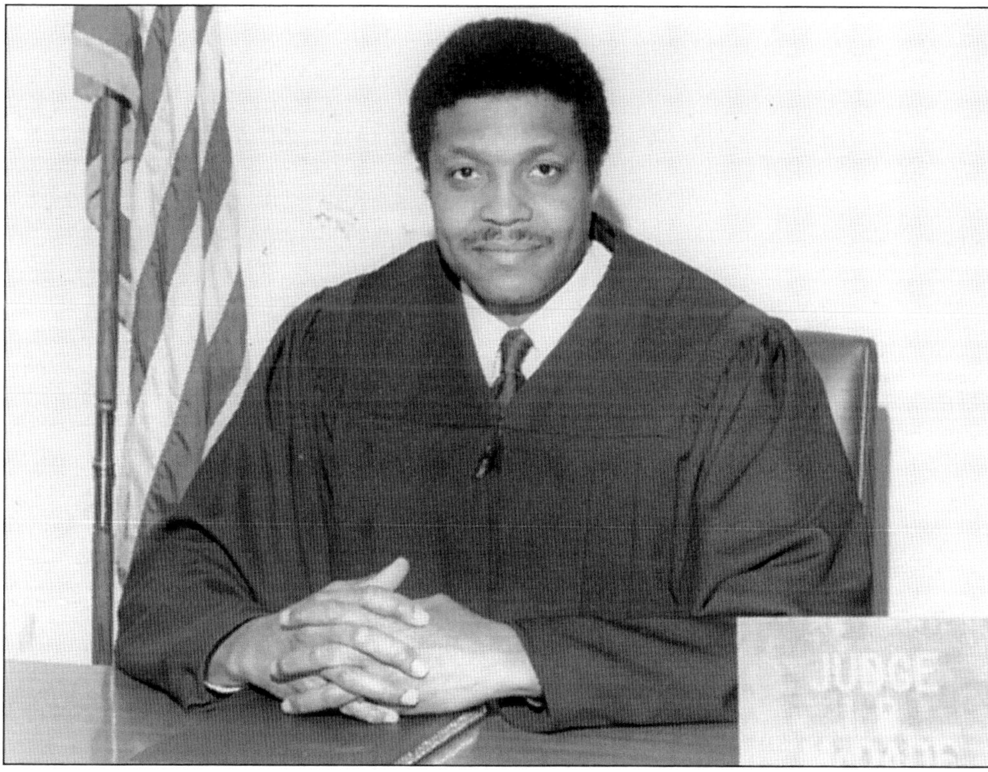

Judge Joe Billy McDade was the first African-American judge to sit on the bench in Peoria. He was a Bradley University graduate and a former student of Dr. Garrett. (Courtesy of the Garrett Collection.)

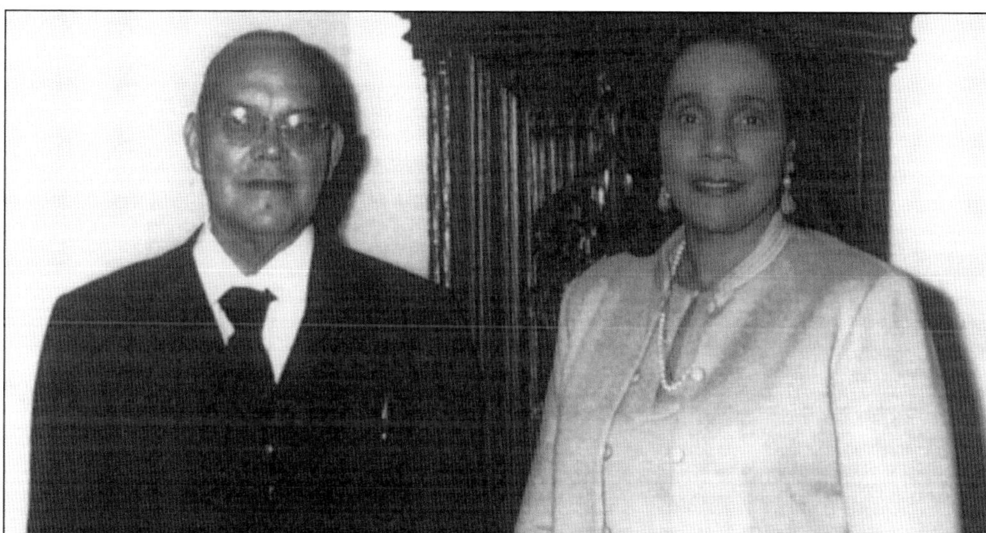

Many American notables sought Dr. Garrett's counsel throughout the nation. Here Dr. Garrett was photographed with civil rights activist and wife of Dr. Martin Luther King Jr., Coretta Scott King. (Courtesy of the Garrett Collection.)

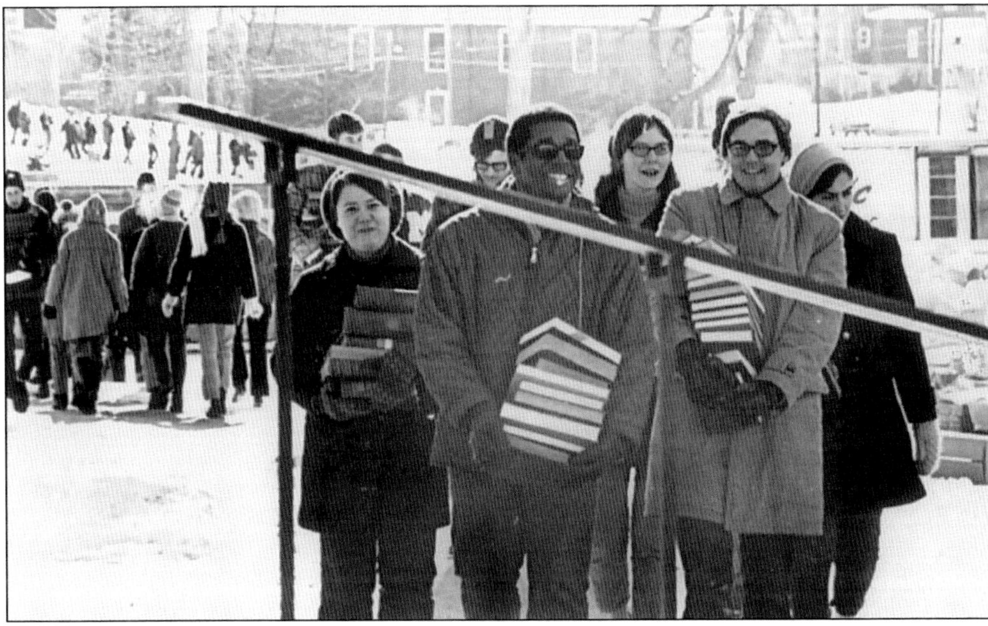

Education, and the opportunity to pursue it, was always a concern amongst African-Americans in west central Illinois. When Monmouth College opened its more modern library in the school year 1969–70, African-American students took part in the moving of the library's collection into its new facilities as this young man makes obvious. (Courtesy of the Monmouth College Library and Archives.)

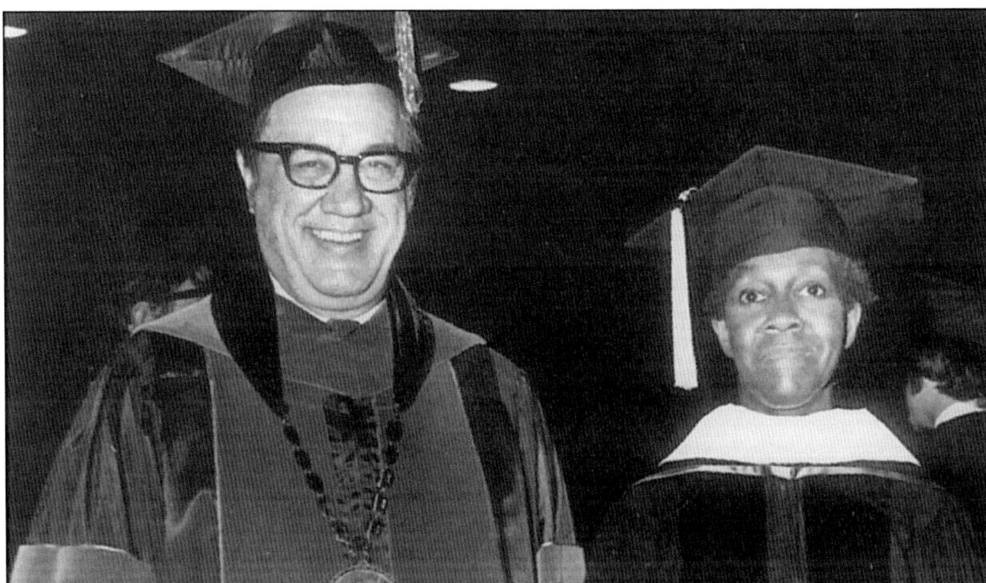

In 1970, Western Illinois University dedicated the Gwendolyn Brooks Cultural Center. Brooks received the first honorary doctoral degree from the institution during the 1971 graduation exercises. Here Brooks is photographed with the president of the university, Dr. John Bernhard. (Courtesy of the Archives and Special Collections, Western Illinois University Library.)

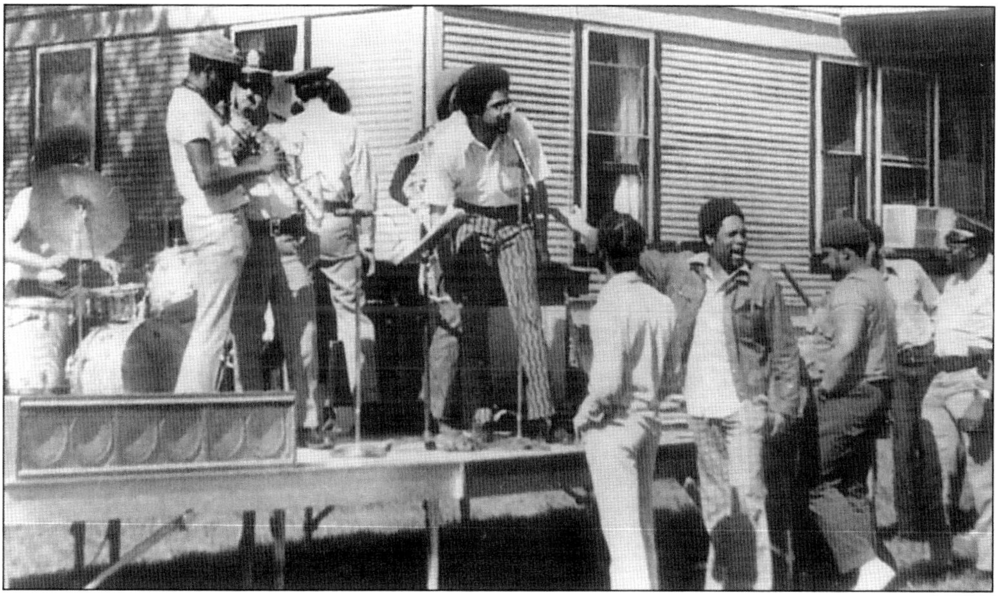

The students of Western Illinois University made much use of the Brooks Cultural Center over the years following 1970, particularly the African-American students of Western Illinois University. It was referred to early on in its existence as the "black house." (Courtesy of the Archives and Special Collections, Western Illinois University Library.)

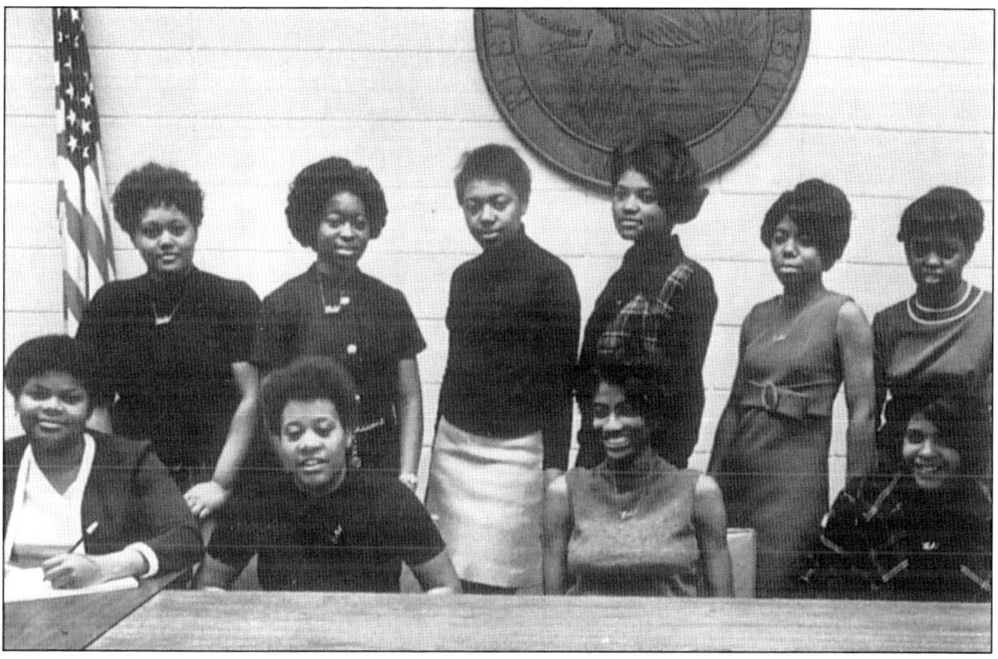

Fraternities, sororities, and other black student social groups grew more prevalent in college life throughout west central Illinois by the 1970s. More African-American students began to take advantage of the recent affirmative action legislation that was passed in 1969. These young women represented the Tiaka Club at Western Illinois University. (Courtesy of the Archives and Special Collections, Western Illinois University Library.)

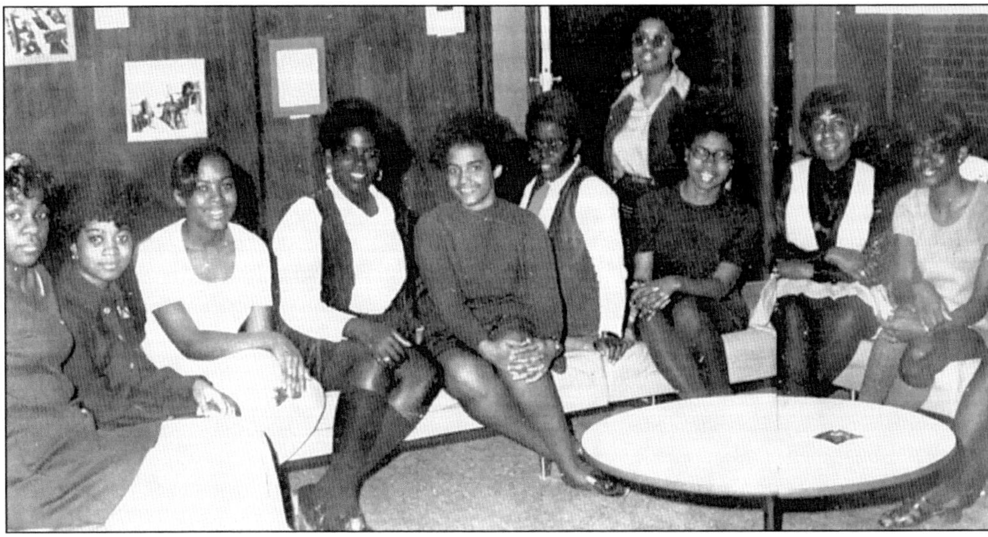

This group of young women were members of Ijema Social Club at Western Illinois University. (Courtesy of the Archives and Special Collections, Western Illinois University Library.)

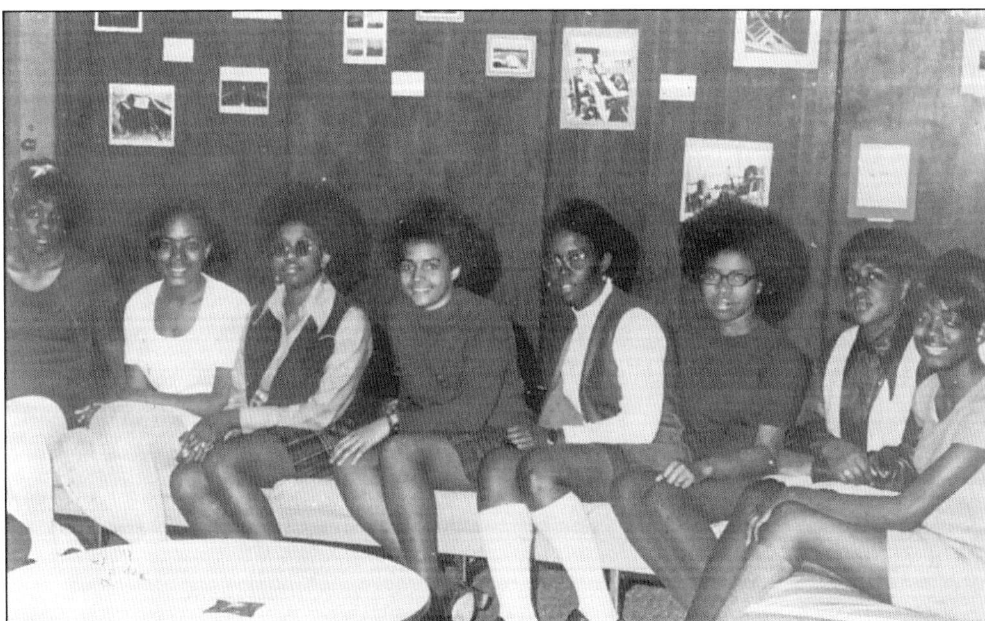

This group of young women were members of Delta Sigma Theta Sorority of Western Illinois University in 1970–71. (Courtesy of the Archives and Special Collections, Western Illinois University Library.)

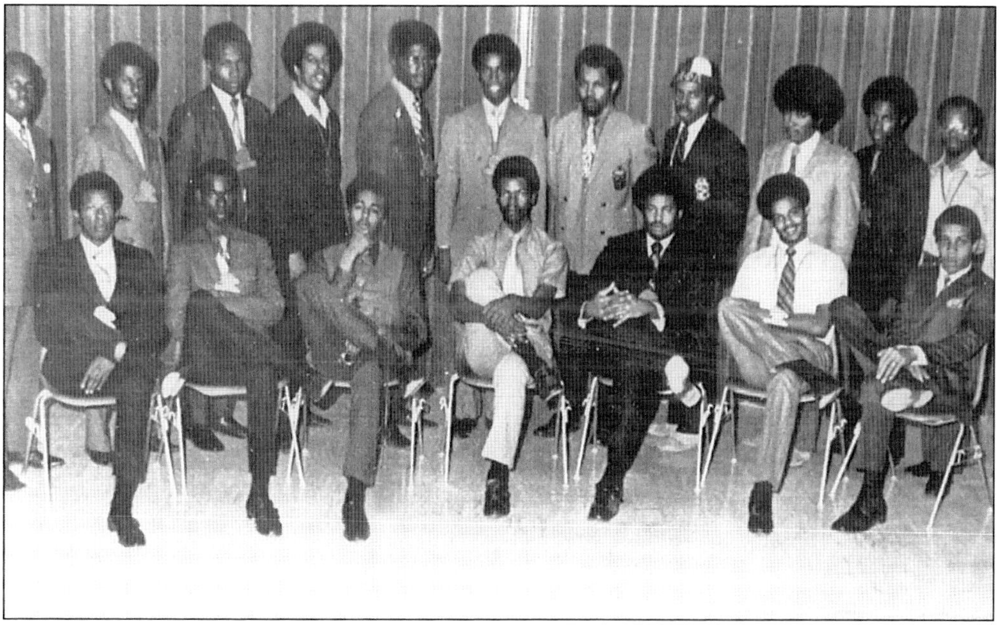

These young men were members of Alpha Phi Alpha Fraternity of Western Illinois University, the oldest African-American fraternity in the United States. (Courtesy of the Archives and Special Collections, Western Illinois University Library.)

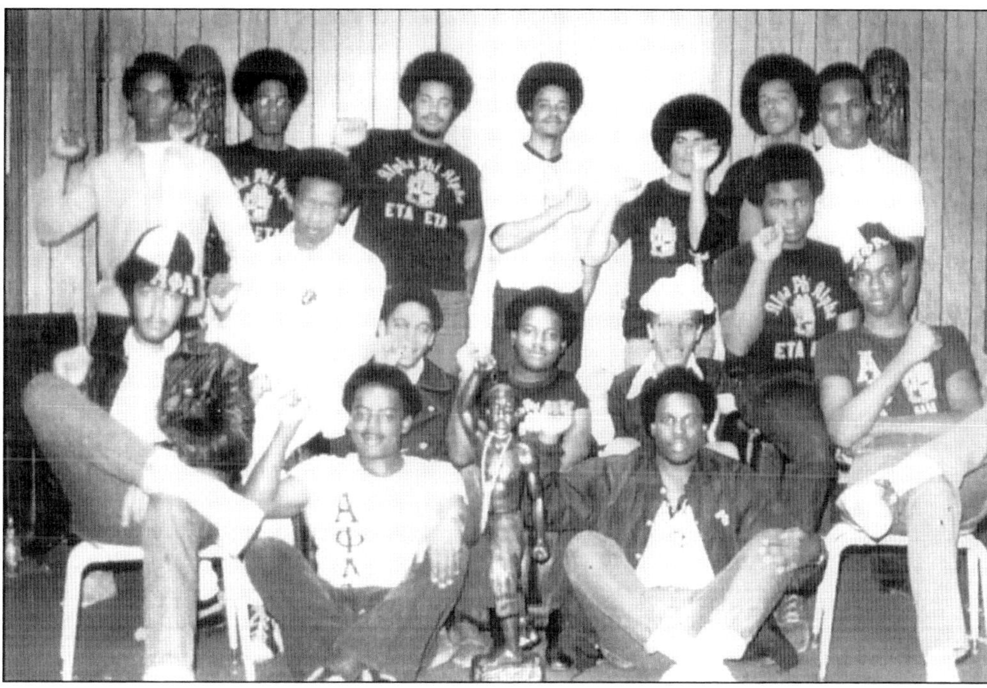

Here the men of Alpha Phi Alpha pose for this group shot at the Brooks Center. The Brooks Center was a popular hangout spot for all the African-American students at Western Illinois University in the 1970s. (Courtesy of the Archives and Special Collections, Western Illinois University Library.)

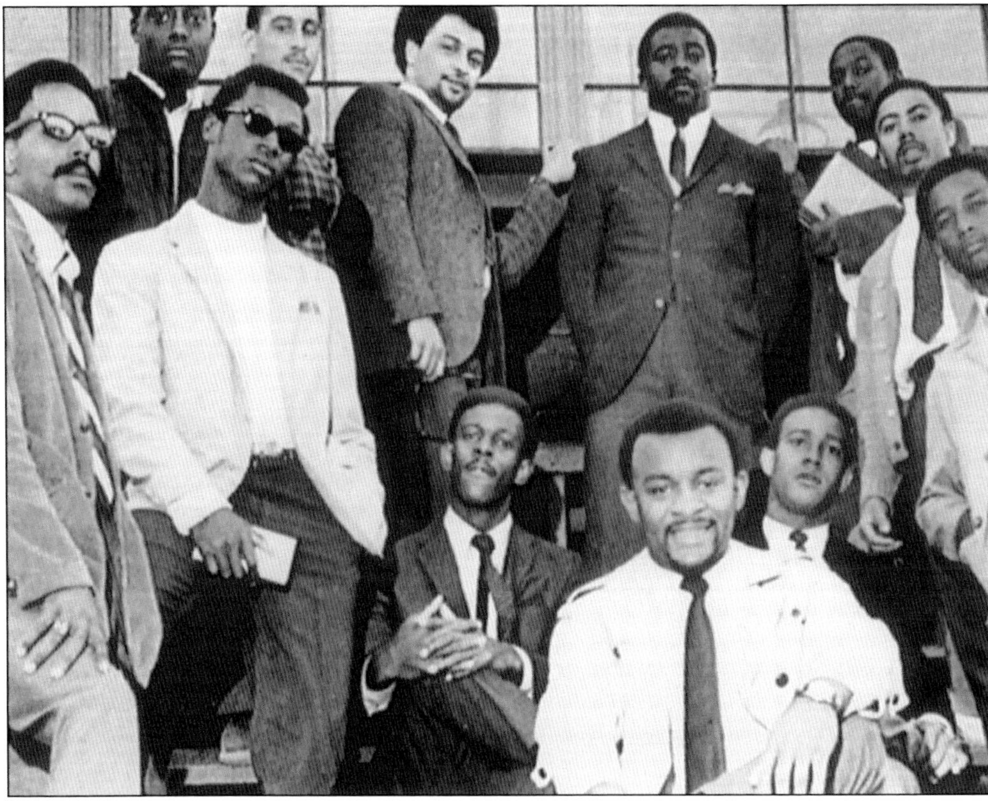

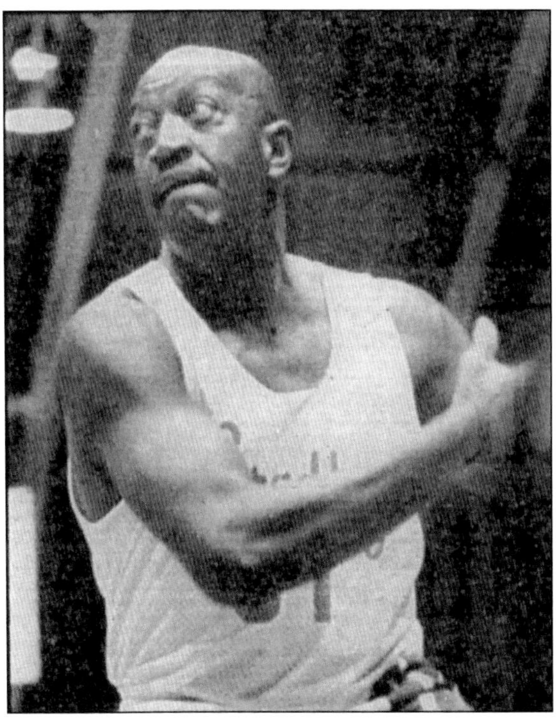

The men of Kappa Alpha Psi Fraternity were also another group of noted young African-American students on the campus of Western Illinois University in the 1970s. (Courtesy of the Archives and Special Collections, Western Illinois University Library.)

Though African-American students often persevered at numerous colleges throughout west central Illinois, they often endured racial slights and insults. Former Bradley University basketball star and alumni Levern Tate stated to the *Peoria Journal Star* in February 1991, that "he heard racial slurs directed at him but he got his revenge on the floor." (Courtesy of the Garrett Collection.)

Five

Business Ventures

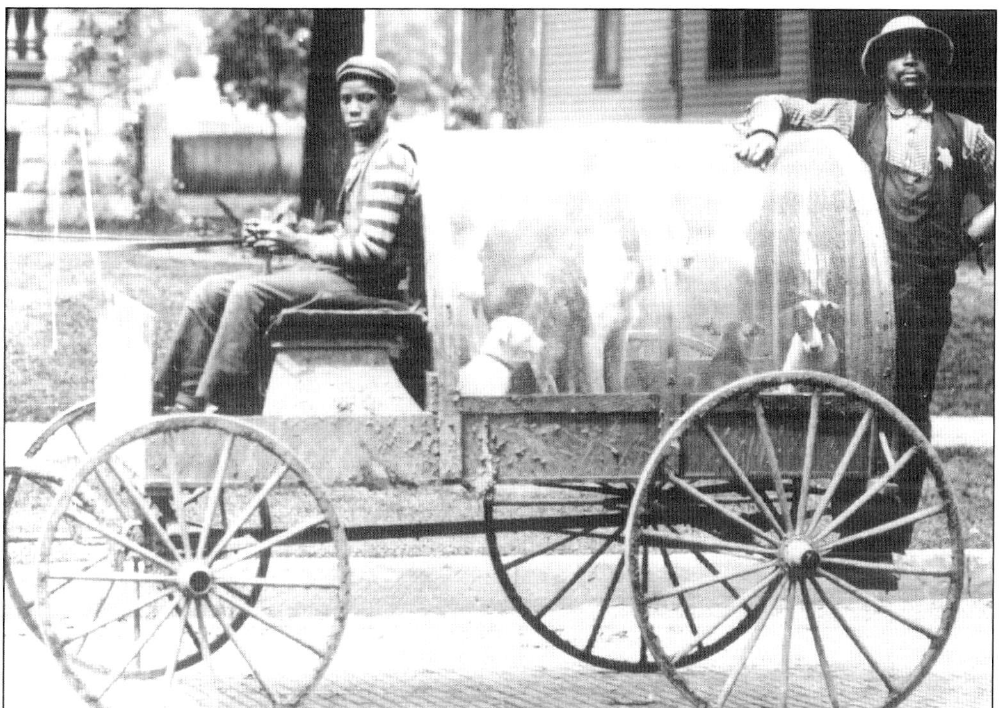

These gentlemen were known throughout the Galesburg area as the dogcatchers. This business thrived early in the twentieth century. (Courtesy of Knox College Archives.)

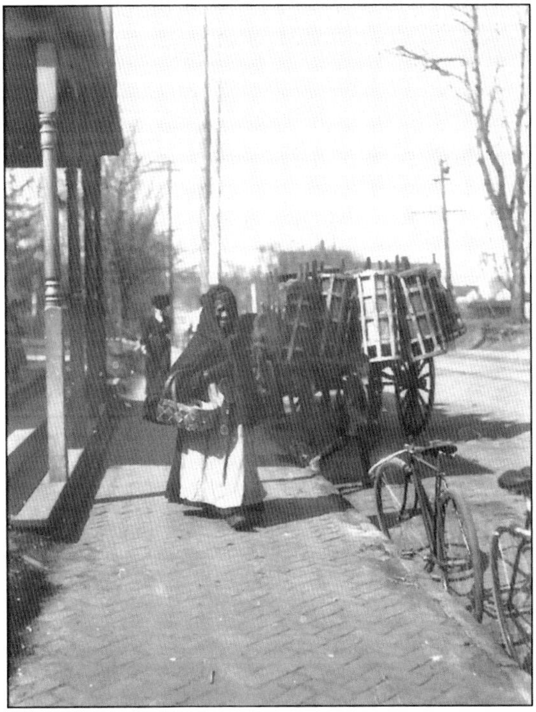

This photograph is of an African-American woman from Galesburg, late in the nineteenth century or at the start of the twentieth century. Legend has it that she was referred to as "Aunt Lucy," and she walked the streets of Galesburg selling her homemade goods to the local people. (Courtesy of Knox College Archives.)

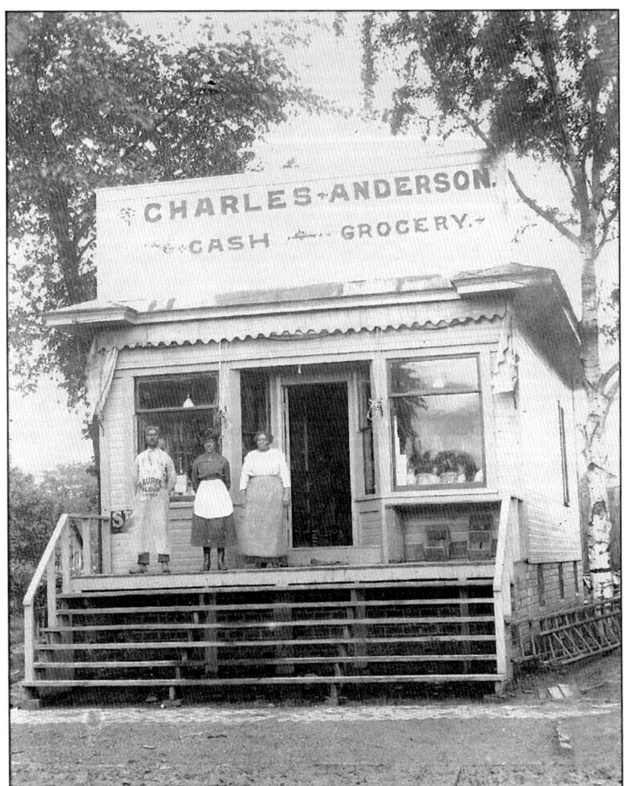

This black-owned-and-operated business was the property of Charles Anderson, a grocer in Galesburg early in the twentieth century. The establishment was referred to as Anderson Grocery. (Courtesy of Knox College Archives.)

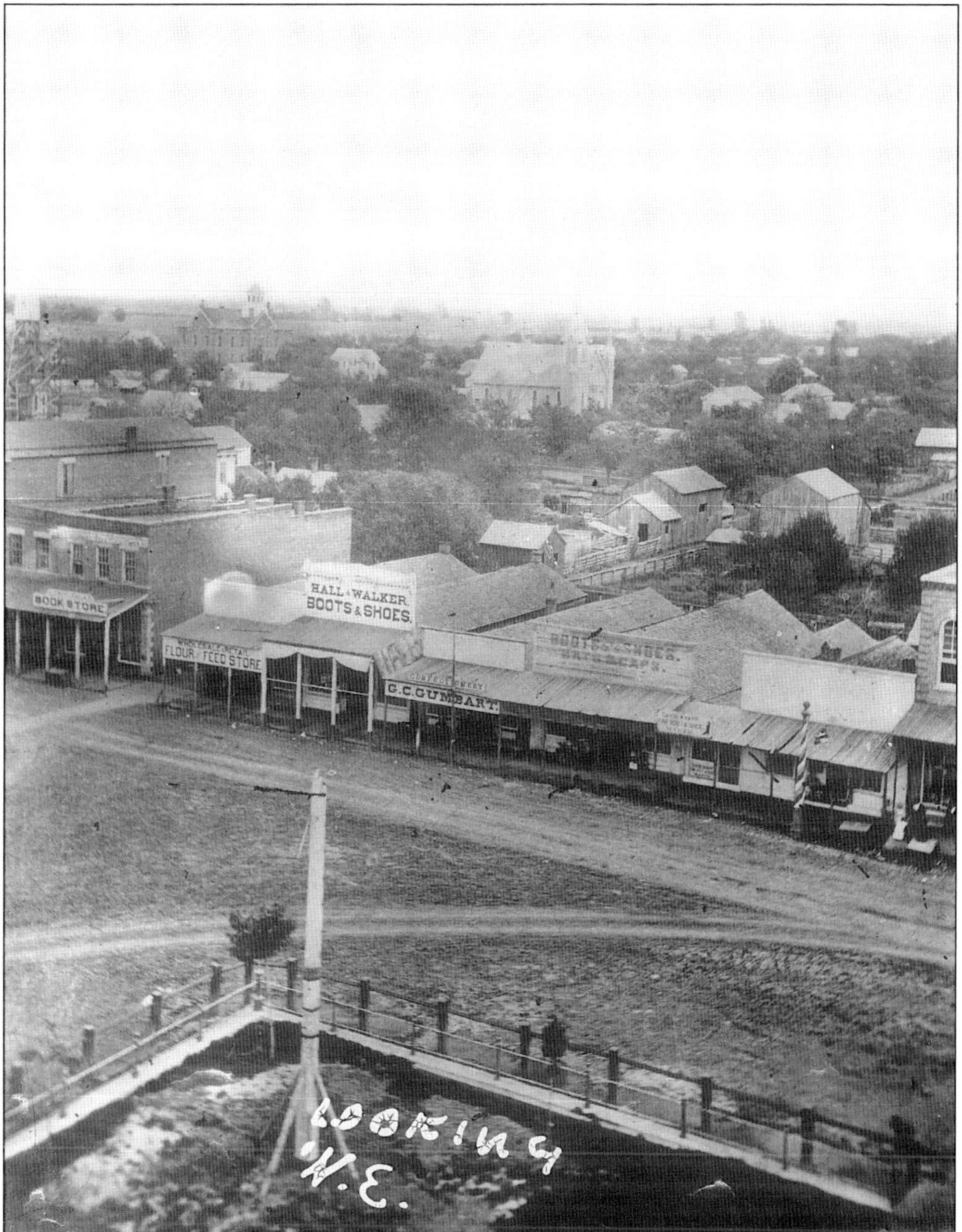

Shortly after the close of the Civil War, the first and only black-owned-and-operated black business was opened on the Courtyard Square in Macomb. This view of the barber's pole is from atop the McDonough County courthouse looking northeast. (Courtesy of the Archives and Special Collections, Western Illinois University Library.)

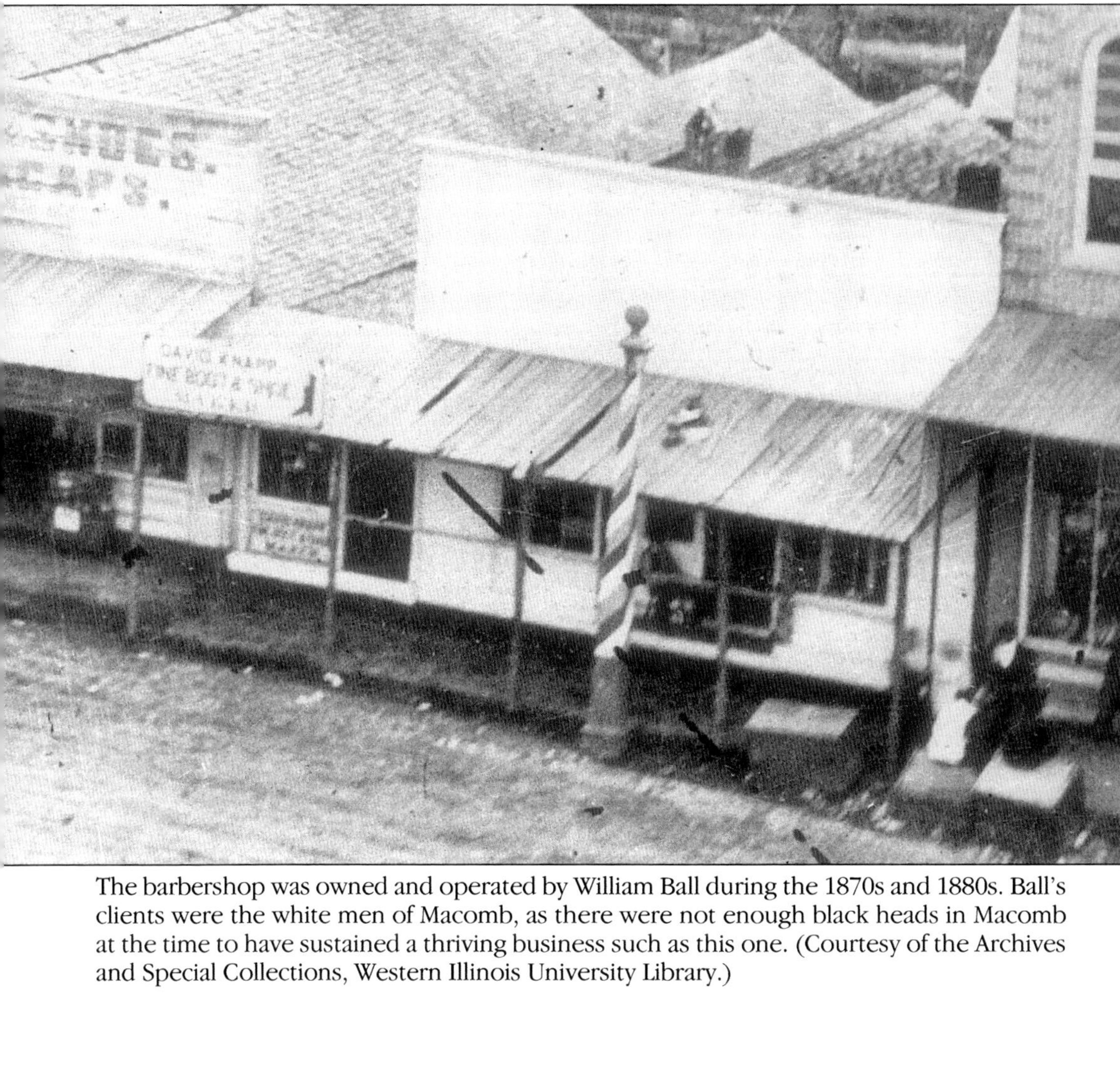

The barbershop was owned and operated by William Ball during the 1870s and 1880s. Ball's clients were the white men of Macomb, as there were not enough black heads in Macomb at the time to have sustained a thriving business such as this one. (Courtesy of the Archives and Special Collections, Western Illinois University Library.)

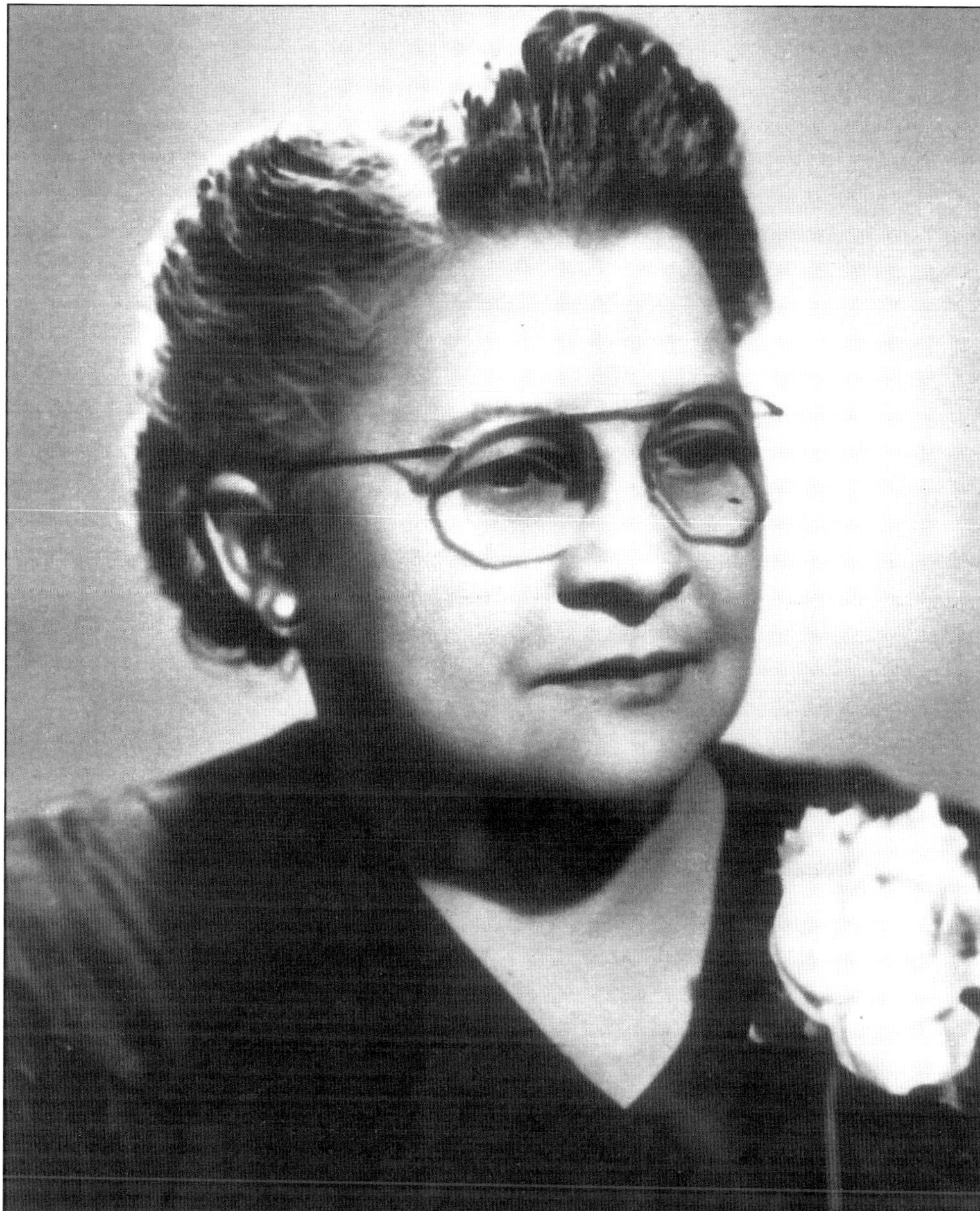

Madeline Owens, who lived from 1895–1960, is one of the first known female black business owners of Peoria. She was co-owner of Owens Cleaners and Dyers Company. (Courtesy of the Garrett Collection.)

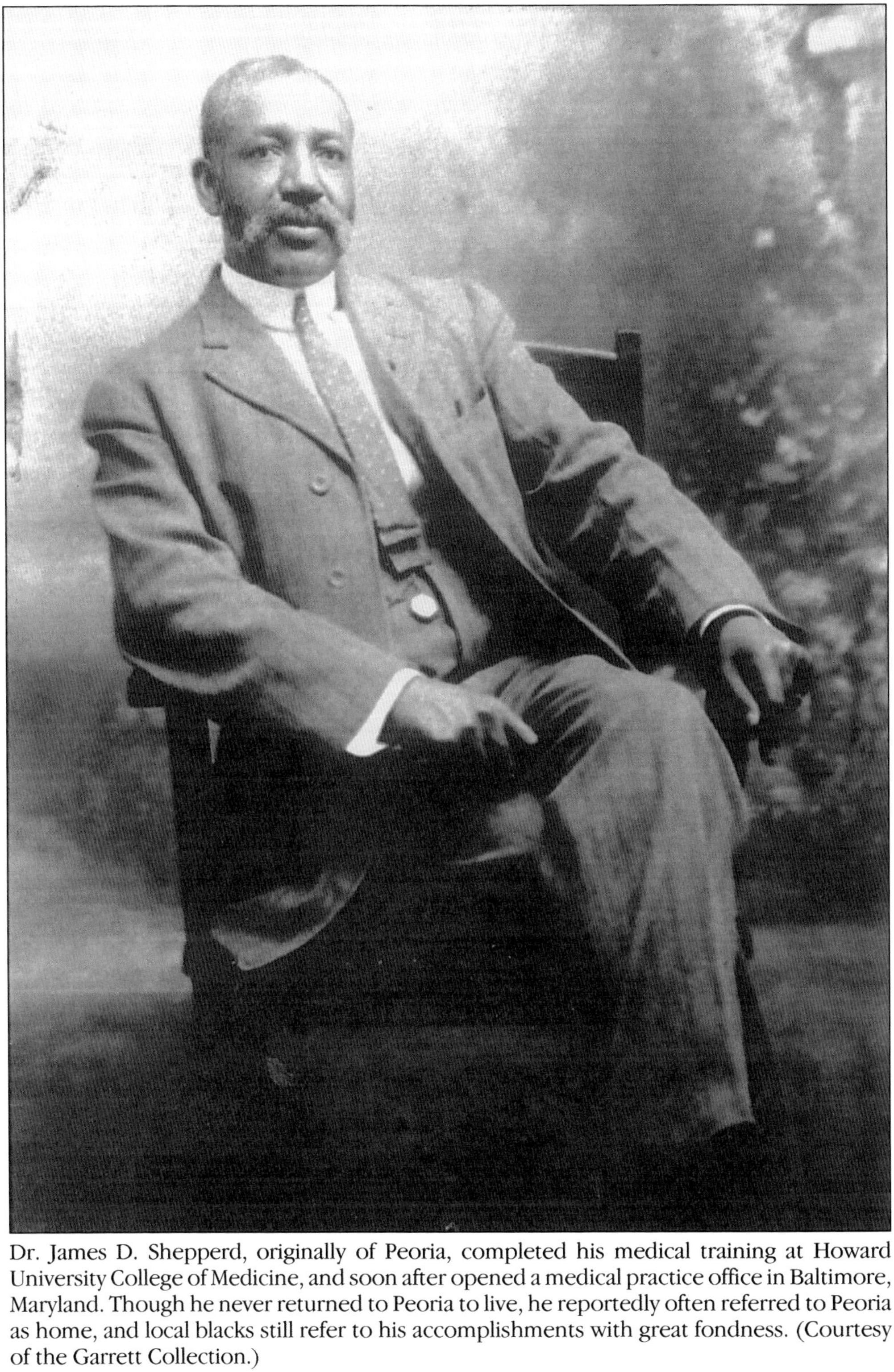

Dr. James D. Shepperd, originally of Peoria, completed his medical training at Howard University College of Medicine, and soon after opened a medical practice office in Baltimore, Maryland. Though he never returned to Peoria to live, he reportedly often referred to Peoria as home, and local blacks still refer to his accomplishments with great fondness. (Courtesy of the Garrett Collection.)

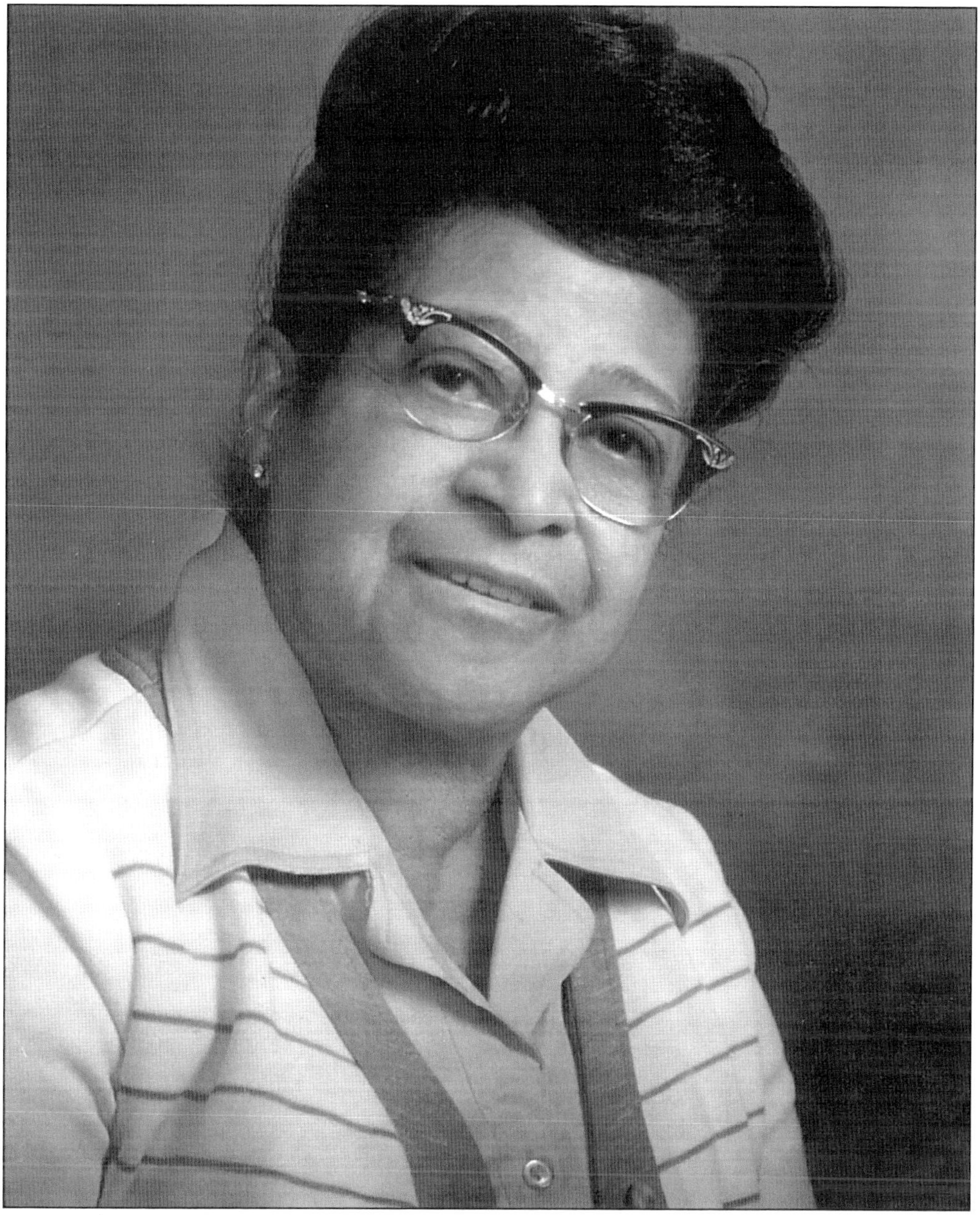

Dr. Maude Sanders arrived in Peoria in 1942, armed with a medical degree from Meharry Medical College in Nashville, Tennessee. Despite the double-exclusivity of race and gender, she overcame much adversity and practiced medicine in Peoria for 50 years. Dr. Sanders was also a charter member of the local chapter of the NAACP in Peoria. (Courtesy of the Garrett Collection.)

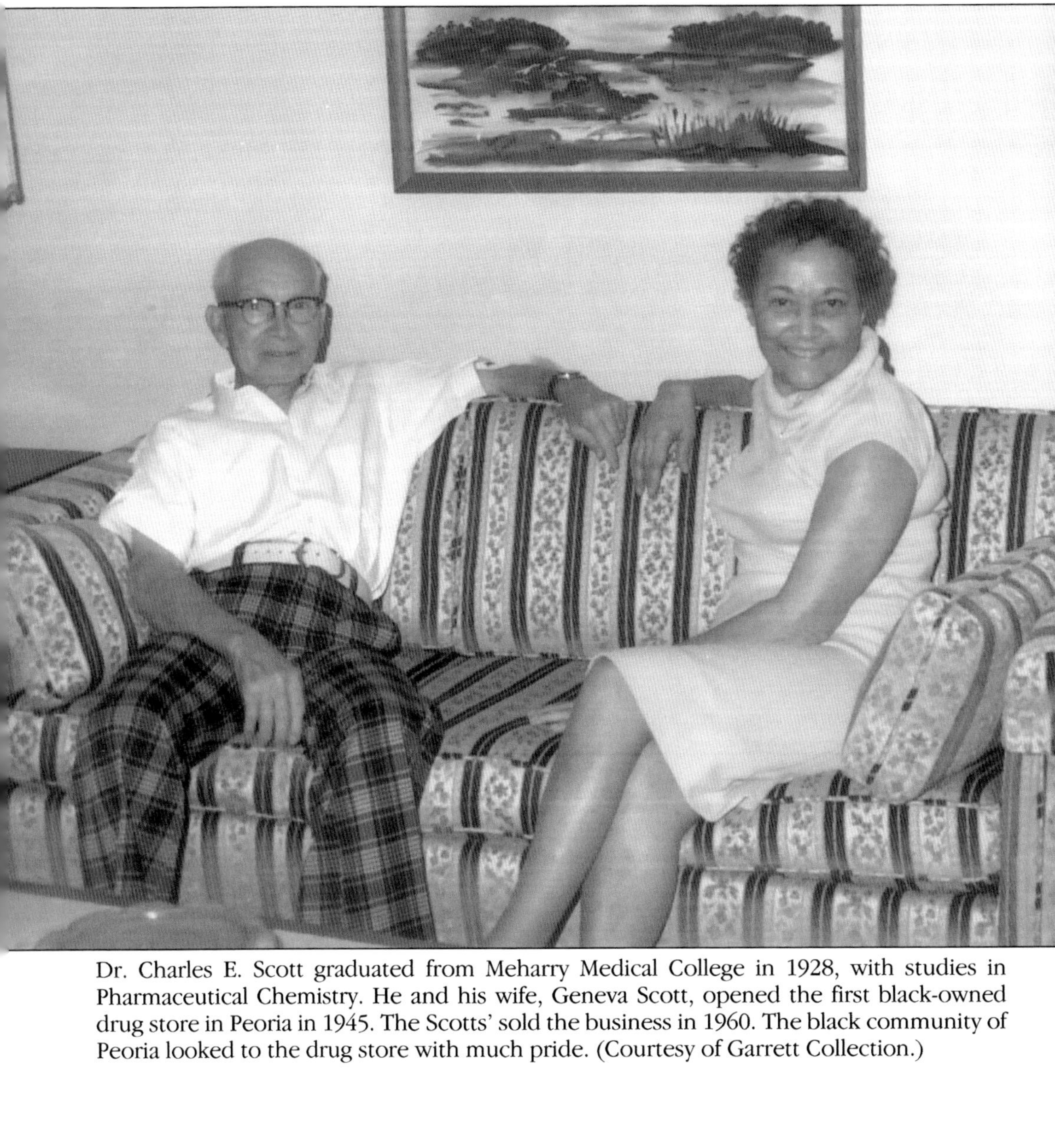

Dr. Charles E. Scott graduated from Meharry Medical College in 1928, with studies in Pharmaceutical Chemistry. He and his wife, Geneva Scott, opened the first black-owned drug store in Peoria in 1945. The Scotts' sold the business in 1960. The black community of Peoria looked to the drug store with much pride. (Courtesy of Garrett Collection.)

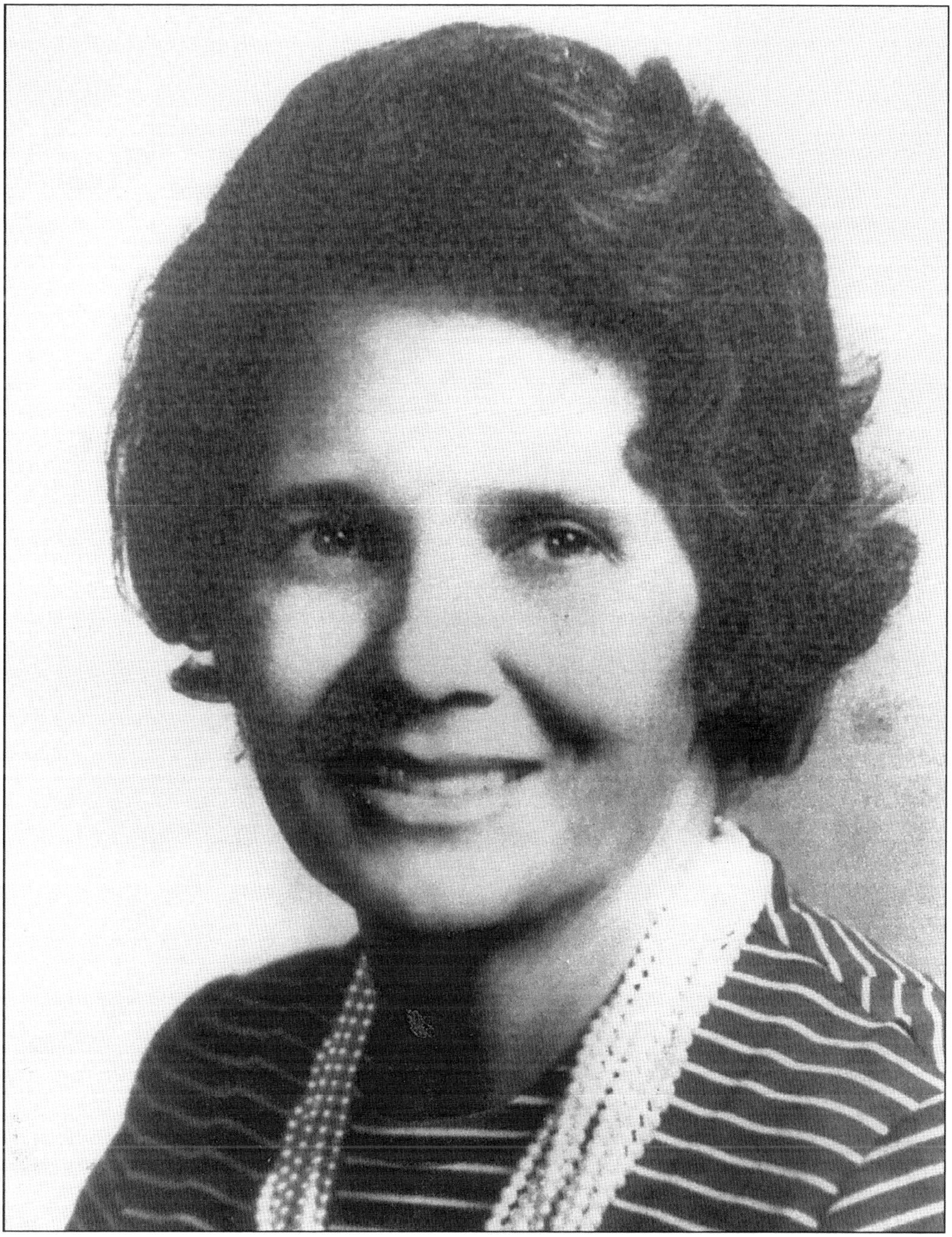

Elise Allen was born in Peoria in 1921. Allen was the editor and publisher of *The Traveler Weekly Newspaper*; Peoria's only black-based newspaper for 40 years. The purpose of the paper: "We propose to have a paper dedicated to the truth and thereby the common good. Our goal is too have a paper of note and dignity and to be interesting. Get the news. Fight for our opinions, but will not believe they contain the whole truth, or the only truth. Above all, we will remain to know that humanity is advancing that there is progress in human life and human affairs; and that, as sure as God lives, the future will be greater and better than the present and the past." (Courtesy of the Garrett Collection.)

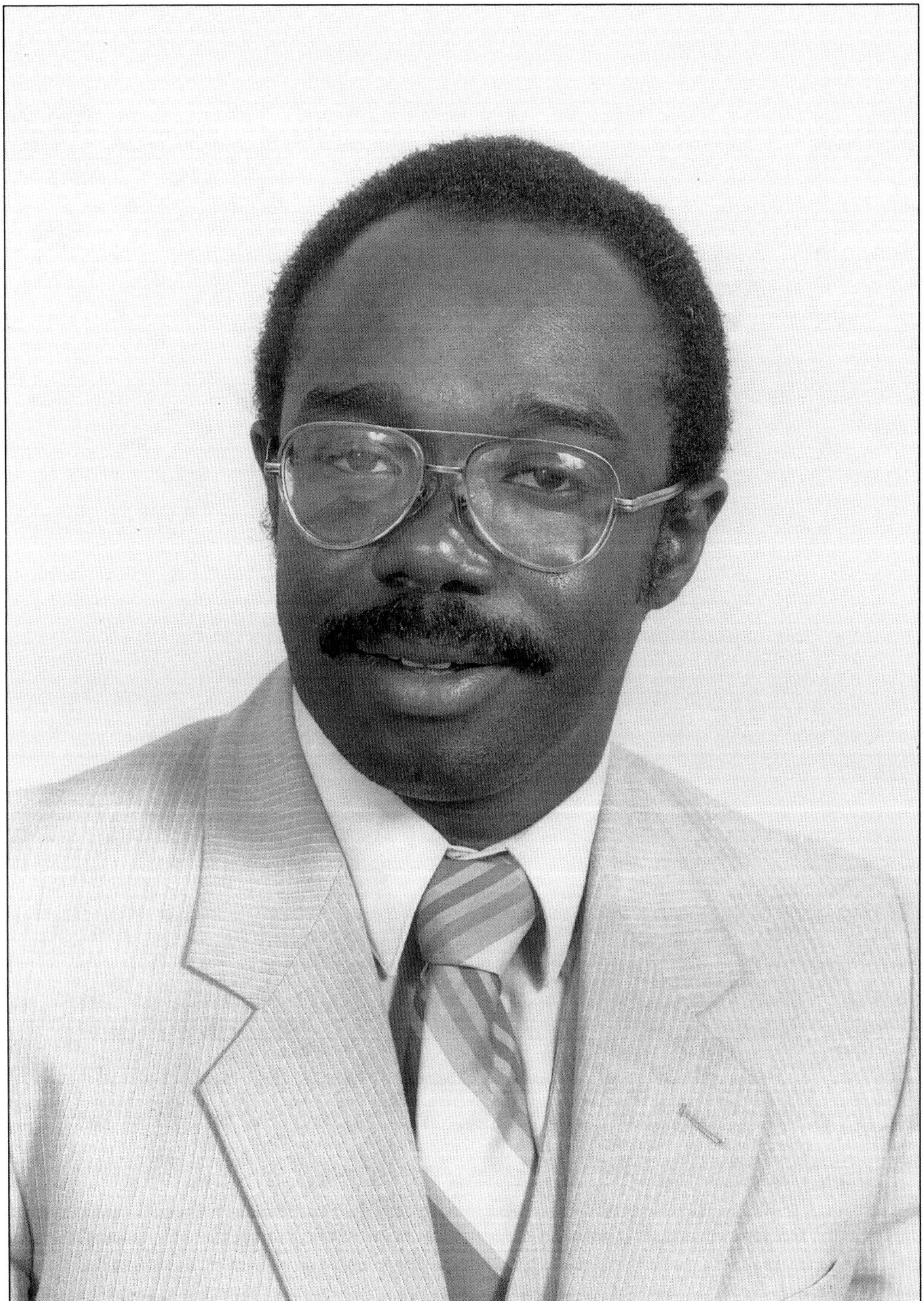

Earl Bracey graduated from the University of Southern Illinois at Carbondale College of Law and is the first and only African American to practice law in McDonough County. (Courtesy of the Archives and Special Collections, Western Illinois University Library.)

Six

Local People and Activism

African Americans throughout west central Illinois endured despite major insults to their social and cultural events. The *Macomb Journal* ran the following announcement (lower right) in April 1906. "Colored Jubilee: Old Fashioned Colored Jubilee Will Be Given by Macomb Negroes April 24th." The newspaper referred to the event several times as an "old-fashioned darkey jubilee." (Courtesy of the Archives and Special Collections Western Illinois University Library.)

Following the Springfield Riot of 1908, African Americans in Macomb pledged their loyalty, denounced the rioters, and encouraged the stance of the *Journal*. (Courtesy of the Archives and Special Collections, Western Illinois University Library.)

1908 – 8

TUESDAY, AUGUST 25, 1

MACOMB COLORED PEOPLE

Pledge Their Loyalty—Denounce the Rioters and Commend Stand of The Journal.

Macomb, Ill., Aug. 24.—In view of the Springfield riot, and upon suggestion of Rev. Wm. M. Collins Sunday evening at the close of services, a call was made for the Afro-Americans of the city of Macomb to meet Monday evening in Brown chapel, A. M. E. church.

On the above date at 8:30 p. m. the meeting was called to order by Rev. Collins. A song was sung and prayer was offered by Rev. Sears, and the first eight verses of the first chapter of the general Epistle of James was read.

On motion Rev. Sears was elected chairman and Oliver Daniels was elected secretary. The following committee on expression and resolutions was appointed by the chairman: Rev. Wm. M. Collins, S. F. Daniels, Thos. Top, W. H. Hawkins, Milford Daniels.

The committee reported the following expressions and resolutions:

"Macomb, Ill., Aug. 24, 1908.—To His Excellency, the Governor or Guardian of the State of Illinois, Charles S. Deneen, and all Associates in Maintaining Law and Order in State, County and City of Springfield, or Counties or Cities of Said State: We, the Afro-American citizens in Macomb, in mass meeting assembled, commend your highness as governor and as a citizen of our state.

"We condemn uncompromisingly the rapist and assaulter of womanhood and brand them as hell-bred blots upon civilization, be they black, white, or what not. We also, without compromise, condemn the leaders and participants of mobs and riots.

"We further note, with much appreciation and encouragement, many of the leading journals of our country, and with pride in the papers of our own city, particularly the Macomb Journal, editorially and otherwise, in speaking out for fairness and justice for all people, of whatever class or color, and equally condemning their crimes and wrongs.

"We are opposed to lawlessness in any form. We stand for the law and order of our community and country.

"We furthermore herein resolve, collectively and individually, to stand to co operate with and assist those in authority to detect, arrest and punish by laws and courts of our commonwealth the transgressors of law.

"We also deeply regret and deplore and share with you and all who feel a sense of the disgrace and blush at the assault on womanhood and the wanton crimes committed by the mob and rioters of the city of Springfield, the capital of Illinois.

"We will ever pray for you and all those who strive to uphold the laws of our land, and peace to all men, and that the God and Father of us all will save and protect our lives.

"(Signed) W. H. HAWKINS,
"MILFORD DANIELS,
"Committee."

The same were, on motion, adopted unanimously.

After some other business the meeting adjourned.

REV. SEARS, Chairman.
Oliver Daniels, Sec'y.

COLORED JUBILEE.

p. 4
4/11/1906

Old-Fashioned Colored Jubilee Will Be Given by Macomb Negroes April 24th.

There is a treat in store for the local show-goers and music lovers in the coming home talent event to be given by the colored people in this city. The rehearsals are at present under way and a regular old-fashioned darkey jubilee will be given in the local opera house about April 24th.

The enterprise is under the direction of Miss Edna Hammer, who is visiting with Mrs. James of this city. Miss Hammer is a singer and entertainer of considerable talent and for several years was a member of the Williams & Walker company, of national reputation. Twenty-five of the best negro singers and dancers of the city will take part and the entertainment is sure to be one of merit. The nature of the event will be a

COLORED MENS BUSINESS CLUB TONIGHT

Important Meeting for the Colored Women as Well as Men—Why They Should Vote.

The Colored Men's Business club will meet at the Second Baptist church tonight. Please come early, for all business must be passed upon each night this week. Rev. A. J. Cromwell and some leaders of the colored women wish to see every colored woman of this city to explain to them why every colored woman should vote. It is also understood that all colored men should be present at this meeting. A good program will be rendered. Watch for the date and place.

Mrs. Mattie Sears of this city, one of the leaders in promoting the progress of her race, is in touch with the Colored Women's club of Chicago, Ill. She has lately received from them some very important pamphlets stating why every colored woman that can should vote. See her or any member of the Colored Men's Business club for the same.

Soon after the turn of the twentieth century, African-American men and women established "Business Clubs" to begin addressing the issue of voting rights. African Americans in Macomb met to discuss the voting rights of black women. (Courtesy of the Archives and Special Collections, Western Illinois University Library.)

COLORED WOMEN'S CULTURE CLUB

Interesting and Instructive Meeting—Questions of the Day Discussed—Social Time Enjoyed.

Mrs. Violet Newsome was hostess to the Colored Women's Culture Club at her home on North Monroe street, in honor of Mrs. Robert Sloan of Denver, Colo., who is visiting here.

A fine miscellaneous program was rendered as follows:

Victrola Selections.

Introduction of Visitors.

Address of Welcome—Mrs. Nathan Thorpe, Pres.

Condition of the Race and Woman's Suffrage in Denver—Mrs Robert Sloan.

Political Condition—Miss Olire Ringer.

Child Labor—Mrs. Frank Russell.

Condition of Race in the South—Mrs. Florence McBride Sledge.

How to Vote—Nora Josie Jacobs.

Racial Condition—Mrs. Mattie Mayo.

Duet—Mesdames Florence Sledge, Iva Forth.

Report of State Federation—Mrs. Violet Newsome.

Light refreshments of ice cream and chocolate cake were served.

Those present were: Miss Olive Ringer and Mesdames Robert Sloan, Nathan Thorpe, Mattie Mayo, Katie Williams, Mary McBride, Frances Barnett, Mary Derrick, Nettie Hyde, Ethey Thorpe, Anna Johnson, Garnet McGruder, Joseph Sloan, Albert Derry, Violet Newsome, Frank Russell, Josie Jacobs, Hazel Johnson Ashford and Stella McBride Johnson of Peoria, Florence McBride Sledge, Huston, Tex., Gertrude McBride Groff, Cedar Rapids, Ia., Iva McBride South, Galesburg, and Edna Ashby King, Denver, Colo.

African-American women in west central Illinois established "colored women's clubs," just as black women were doing all over the country early in the twentieth century. This group was of Macomb, Illinois. (Courtesy of the Archives and Special Collections, Western Illinois University Library.)

What Will Macomb do For Cooper.

The above question is being asked daily by those who know Henry Cooper, the negro, who graduated with second honors from our High School. He is the first real Macomb colored boy who has ever graduated here. He was born, reared and educated here, while all other colored graduates were born elsewhere. His father, Granville Cooper, is an old and respected citizen of Macomb. Much interest is being taken in his boy. White clerks, copyists, etc., are being employed by the Macomb business houses and schools are being given out, but will Henry Cooper, who has proven his worthiness, be given a place? Is it possible that Macomb will refuse her own son because he is of negro origin? A few of us are watching and hoping for his success. May we appeal to the influential citizens for a little recognition for our boy who, like the white boys, is worthy of success. 6/16/96 REV. G. W. BROWN. p. 3

Henry Cooper of Macomb graduated second in his class from the local high school in 1896, and the black community questioned whether the community would grant him suitable employment. (Courtesy of the Archives and Special Collections, Western Illinois University Library.)

William Pickens of the NAACP national office made a lecture appearance in Galesburg, Illinois, in July 1915. (Courtesy of Knox College Archives.)

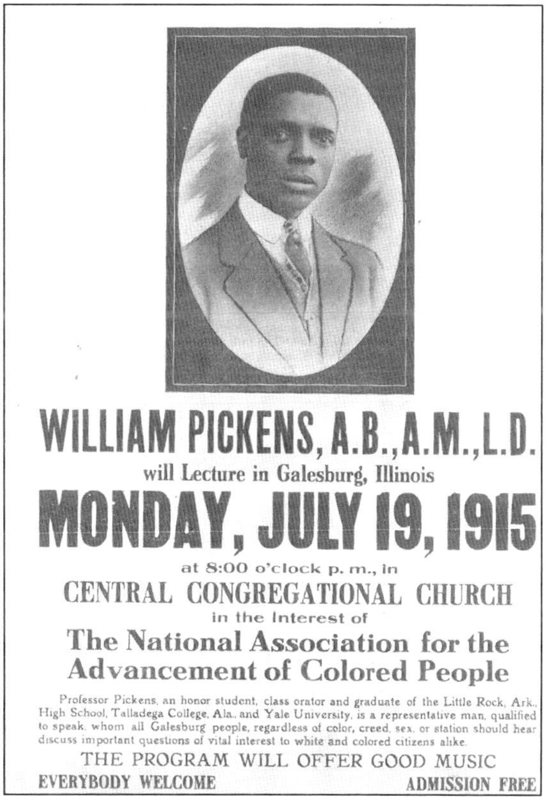

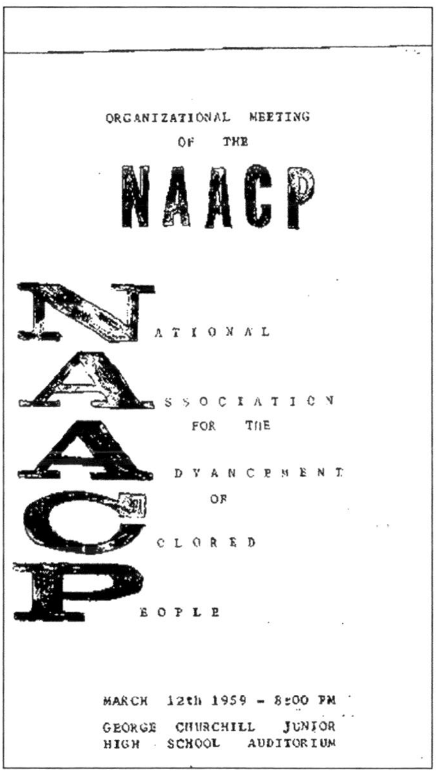

In March 1959, the African-American citizens of Galesburg held an organizational meeting of the NAACP. (Courtesy of Knox College Archives.)

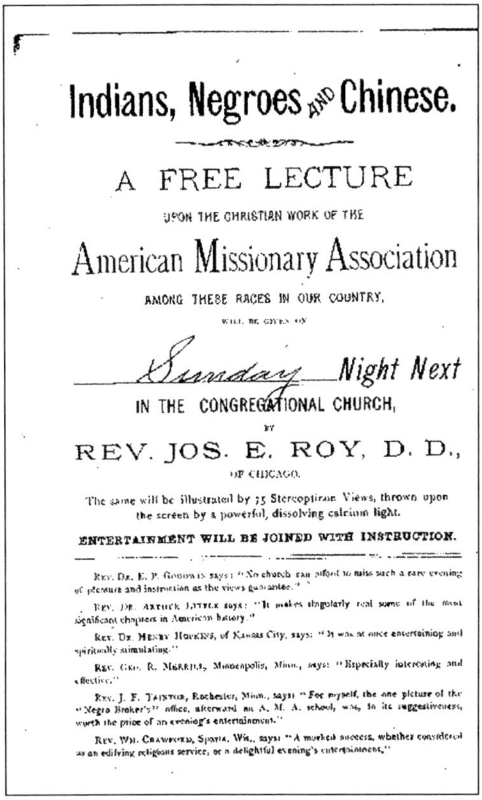
Indians, Negroes and Chinese.

A FREE LECTURE

UPON THE CHRISTIAN WORK OF THE

American Missionary Association

AMONG THESE RACES IN OUR COUNTRY,

WILL BE GIVEN ON

Sunday Night Next

IN THE CONGREGATIONAL CHURCH,

BY

REV. JOS. E. ROY, D. D.,

OF CHICAGO.

The same will be illustrated by 75 Stereopticon Views, thrown upon the screen by a powerful, dissolving calcium light.

ENTERTAINMENT WILL BE JOINED WITH INSTRUCTION.

REV. DR. E. P. GOODWIN says: "No church can afford to miss such a rare evening of pleasure and instruction as the views guarantee."

REV. DR. ARTHUR LITTLE says: "It makes singularly real some of the most significant chapters in American history."

REV. DR. HENRY HOPKINS, of Kansas City, says: "It was at once entertaining and spiritually stimulating."

REV. GEO. R. MERRILL, Minneapolis, Minn., says: "Especially interesting and effective."

REV. J. F. TAINTOR, Rochester, Minn., says: "For myself, the one picture of the 'Negro Broker's' office, afterward an A. M. A. school, was, in its suggestiveness, worth the price of an evening's entertainment."

REV. WM. CRAWFORD, Sparta, Wis., says: "A marked success, whether considered as an edifying religious service, or a delightful evening's entertainment."

The American Missionary Association hosted a free lecture in Galesburg concerning the question of "Indians, Negroes, and Chinese" peoples of that city. The lecture was to address "stereotypical views thrown upon the screen by a powerful dissolving calcium light." (Courtesy of Knox College.)

Throughout the 1930s, African Americans suffered the stereotypical images that were popular in white America. This 1936 stage performance at Monmouth College depicted whites in black face, which was sweeping the country during this era. (Courtesy of Monmouth College Archives.)

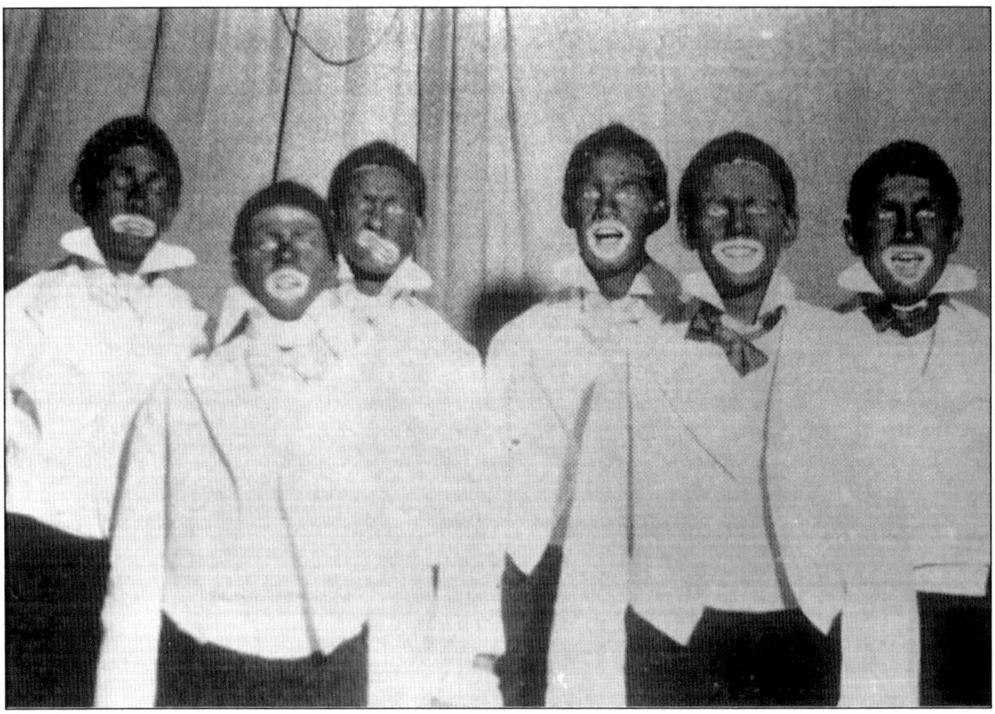

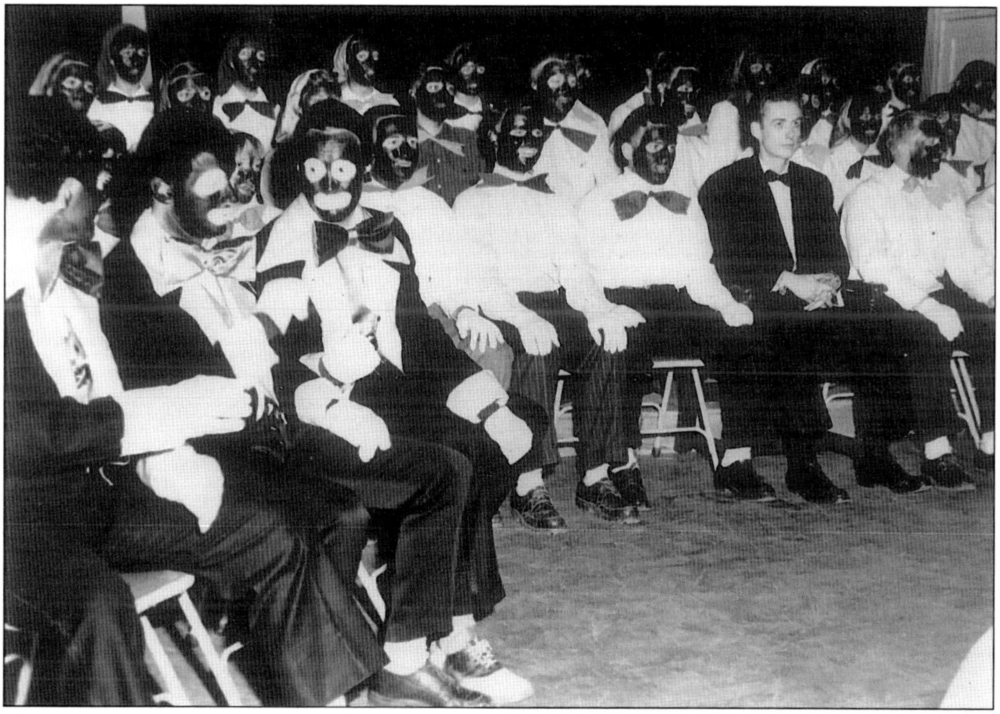

This was an entire audience of whites in black face in the 1930s at Monmouth College. (Courtesy of Monmouth College Archives.)

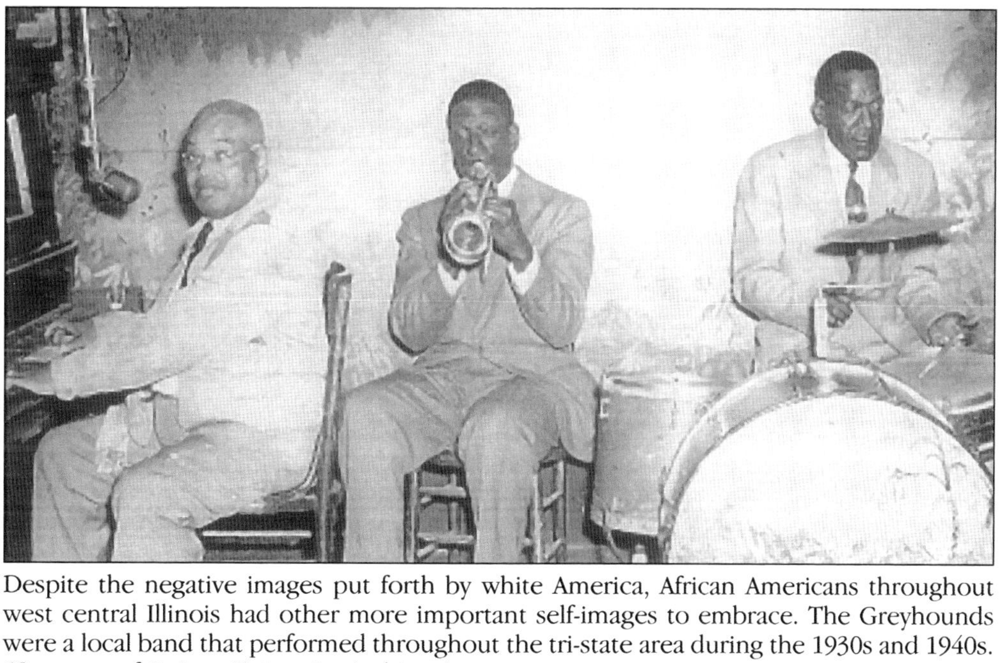

Despite the negative images put forth by white America, African Americans throughout west central Illinois had other more important self-images to embrace. The Greyhounds were a local band that performed throughout the tri-state area during the 1930s and 1940s. (Courtesy of Quincy University Archives.)

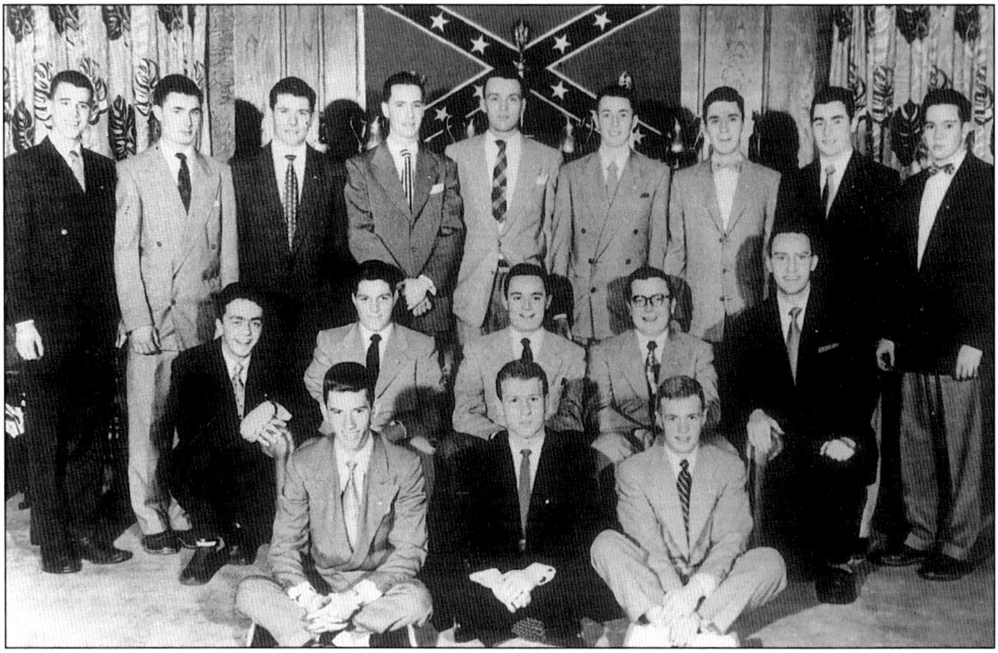

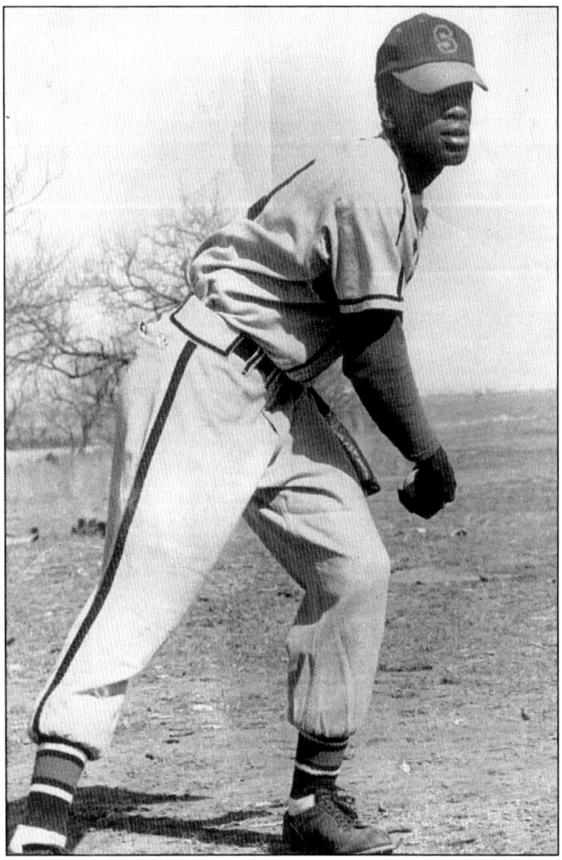

As late as 1953, white male student groups posed before the confederate flag at Monmouth College. (Courtesy of Monmouth College Archives.)

Keith F. Kelley, upon graduating in 1950 from Peoria Central High School, signed with the Brooklyn Dodgers and later with the Los Angeles Dodgers before he enlisted into the United States Air Force. (Courtesy of the Garrett Collection.)

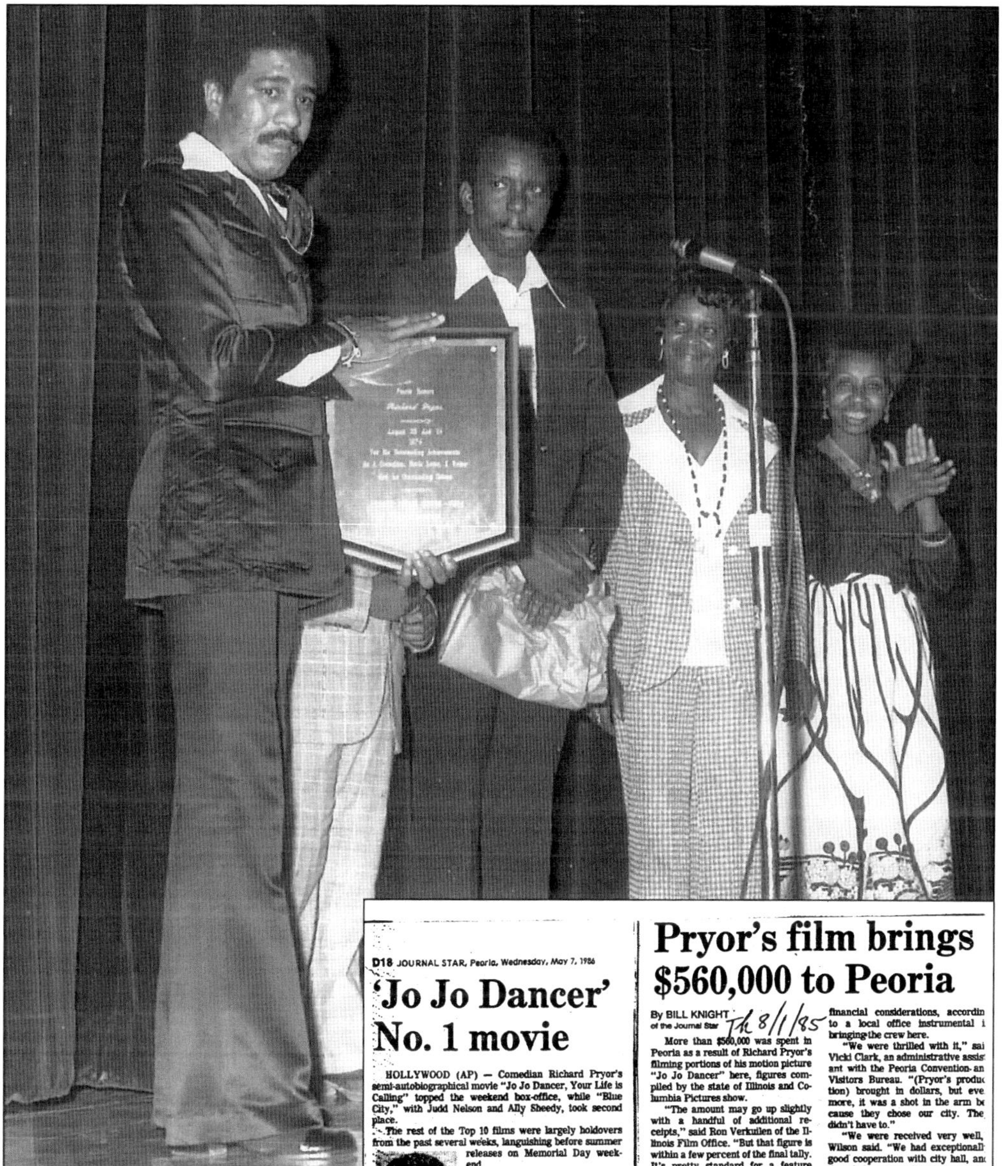

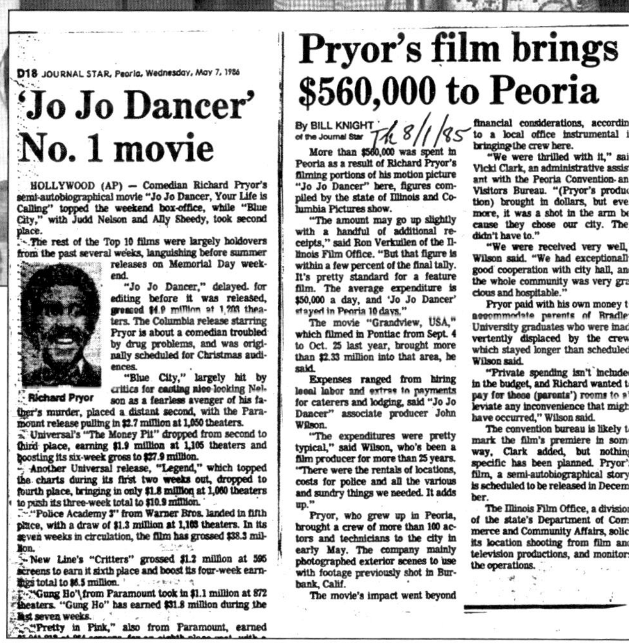

D18 JOURNAL STAR, Peoria, Wednesday, May 7, 1986

'Jo Jo Dancer' No. 1 movie

HOLLYWOOD (AP) — Comedian Richard Pryor's semi-autobiographical movie "Jo Jo Dancer, Your Life is Calling" topped the weekend box-office, while "Blue City," with Judd Nelson and Ally Sheedy, took second place.

The rest of the Top 10 films were largely holdovers from the past several weeks, languishing before summer releases on Memorial Day weekend.

Richard Pryor

"Jo Jo Dancer," delayed for editing before it was released, grossed $4.9 million at 1,208 theaters. The Columbia release starring Pryor is about a comedian troubled by drug problems, and was originally scheduled for Christmas audiences.

"Blue City," largely hit by critics for casting nice-looking Nelson as a fearless avenger of his father's murder, placed a distant second, with the Paramount release pulling in $2.7 million at 1,050 theaters.

Universal's "The Money Pit" dropped from second to third place, earning $1.9 million at 1,105 theaters and boosting its six-week gross to $27.9 million.

Another Universal release, "Legend," which topped the charts during its first two weeks out, dropped to fourth place, bringing in only $1.8 million at 1,060 theaters to push its three-week total to $10.9 million.

"Police Academy 3" from Warner Bros. landed in fifth place, with a draw of $1.3 million at 1,103 theaters. In its seven weeks in circulation, the film has grossed $38.3 million.

New Line's "Critters" grossed $1.2 million at 595 screens to earn it sixth place and boost its four-week earnings total to $6.5 million.

"Gung Ho" from Paramount took in $1.1 million at 872 theaters. "Gung Ho" has earned $31.8 million during the last seven weeks.

"Pretty in Pink," also from Paramount, earned [illegible]

Pryor's film brings $560,000 to Peoria

By BILL KNIGHT
of the Journal Star

Th 8/1/85

More than $560,000 was spent in Peoria as a result of Richard Pryor's filming portions of his motion picture "Jo Jo Dancer" here, figures compiled by the state of Illinois and Columbia Pictures show.

"The amount may go up slightly with a handful of additional receipts," said Ron Verkuilen of the Illinois Film Office. "But that figure is within a few percent of the final tally. It's pretty standard for a feature film. The average expenditure is $50,000 a day, and 'Jo Jo Dancer' stayed in Peoria 10 days."

The movie "Grandview, USA," which filmed in Pontiac from Sept. 4 to Oct. 25 last year, brought more than $2.33 million into that area, he said.

Expenses ranged from hiring local labor and extras to payments for caterers and lodging, said "Jo Jo Dancer" associate producer John Wilson.

"The expenditures were pretty typical," said Wilson, who's been a film producer for more than 25 years. "There were the rentals of locations, costs for police and all the various and sundry things we needed. It adds up."

Pryor, who grew up in Peoria, brought a crew of more than 100 actors and technicians to the city in early May. The company mainly photographed exterior scenes to use with footage previously shot in Burbank, Calif.

The movie's impact went beyond financial considerations, accordin to a local office instrumental i bringing the crew here.

"We were thrilled with it," sai Vicki Clark, an administrative assis ant with the Peoria Convention an Visitors Bureau. "(Pryor's produc tion) brought in dollars, but eve more, it was a shot in the arm be cause they chose our city. The didn't have to."

"We were received very well, Wilson said. "We had exceptionall good cooperation with city hall, an the whole community was very gra cious and hospitable."

Pryor paid with his own money t accommodate parents of Bradle University graduates who were inad vertently displaced by the crew which stayed longer than scheduled Wilson said.

"Private spending isn't include in the budget, and Richard wanted t pay for those (parents') rooms to al leviate any inconvenience that migh have occurred," Wilson said.

The convention bureau is likely t mark the film's premiere in som way, Clark added, but nothing specific has been planned. Pryor's film, a semi-autobiographical story is scheduled to be released in Decem ber.

The Illinois Film Office, a divisior of the state's Department of Com merce and Community Affairs, solic its location shooting from film an television productions, and monitor the operations.

ABOVE: In 1974, the city of Peoria welcomed home and honored its native son, Richard Pryor. (Courtesy of the Garrett Collection.) RIGHT: In 1986, Pryor's film *Jo Jo Dancer* was named the number one movie. The Peoria *Journal Star* profiled Pryor and the movie. (Courtesy of the Garrett Collection.)

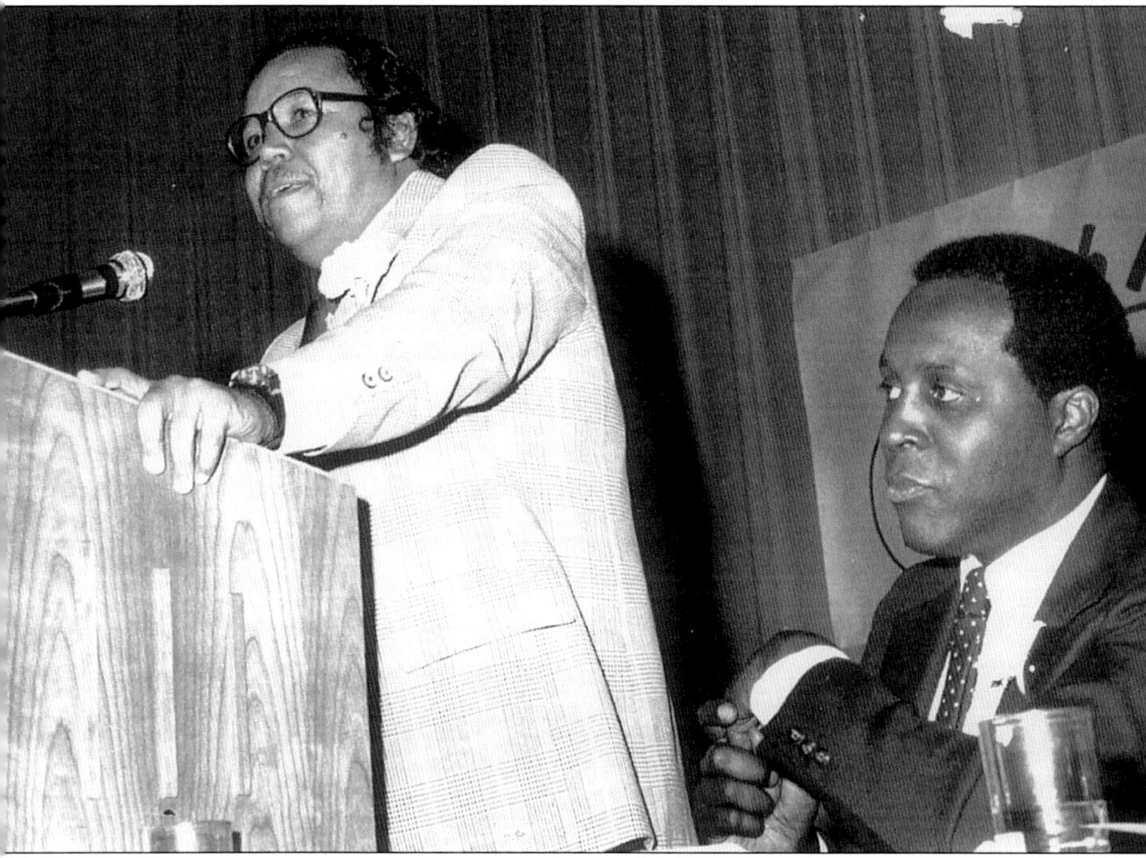

Frank Campbell, the director of the Tri-County Urban League, addressed the audience as Vernon Jordan, executive director of the National Urban League, looked on. (Courtesy of the Garrett Collection.)

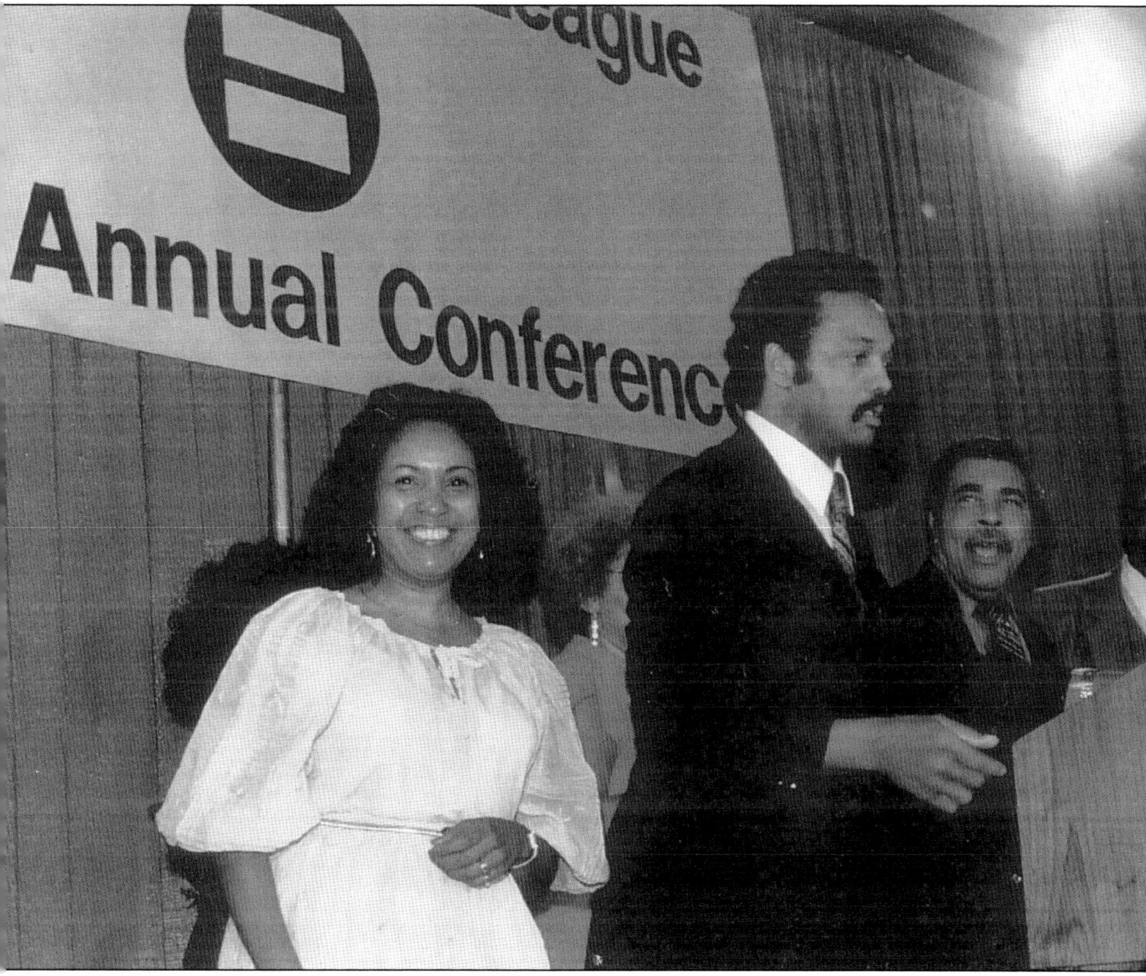

Jessie Jackson addressed the 82nd annual conference of the National Urban League, held in Peoria, Illinois, during the 1970s. Dr. Barbara Penelton of the Department of Education at Bradley University shared the podium with him. (Courtesy of the Garrett Collection.)

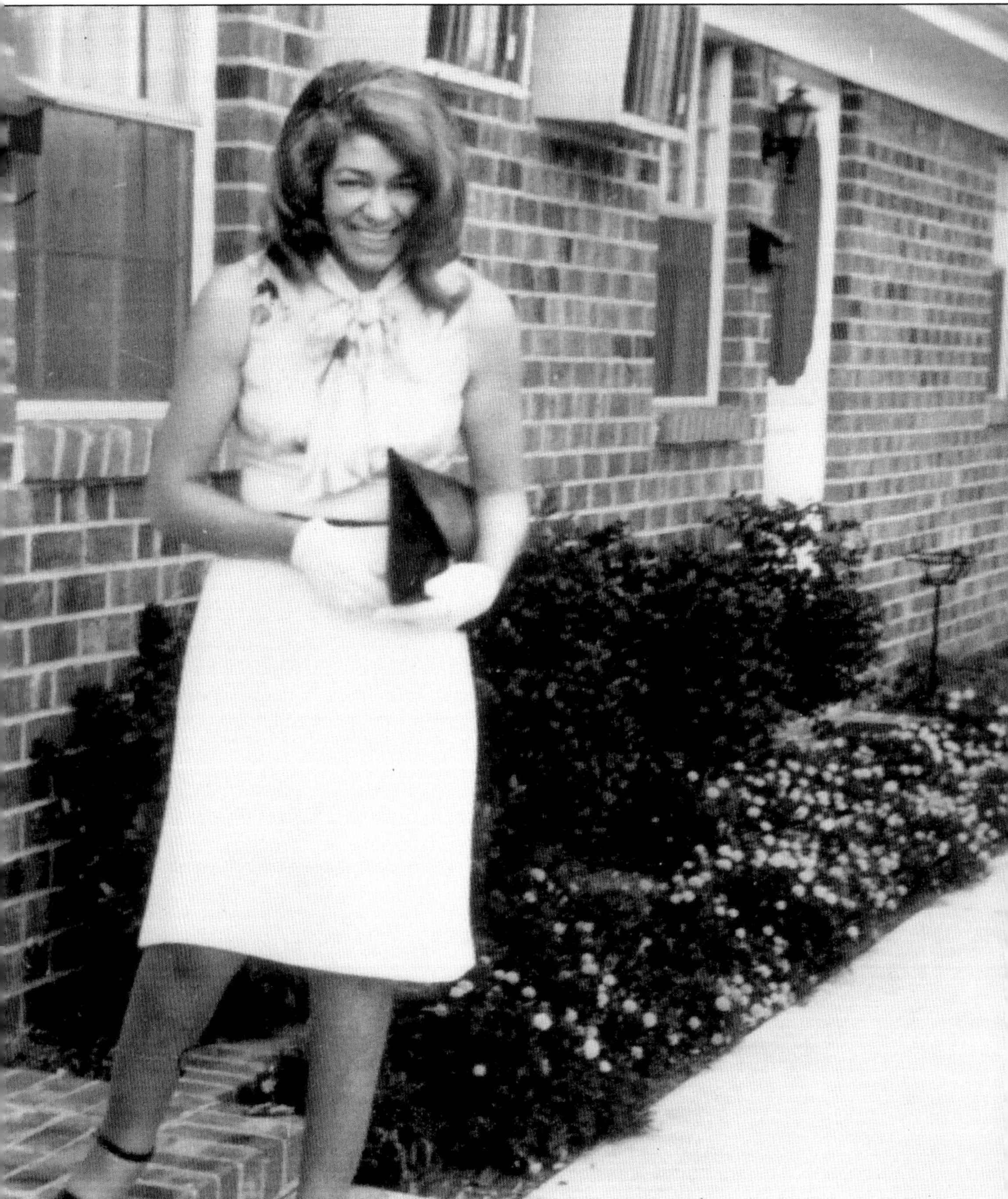

Eva Cox is reported to have been the first noted African-American artist of Peoria, Illinois. (Courtesy of the Garrett Collection.)

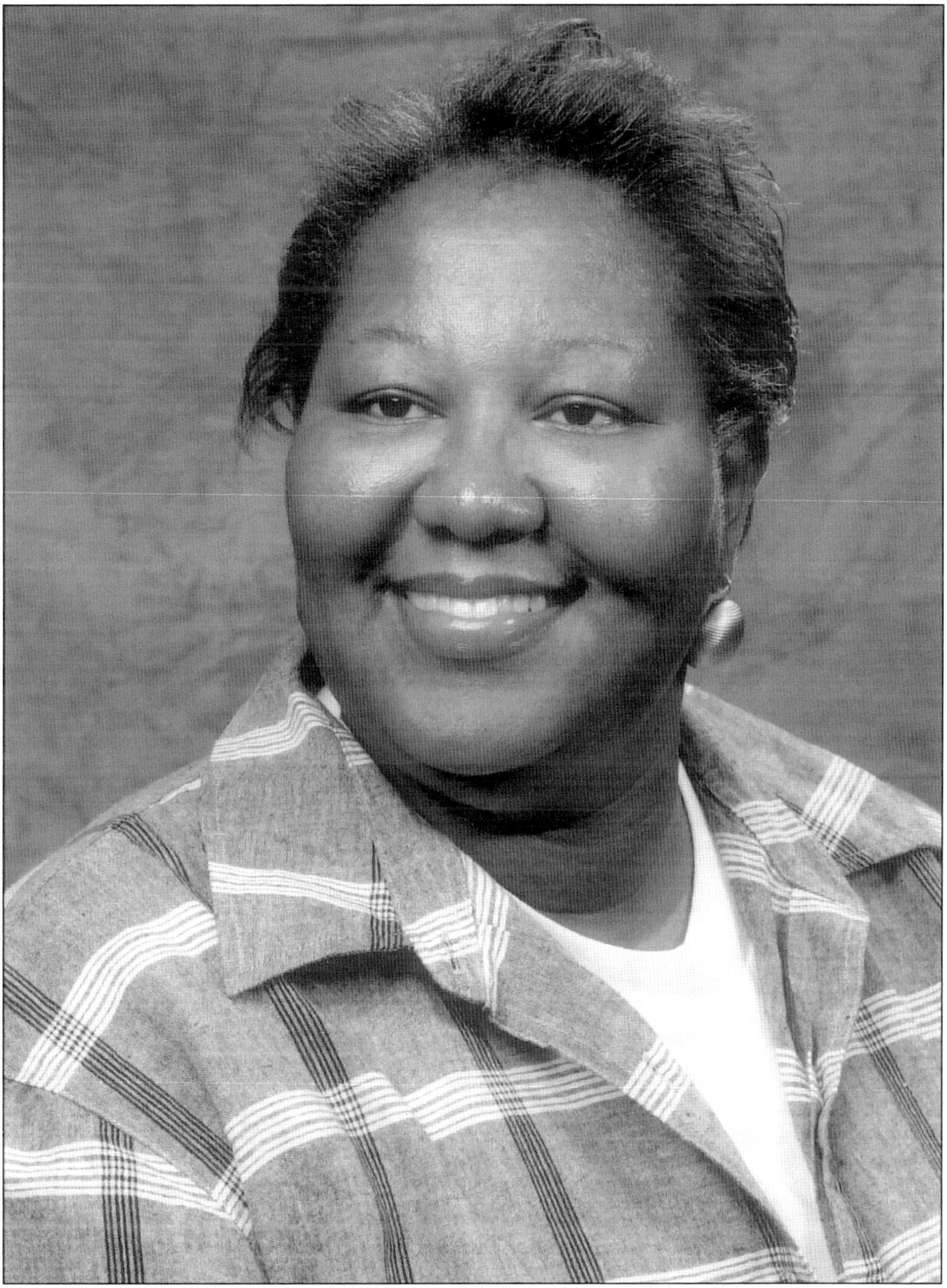

Belinda J. Carr is the first African American to be elected to the McDonough County Board. She was elected in 2000. (Courtesy of the Archives and Special Collections, Western Illinois University Library.)

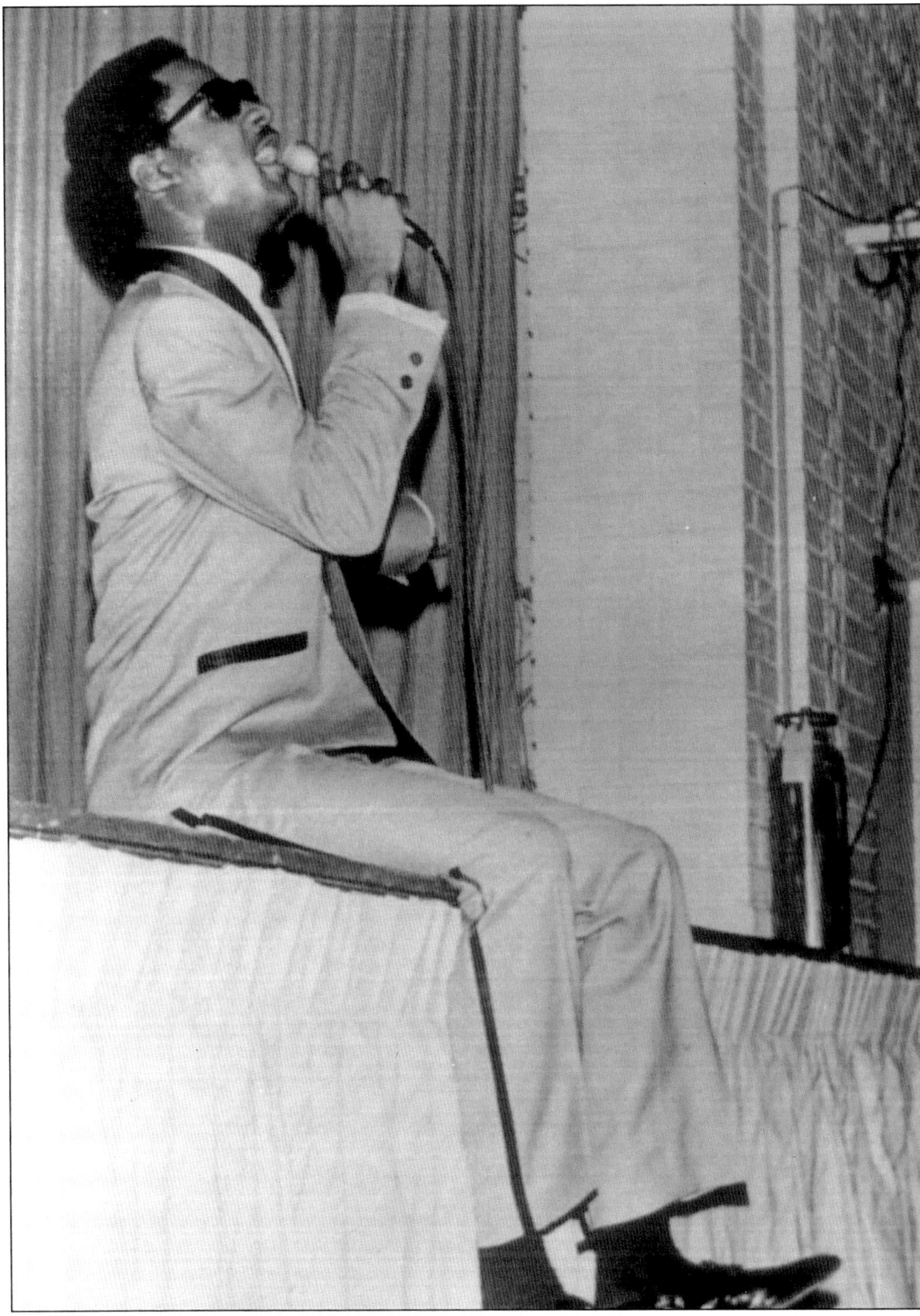

Stevie Wonder performed at Monmouth College in 1970, during the college's homecoming activities. (Courtesy of Monmouth College Archives.)

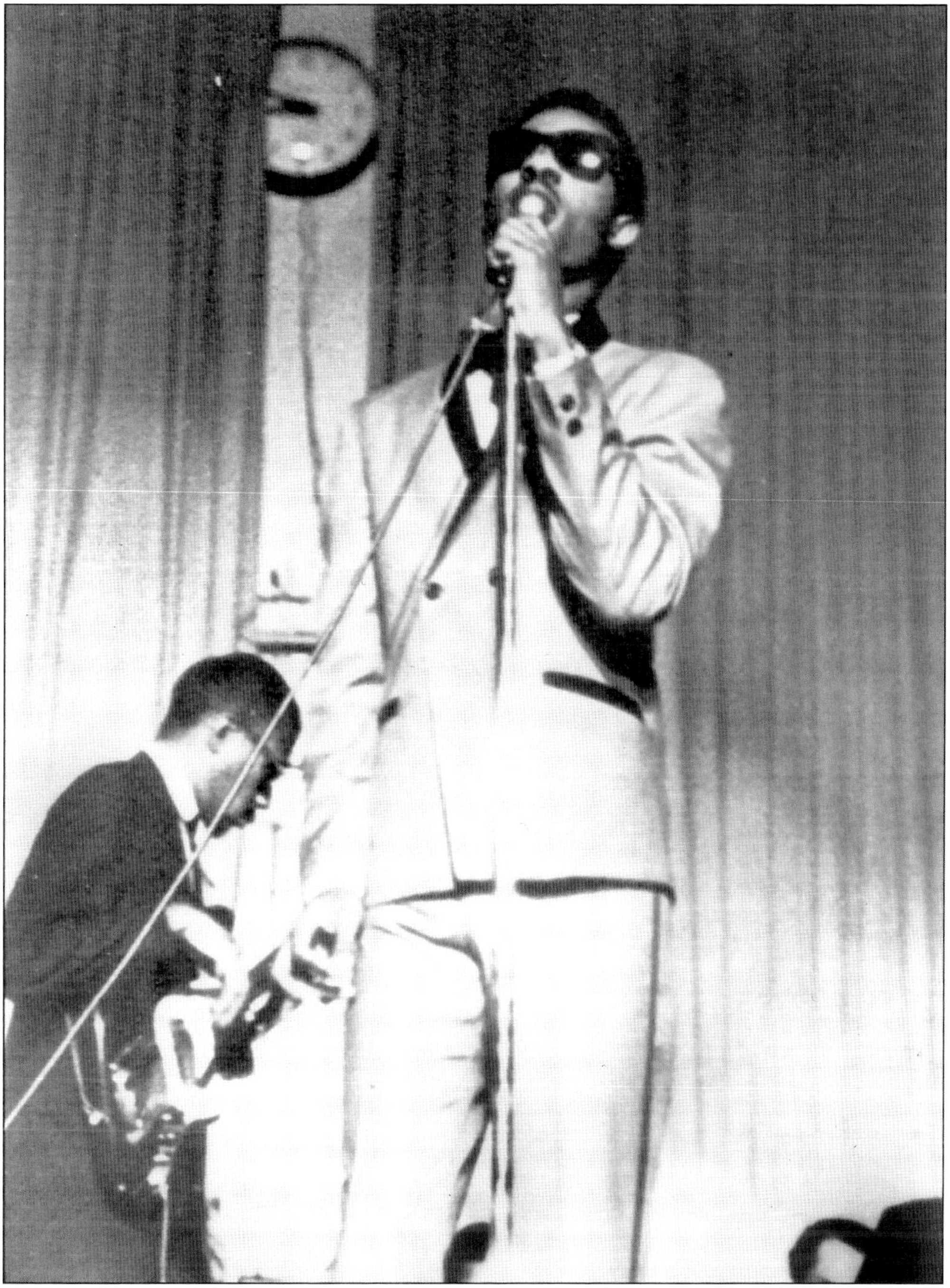

This image depicts the Stevie Wonder concert held at Monmouth College in 1970. (Courtesy of Monmouth College Archives.)

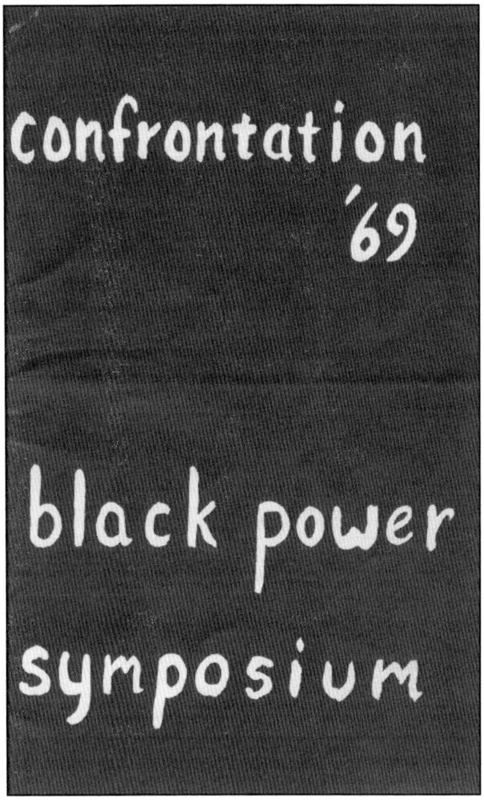

In 1969, the fever of "black power" swept the country, as college students demanded a new day in higher education. This was the front cover of the program that accompanied the black power symposium held at Augustana College in 1969. (Courtesy of Special Collections, Augustana College Library.)

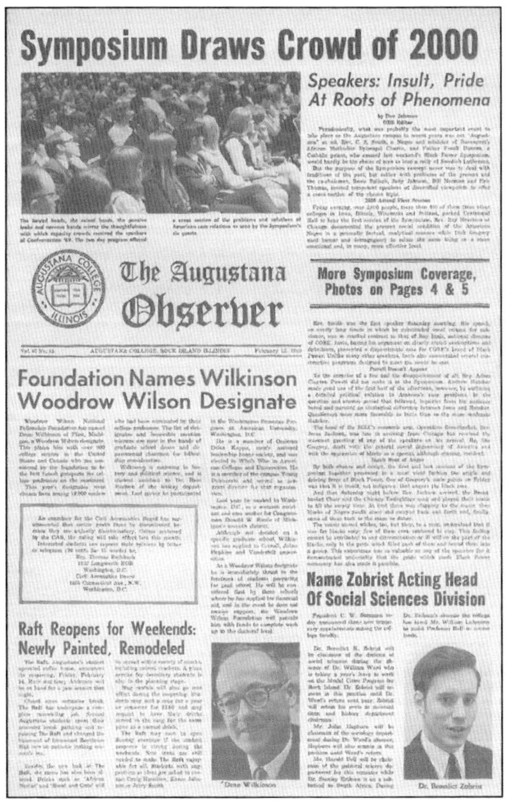

Symposium Draws Crowd of 2000

Speakers: Insult, Pride At Roots of Phenomena

The Augustana Observer

More Symposium Coverage, Photos on Pages 4 & 5

Foundation Names Wilkinson Woodrow Wilson Designate

Name Zobrist Acting Head Of Social Sciences Division

Raft Reopens for Weekends: Newly Painted, Remodeled

Dean Wilkinson

Dr. Benedict Zobrist

The black power symposium reportedly drew a crowd of 2,000 attendees. (Courtesy of Special Collections, Augustana College Library.)

Dick Gregory addressed a packed audience of the symposium. (Courtesy of Special Collections, Augustana College Library.)

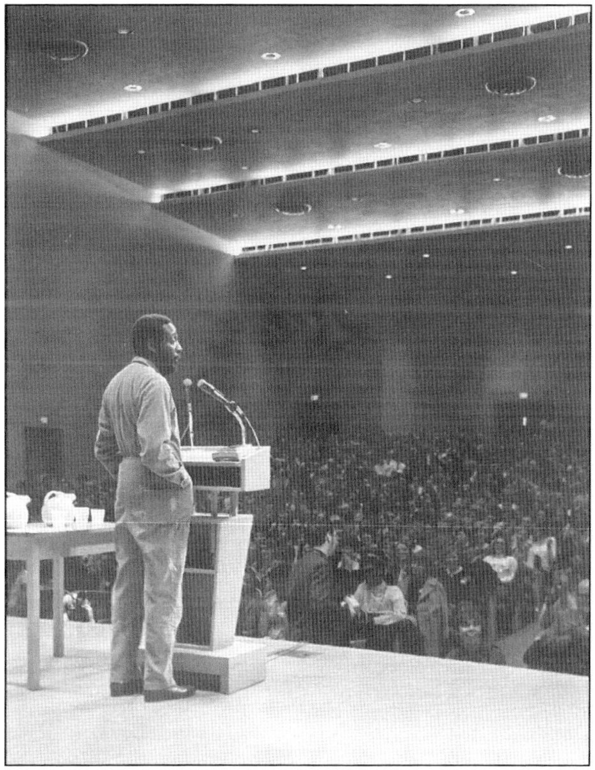

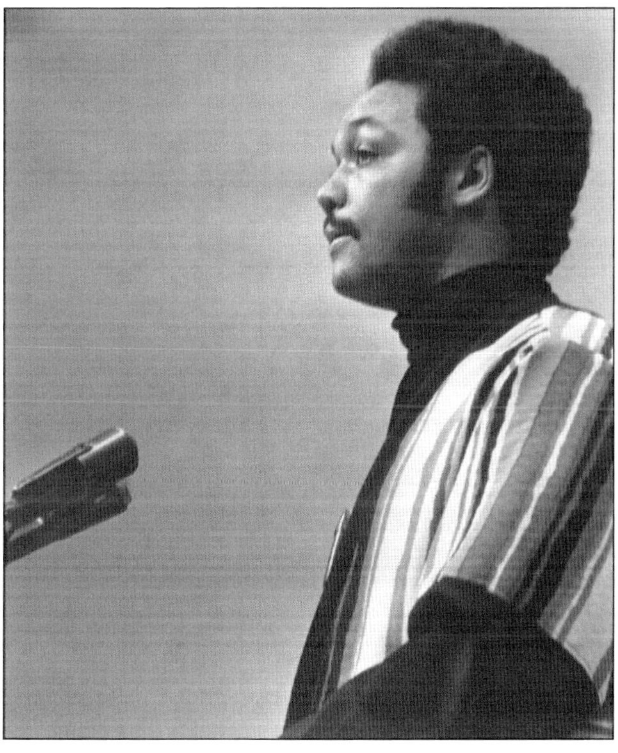

Jessie Jackson also headlined during the symposium at Augustana College in 1969. (Courtesy of Special Collections, Augustana College Library.)

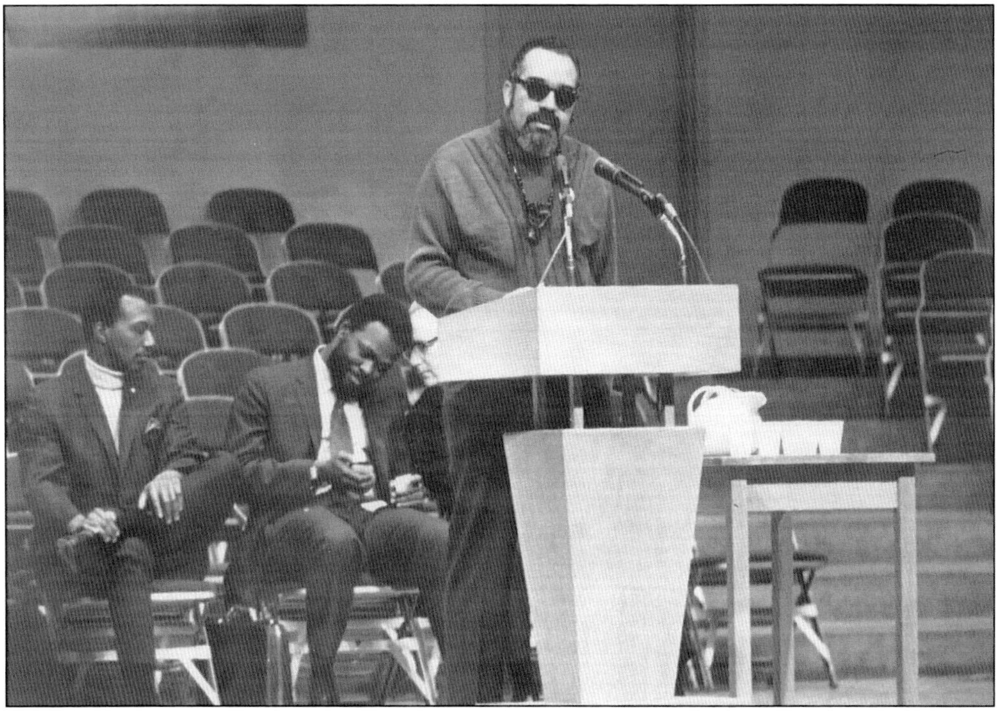

Rev. C.S. Smith, Pastor of the A.M.E. Church of Davenport, Iowa, and head of Project NOW addressed the symposium of 1969, as Roy Innis listened from the platform. (Courtesy of Special Collections, Augustana College Library.)

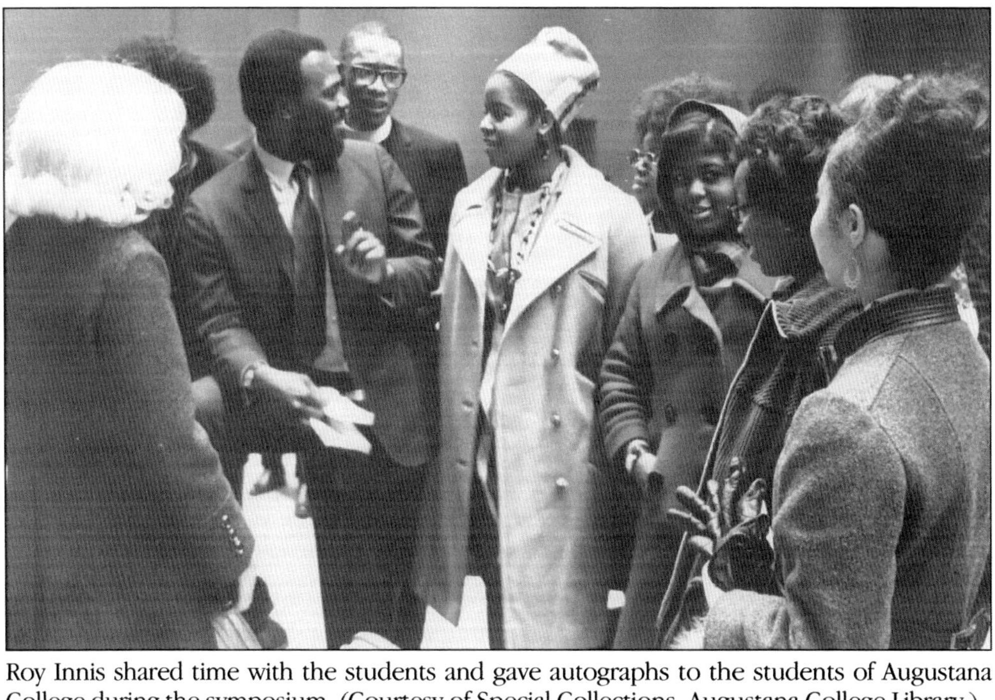

Roy Innis shared time with the students and gave autographs to the students of Augustana College during the symposium. (Courtesy of Special Collections, Augustana College Library.)

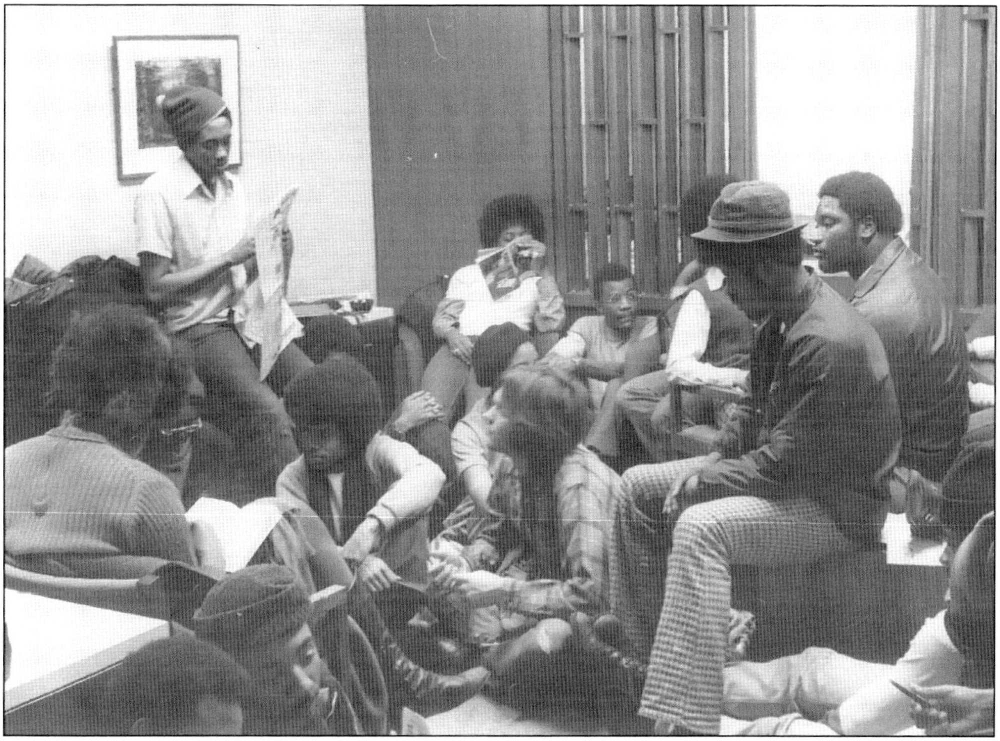

In 1972, the students of Augustana College sat in at the president's office to demand a change of the curriculum during the struggle over black power. (Courtesy of the Moline Dispatch Publishing Company.)

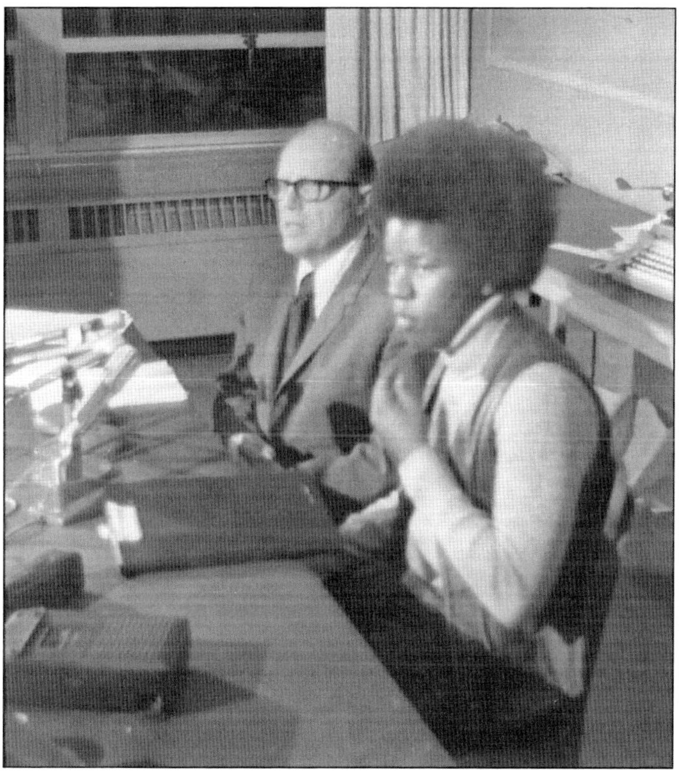

Eric Thomas, black student body representative of Augustana College, held a press conference with President Clarence Woodrow Sorensen and addressed the student concerns. (Courtesy of Moline Dispatch Publishing Company.)

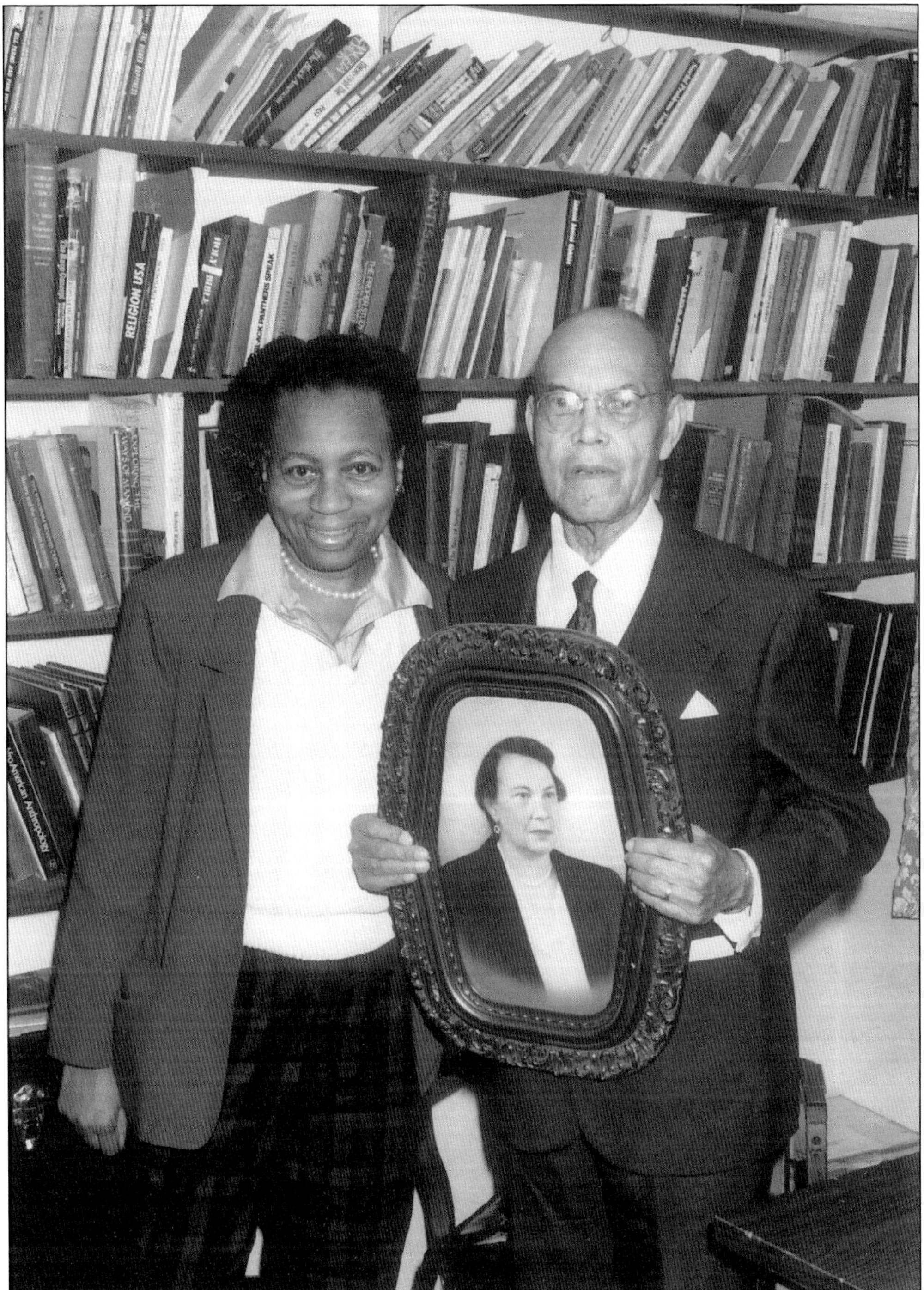

Ms. Millie Hall, who continues to be tireless working in black history preservation, and Dr. Romeo B. Garrett, to whom this book is dedicated for all his pioneering work on black history in Peoria and west central Illinois, are pictured here. (Courtesy of Ms. Millie Hall.)